The Quebec and Acadian Diaspora in North America

The Quebec and Acadian Diaspora
in North America

edited by
Raymond Breton
and
Pierre Savard

1982
The Multicultural History Society of Ontario
Toronto

ISBN 0-919045-11-1

The Multicultural History Society of Ontario
43 Queen's Park Crescent East
Toronto, Ontario M5S 2C3

Contents

French in the Canadian West

Franco-Ontarians

Preface

Robert F. Harney

This conference is one of a series of ethnic studies meetings that the Multicultural History Society of Ontario has sponsored over the last three years. We have convened large conferences on the Finns in North America, the Poles in North America and the State of the Art of ethnic and immigration studies. Smaller convocations have dealt with Dutch immigration and Little Italies, and plans for conferences on the Mennonites in Canada and Jews in North America are almost complete. There is no special logic to the scheduling or ethnic sequence of our symposia. They occur because scholars of a given ethnic group believe the time is right to review the state of study, because the Society learns of valuable ferment or discourse in a field such as that which took place among scholars of Franco-America at Assumption College in Worcester last year. Since most ethnic groups have a North American experience, no matter how localized their patterns of migration and settlement, we in Canada know that we can learn from American historiography. We also know that awareness of Canadian immigrant and ethnocultural history will enrich American ethnic studies. In this instance, we saw that a conference on the ethnic identity of francophones and their descendants outside of Quebec and Acadia would offer interesting comparative perspectives on Franco-Americans, French Canadians, Cajuns, Quebecois and Franco-Ontarians.

The conference went from idea to reality more quickly than its predecessors. That was so partly because of the energy of Professors Breton and Savard and their knowledge of the field and the people in it, but also because of my own naiveté. I assumed that such a gathering would be as easy to convene as our earlier conferences on the Finns and Poles. Both of those immigrant groups have produced young scholars in the second and third generation who have grafted new social scientific study onto the older filio-pietist histories of their groups. I was misled by the vibrancy of Quebec's political culture and the ubiquitous nature of the new ethnicism in the United States into believing that Franco-American scholarship—indeed the study of Quebecois and Acadians anywhere in North America—would be flourishing too. I did not then comprehend the aspects of Quebec's assertions of nationhood that have led to a scholarly neglect of the diaspora. From my Massachusetts upbringing, I should, however, have understood the reasons French Canadians in New England had not flocked to the "new ethnicity."

A few years ago, a book appeared about the French Canadians in Toronto entitled *The Invisible French*. Its thesis, obvious from its title, might be true, I reasoned, for polyglot Toronto, but it could not be so for New England or Manitoba. In those places, people knew about Franco-North American ethnicity, about the history of St. Boniface or of the "Little Canadas" in every mill town. To acquaint myself with the current literature in the field, I turned to the entry on French Canadians in the new *Harvard Encyclopaedia of American Ethnic Groups*. That article offered a good analysis of the demographic base of the ethnic group but no insight into the boundaries, intensity or evolving emblematics of French identity outside of Quebec and l'Acadie. I might add that it seemed to me a small advance over invisibility that the entry on French Canadians in that encyclopaedia was only one column longer than that on the much smaller, sporadic and less significant immigration of French from France to the United States. In Gerard Brault's paper, "Etat présent des études sur les centres franco-américains de la Nouvelle-Angleterre," delivered at the Premier colloque de l'Institut français du College de l'Assomption in 1980, I did find confirmation that serious scholarship about the social and cultural history of French Canadian enclaves in New England exists. However, much of it was unpublished.

The absence of an awareness of Franco-American ethnic history in our textbooks—no matter if it befits a people who have avoided ideological ethnicism and gone their own way, practising quiet tactics of *survivance* or equally quiet tactics of accommodation and acculturation—is a reprehensible failure by scholars of social and ethnic history. The Franco-American role has been too great in the making of New England, the Franco-Ontarian role too great in the opening of northern Ontario and the paradox of rural people flowing from Quebec away from their mother culture while thousands of European immigrants replaced them is too striking for the story of the French Canadian diaspora to be but a footnote in the writing of other peoples' histories. Yet it remains little more than that.

To my knowledge, only one thesis on the French outside of Quebec has ever been presented to the Department of History at the University of Toronto. In my undergraduate days at Harvard, I recall mention of the Franco-Americans only in the context of Senator Henry Cabot Lodge's restrictionism, or their strike-breaking activities. The entry on the French Canadians in the new *Harvard Encyclopaedia of American Ethnic Groups* is one of the few on a major group where the author is not a member of that ethnoculture. That is not improper, but it does suggest a lack of historical scholarship within the ethnic group. Franco-Americans are "ethnics" but not in the mainstream of ethnic and immigration studies; Little Canadas were, or are, a salient feature of dozens of New England cities but far less understood or studied than other ethnic enclaves. I suppose that neatly fits Barbara Solomon's remark that the issue of French Canadian immigrants aroused little interest and only led to limited discourse in New England. There is in all of this scholarly neglect a remarkable parallel to Franco-Ontarians who are caught between seeing themselves as inhabitants of a *terra irredenta* of Quebec, or as a founding race of Canada, or now as one of Ontario's immigrant ethnic groups. However they choose to negotiate their ethnic status, the result, for scholarship, is not flux but paralysis. With the exception of the Centre de recherche en civilisation canadienne-française (Ottawa) and the Institut Franco-Ontarien at Laurentian University, there is a failure of either social or ethnic historical work to focus on the French fact of settlement, niching and *survivance* in the province.

This gathering has, as its first purpose, to raise concern for the recording and studying of the Quebec and Acadian diaspora throughout North America. There already exist some serious, if fugitive, monographic works about certain Little Canadas in the United States, a worthwhile demographic literature emanating from Quebec and the usually much criticized — but always borrowed from — filio-pietistic studies and *petit-histoires* of settlement. What is needed, I believe, is some assertion that the study of the diaspora should move to the mainstream of North American ethnocultural, social and labour history. Such a move requires contact with and knowledge of the scholarship and methodology current in the study of other ethnic groups and a revival of scholarly interest in emigrants among Quebecois scholars.

Losing invisibility and coming into the mainstream has its risks. There is the danger that Quebecois scholars, freeing them- selves from the foolish ideological frame which makes study of the diaspora unpopular, will begin to love the New England and Ontario French to death. By viewing them as lost Quebecois, or a "lost tribe" to be studied like Cajuns, they will reduce history either to contemporary politics or folklore. There is also a disturb- ing drift among American labour and social historians which treats Franco-Americans not in the fullness of their ethnoculture, *mentalités* and ethnic socio-economy but merely as a segment of the mill work-force, a variant group through which to raise issues about comparative modernization and the uneven development of proletarian consciousness. Much of the new social history—Wal- kowitz's *Worker City, Company Town, Iron and Cotton Workers Protest in Troy and Cohoes* and Hareven's *Amoskeag. Life and Work in an American Factory-City*—while effective for its own purposes, seems to nullify the significance of a Franco-American ethnoculture. Either because of their lack of appropriate "tracking tools" or an unwillingness to hear the ethnic voice in oral testi- mony, such studies, it seems to me, generalize rural, migrant and familial conditions and traditions as they affect the work-force and the work place but ignore the real history of Quebec emigra- tion and distort the communal history of French Canadians and the Little Canadas they created in order to survive.

During the 1980 conference entitled "Situation de la Recherche sur la Franco-Américanie," at Assumption College, Claire Quin- tal, the director of the Institut français there, remarked that, "il existe bel et bien une realité franco-américaine," and that, "il y a un avenir pour les études franco-américaines." Our conference, I hope, will show not only that there is such a future, but that revived Franco-American studies form a necessary comparative base for the study of the French as an ethnic group outside of Quebec and Acadia in Canada. Without making the Franco- Ontarians just another immigrant group in Ontario's multicultural mosaic, or threatening the Franco-American's honorary status as francophone Yankees, scholars must bring the history of the Quebec and Acadian diaspora into the context of North Ameri- can immigrant and ethnic studies.

On behalf of the Multicultural History Society of Ontario and the University of Toronto's Ethnic and Immigration Studies Program, I would like to welcome you to this conference on the Quebec and Acadian diaspora in North America and to thank Professors Pierre Savard and Raymond Breton for planning the conference and the staff of the Society who helped organize it. I also wish to thank Anne McCarthy, the associate editor of the Multicultural History Society, who has assumed the responsibility for copy editing and producing, with the assistance of Michèle Breton, the volume of essays that will result from this conference.

Introduction

Raymond Breton and Pierre Savard

Within the last decade, political debates and the development of ethnic studies have focused attention on the francophones in North America, descended from Quebecois and Acadian immigrant families. To be sure, these minority groups had never been forgotten. An entire literature, polemical and filio-pietist in nature, exists. And the tone of these stories can still be found in the writing of today. Aside from tourist publicity, propaganda and family albums, studies have been published in recent years which are based on surer and newer methods of social science research. We hope that this conference will reflect that trend and its spirit.

In less than two days, it is not possible to cover all the concerns of this group, nor every region of this continent where francophones can be found in number. Thus, our publication reveals more fallow ground than cultivated land. Areas such as British Columbia and California will not be discussed. The prairies will only be glanced at. Other regions like Manitoba, with firmly established francophone settlements, are mentioned only in regard to recent developments. The most significant problems of the Franco-Ontarian community, past and present, will be introduced, as will those of the Acadians—a people without a state, even at the provincial level. What should be sought in these pages is not an encyclopaedia or compendium of knowledge, but rather paths that will lead us in different directions through the human sciences, ranging from demography to literary history, and including geography, sociology and history.

A considerable range of questions are discussed and documented in these essays. Many of the hypotheses examined and the findings presented, however, raise a number of additional questions for research critical to any understanding of the evolution of the Quebec and Acadian diaspora in North America. For instance, Robert Choquette's paper, which deals with the separation of Irish Canadian Catholicism from the dominance of French Canada, may raise similar reflections about religious developments in the west. Gaetan Vallières' article reminds us that migration between Quebec and Ontario cannot be studied without reference to the population movements in New England and western Canada. For his part, David Hayne stresses that emigration and the colonization of Quebec are two indissoluble phenomena in the works of nineteenth-century francophone writers, and that each sheds light on the other. If the demographic-linguistic data and comments of Charles Castonguay allow us an overview of language transfers, then Donald Cartwright's paper should enable us to see the spatial developments of francophone and anglophone communities in a given area, namely, Ontario. Gerald Gold examines changes in social organization and related linguistic patterns. Danielle Juteau-Lee and Gilbert Comeault deal with the transformation of the internal political organization of francophone communities and their relationship with the centres of power. Our host, Robert Harney, shows how personal memory and social science scholarship can come together to suggest the *mentalités* of a Little Canada. And the occupational distribution of Franco-Americans, compared to the rest of the work-force, is considered by Madeleine Giguère.

The extensive linguistic assimilation documented by Castonguay raises important questions that are not dealt with in the existing research literature: What has happened or is happening to all those individuals and families who are linguistically assimilated? How has the language loss affected their ethnocultural identity? To what extent and in what ways do they feel they belong to the francophone community? Do they feel rejected? How has the loss of language affected their social networks, their social participation and the cultural content of their behaviour and social relationship? How do they differ in this regard from those who have retained the French language and use it in their homes and in public domains? Differences in identity, sense of belonging, social participation, cultural experience and social network would be worth examining, but so would differences in socio-economic mobility, involvement in the larger political system, socio-political ideology, religious participation, and so on. Needless to say, such a comparative analysis would need to differentiate what happens at the level of elites and non-elites in the various segments of the francophone population of Quebecois or Acadian origin—those in large metropolitan areas in comparison with those in small towns; those in lower, middle and professional classes; those of various age categories and so on.

Some of the results presented suggest that one cannot simply assume that with linguistic assimilation the French identity—individual and collective—disappears. However, variations in the extent to which the emphasis has historically been placed on language as the critical component of ethnocultural identity among francophone communities should, perhaps, be ascertained.

The impact of linguistic assimilation on those who retain their language should also be studied. How do they perceive and react to the loss of language within their own families, among neighbours and in the larger, regional community? How does the ongoing assimilation affect their collective identity, their views of the future and their own participation in community affairs? At another level, future research might consider whether or not there is a shift from a linguistic group identity to that of an ethnocultural group or, as Juteau-Lee states, from a "groupe nationalitaire" to an ethnic group.

Finally, the extent and nature of the interconnections between these two segments of the Quebec and Acadian diaspora should be examined. What patterns of interpersonal relationships exist between them, including intermarriage? (Castonguay has suggested that the linguistically assimilated still have a propensity to marry within their own ethnic group.) What is the relationship between francophone associations and institutions and the linguistically assimilated?

Another area of study to which the papers direct our attention concerns the social and political organization of francophone communities, and their evolution. More specifically, one's attention is drawn to the question of the transformation of community institutions. What role are the traditionally important institutions, such as the church, now playing? It should not simply be assumed that they have disappeared from the scene. That their role has changed seems quite evident; but this does not mean that they have not defined a new role for themselves in response to the changing circumstances. The transition process of these traditional institutions needs more careful examination. Some of the essays point to the emergence of new institutions and associations. What types of organizations are they? Who controls them? What roles are they defining for themselves? What seems to be their impact? For instance, Gold argues that his research has consistently shown that the major organized force for language change (in Louisiana) has been peripheral to regional manifestations of cultural change, whether it be a revival of popular culture or the ability of certain occupational groups to retain and even extend the use of French despite extensive modernization.

Research should also explore the relationship between the traditional and the new organizations and their respective elites. What patterns of conflict, accommodation and complementarity do they have with each other? How do these patterns affect the social structure of the community and its ability to act in a concerted way? The emergence of intercommunity networks of organizations should also be probed. To what extent is there an "extension of local networks to the national folklore circuit and to the folklore circuit of the francophone industrial nations" (Gold)? What is the social and political impact of such networks? Do they involve only a small segment of the various community elites, or are they ramified throughout the cultural life of various localities?

The comparative study of the evolution of communities raises the question of the impact of the socio-economic, demographic and political context in which those communities have evolved. It cannot be assumed that industrialization and urbanization had a uniform effect on all francophone communities in the different regions of North America. Nor can it be assumed that, even though a minority-majority situation probably has some constant structural features, the relationship of the linguistic minority with the dominant group and its institutions has been the same across the various regions or over time within a given region.

In this regard, several papers have raised questions concerning the role of the state and its effect on the situation of linguistic minorities. Whether the importance of the state in relation to such minorities in North America is growing or declining is far from clear; it appears, however, that it is changing. Again, only comparative research can bring reliable answers to questions about variations in state policies, over time and across regions, and their impact. Among the questions to be probed are those about the degree of variations in political phenomena and their consequences:

(a)   Variations in officially supported ideologies concerning ethnocultural diversity, in general, and linguistic maintenance in particular;

(b)   Variations in legislation, programs, services, administrative and electoral practices;

(c)   Variations in direct attempts by state agencies to organize or influence the organizational structure of francophone communities and their socio-cultural and political activities;

(d)   The extent and ways in which francophones have penetrated political parties and government bureaucracies at various levels;

(e)   Variations in the strategies and tactics used by the linguistic minorities: Has more importance been given to legal strategies and tactics or to those of a political, electoral and bureaucratic nature?

Needless to say, when examining the relationship of minorities with the state, the extent of their power (or weakness) and its basis need to be taken into account whether it be moral, organizational, demographic or cultural.

An issue raised by a number of authors, and perhaps especially by Comeault, pertains to the extent to which cultural and linguistic maintenance has come to depend on planned as opposed to spontaneous processes. Can linguistic communities survive without constitutional provisions, legislation, or governmental programs and services? In other words, are the social, demographic, spatial, economic and political processes, operating in favour of linguistic maintenance, sufficient? Are they so weak that they need to be constantly buttressed by systematic intervention on the part of the state and its organizational apparatus? What are the forces leading to assimilation, and can they be resisted through state intervention? Are they so strong that the cultural basis and social organization of the communities are bound to become progressively eroded through assimilation?

In this connection, it should be noted that research such as that suggested above would help to show whether the evolution of francophone communities supports a linear model of social change or rather a dialectic model in which various changes—both within and outside the communities—trigger reactions which, in turn, set in motion processes of social reconstruction either at the individual level, the collective level, or both. At least some of the papers presented suggest that the evolutionary processes are rather complex, and that it would be misleading to assume a linear evolution. There is evidence to suggest that there are some counter-processes that occur at least in certain circumstances. This needs to be explored more thoroughly.

In addition, reading these essays leads us inevitably to the important question of the sources for the study of these *membra disjecta* scattered over the continent—ethnocultural communities without a political state and whose boundaries often remain hard to define. The Linguistic statistics of the American and Canadian federal governments constitute, of course, a major source. Used with skill (Castonguay, Cartwright, Vallières), they are a necessary starting point. They can also tell us a lot about the social and professional behaviour of the communities (Giguère). It is unfortunate that the measurement of popular, learned and traditional cultural practices (i.e., watching television or reading) is still in its infancy. Such measurement would undoubtedly tell us a good deal about behaviour. It is the intelligent questions formulated by researchers that do the most for the refinement of these census instruments, provided, of course, that their formulation is not forbidden for reasons of petty politics.

The Acadian and Quebec diaspora communities do not have a state of their own and, consequently, no public archives, as we have mentioned. For a few years and with new vigour, they have been making up for this by collecting the archives of national ethnocultural organizations, for example, those of the Association canadienne-française de l'Ontario kept at the Centre for Research on French Canadian Culture of the University of Ottawa (Vallières). Besides these numerous collections, there are also documents from individuals like Félix Albert, ingeniously utilized by Frances Early; the correspondence of politicians and administrators kept in public archives; and the essential and abundant religious archives so important to the study of the *petit peuple* dear to chanoine Groulx (Choquette) and of the Acadians. The latter have undertaken the mammoth task of microfilming all their historical records in Great Britain, France, the United States and elsewhere. Consequently, the Centre d'études acadiennes in Moncton already has a collection of documents of model richness and accessibility to benefit current research (Daigle).

Oral history alone can provide essential data on the history of francophones scattered in the manufacturing towns and on the last colonization land in North America. These sources appear as a watermark, if not a direct reference in certain papers (Gold).

There remains to be mentioned the mass of printed material, for long the most obvious source—countless brochures and action papers, of a tiresome tone, but in the end essential to recreate an ambiance and define problems as the people of the time saw them (Lalonde); government and organization reports that, if read with a critical eye, offer an insight on the rest of the documentation (Vallières); and careful study of the writing of the period should not be overlooked either (Hayne).

While reading through this book, the reader will not fail to note how deficient our knowledge is; such deficiencies being inherent in a history that takes place on the periphery of a world (Quebec) better known than its fringes (New England or French Alberta). Shortcomings are also due to the still embryonic state of research in certain regions that are only starting to collect or exploit their archives. Nevertheless, one feels comforted after reading these essays that put forward bold and stimulating syntheses (Hayne or Castonguay) and monographs with daring and appealing conclusions (Early). As for the multiple contradictions herein that a systematic mind won't fail to point out, they are often due to the vocabulary differences of an ecumenical symposium. These contradictions, where genuine, invite us to further our research. They also initiate fruitful debates that are more than mere academic quarrels over the life and survival of these rather particular French communities.

We hope that these papers will not only contribute to an increased knowledge of francophones outside Quebec and Acadia, but that they will also inspire methodological developments and encourage additional studies aimed at more structured knowledge acquisition concerning these ethnic groups which are among the oldest and most widely dispersed in North America.

Quebec and Acadia as Sources of Emigration

The Acadians: a People in Search of a Country

Jean Daigle

The period between 1604 and 1763 saw the development of the Acadian identity and community.[1] They were the first Europeans to settle in North America, four years before the establishment of Quebec and three years before the founding of Jamestown. Coming from the French region south of the Loire, the old provinces of Poitou (Anjou, Touraine), the Acadian settlers were different from those of New France, who had come mostly from north of the Loire (Normandy, Brittany, Island of France, Saintonge, etc.). The Acadians settled on both sides of the Bay of Fundy where they built communities united in a strong sense of purpose: their autonomous economic and cultural survival as a group.

Until 1713 the French were the only masters of what are now the Maritime provinces. Marginal settlers, the Acadians (as they came to be known) had learned very early to be self-reliant, since the French government had not always looked after their needs.[2] It was on their own initiative that some of them emigrated from the Port Royal region to Beaubassin in the 1670s and to Grand Pré in the 1680s. This attitude infuriated the colonial administrators who considered the Acadians "half republicans." Their independent ways extended even to farming: rather than clearing and then cultivating the uplands, the Acadians preferred to cultivate the land bordering on the sea. From their experience with the salt marshes in France, they constructed a system of dykes which would allow excess fresh water to flow out to the ocean but prevented salt water from invading the alluvial land at high tide.[3]

Trade between the Acadians and the American colonies, although forbidden, still flourished in the seventeenth century. For the Acadians it was a way to dispose of excess grain produce (wheat, barley, etc.) and furs supplied by the Indians, in exchange for manufactured goods (knives, needles, dishes) and foodstuffs from the West Indies (sugar, molasses, rum). In many respects, the French colony on the Bay of Fundy seemed more an economic satellite of Boston than of Versailles.[4] Massachusetts' economic and commercial penetration of Acadia was constant between 1670 and 1710, demonstrating the power of the English colony which considered the area around the Bay of Fundy as their own sphere of interest.

By comparison with the other colonies in North America, Acadia was the weakest. The small population made it easy prey. Its conquest in 1710 gave the English what is now peninsular Nova Scotia. Cape Breton and Prince Edward Island remained French while New Brunswick was disputed territory between England and France. The Acadians were now a conquered people. Various attempts to have them swear an oath of allegiance to England were unsuccessful. Their attitude reflected the belief that the colony would eventually return to French rule because of the relative weakness of the English presence. As all had wearied of the strife, a condition of neutrality was proposed in 1730 (considering Acadia distinct from New France), and from that date the Acadians were known as the "French Neutrals."[5]

Comparative Table of the Populations of New France, Acadia and the American Colonies

Year	New France (Canada)	Acadia	American Colonies
1608	28	10	100
1640	220	200	28,000
1680	9,700	800	155,000
1710	16,000	2,000	357,000
1750	55,000	10,500	1,200,000

Nova Scotia was now an English colony with a French flavour. The Acadians had little contact with the administration, staying within their own self-contained community. The governing policy of tolerance soon led to one of force in the 1740s and 1750s. A recommended solution to the problem of the French presence in North America (the Acadian population alone had multiplied by five between 1710 and 1750) was to "Britannize" Nova Scotia by introducing British institutions and laws and by transporting over 2,000 English colonists to a new settlement called Halifax.[6] This large influx of English Protestants into the colony dramatically changed the balance of power and made possible a future without the Acadian French presence. With the beginning of the Seven Years' War in 1755, all those Acadians who would not bear an oath of allegiance to the English crown were deported. This process, started in peninsular Nova Scotia, extended later to Cape Breton, Prince Edward Island and New Brunswick and lasted until 1763. About 8,000 of the 13,000 Acadians were sent off to the American colonies, England or France.[7]

The life of Augustin Benoit can best illustrate this theme of the wandering Acadian. Born in Acadia, he migrated to Cape Breton in 1750 from where he was deported to France in 1759; in 1763 he was persuaded to follow a group of settlers to the Falkland Islands where he stayed until the abandonment of the colony in 1767. He returned then to France from Spain. In 1775 he requested to be transported to Saint Pierre and Miquelon. Unfortunately for him the support of the islanders for the revolutionary cause of the Americans brought the deportation of its inhabitants to France in 1778 by the British. He finally settled in Archigny, France.[8]

Forced migration compelled the Acadians to make quick decisions. Should they return? Where would they settle? Where would they find members of their families? Those who did return to Nova Scotia discovered their land now occupied by the English, leaving them to settle elsewhere. Groups of displaced Acadians could be found in Nova Scotia, on the banks of the St. Lawrence, in Louisiana, England, France, the Falkland Islands and the Caribbean. In their petitions they acted as part of a separate, identifiable group, requesting action in response to specific needs or trying to prevent crises: the desire to leave Nova Scotia, to obtain monetary compensation or land grants, to find loved ones, etc.[9] The central thread running through all these petitions was the disturbance of family life and loss of property.

Those who came back to the Maritimes settled on unoccupied tracts of land removed from the area of English colonization. If the traumatic experience had taught them a lesson it was a fear of the English and a desire to rebuild a stable community where cherished values could be preserved: the Catholic religion, family and French language. It was a period of new beginnings. For a century (1763-1864) the English had given themselves a sound political and economic identity: the arrival of the Loyalists, the founding of new colonies and religious proselytizing.[10] For the Acadians, however, the local and temporary nature of their own institutions was the dominant community characteristic. They did not have schools, newspapers, lawyers, doctors or institutions of higher learning; in all, they had no collective organizations. Their first task was to obtain land grants, and for many decades the colonial legislatures were besieged with cases of land tenure. Once the grants were obtained, the Acadians turned most of their attention to farming, fishing and lumbering, and the maintenance of a traditional economy. In wishing to remain apart from the English, the Acadians cut themselves off from the political and economic life of the colony. It is, therefore, not surprising to see the low opinion of them which the English majority held, considering them "a halfway house between the Indians and the white people."[11]

As the English colonies required the test oath from all voters, this left the abstaining Acadians without any political rights until 1789, when Nova Scotia abolished the oath for the general public, followed by New Brunswick and Prince Edward Island in 1810; but they still retained it for people who ran for the legislature. The religious oaths were abolished in 1830, and the Catholics were politically enfranchised—of benefit mostly to the Irish and Scottish Catholics who were running for office in Acadian ridings.[12] Until the 1840s an outside observer would scarcely notice the Acadian presence in the Maritimes. In all, relations between the French and English were few; the Acadians, as a collectivity, were not active in politics and as such did not represent a menace to the English majority. Political weakness was the price they had to pay to ensure their cultural security.

During the second half of the nineteenth century, outside recognition was given to the Acadian presence in North America. Henry Longfellow wrote his poem *Evangeline*[13] in 1847 and the Frenchman Edmé Rameau de Saint-Père published, in 1859, an historical account of the Acadians.[14] These two publications signalled the awakening of Acadian self-awareness. Absent from all public debates for a century, they gathered in 1881 to discuss their political and social situation, and during the second meeting held in Summerside, Prince Edward Island in 1884, they chose a national anthem, a flag and a national holiday, which still unite them today.[15]

Because of a high birth rate, the Acadians were already the majority in some counties of New Brunswick. According to the 1871 Census, they constituted 71 per cent of the population of

Gloucester and 58 per cent of Kent and Victoria. The Acadian leadership of the nineteenth century tried to find solutions to its most pressing problems: the teaching of French in public schools, the Acadianization of the Catholic church, journalism and immigration to the United States. On that last issue the editor of *l'Impartial*, a French newspaper in Prince Edward Island, wrote in 1902 that Acadian migration to the United States was "another deportation... the Acadians being this time their own torturers."[16] One of the founders of this newspaper, François Buote, even went to visit New England communities to try to repatriate the Acadian families living there. In 1911 he was happy to announce that eighty-two people had boarded ship in Portland, Maine for Prince Edward Island.[17]

The public meetings, initiated in 1881, served as a forum for Acadian nationalists to discuss their vision of French life in the Maritimes and desire for closer integration with the surrounding community. The industrial age was modifying the traditional Acadian life style. On the one hand, in looking for social mobility they were running the risk of being assimilated; while on the other hand, in maintaining their traditional economic exploitation of the natural resources, they were asking for poverty.[18]

This community awakening also brought a shift in the relations between the Acadians and the English. During most of the nineteenth century the Acadians were able to preserve their values mostly because they lived in remote areas and, as such, had very few contacts with the English. The Acadian revendications, associated with their renewed nationalism, clashed with the English desire to maintain the status quo. With the increasing role of government, the Acadians sought more influence (for example, the teaching of French in public schools), which lead to deteriorating relations between the two groups. In asking for respect of its rights, the Acadians had to face an English backlash on many fronts. But in community projects which did not seek government action, the Acadians, left to themselves, did very well. They developed a system of higher education, and founded three newspapers: *Le Moniteur acadien* in 1867, *Le Courrier des Provinces maritimes* in 1885 and *L'Evangéline* in 1887. Hospitals were built with personnel from the Province of Quebec[19] and the Assomption Insurance Company was created in 1903.[20] As long as they used their own resources, they did not have problems in Acadianizing community sectors considered important. Some of them, feeling there was still one area yet to be Acadianized—politics— founded the Acadian party in 1972. Even though the party gained a lot of publicity by advocating the formation of an Acadian province in New Brunswick, its creation illustrated the desire to have a political platform of Acadian interests within the established governing framework.

The last four decades of the nineteenth century were ones of transition from an age of wood, wind and sail to one of iron, coal and rail. This dramatic economic development brought profound changes to the Maritimes: the "persistent depression and economic dislocation which characterized these years ... in much of the Maritimes provided the overriding motives for out-migration."[21] The coastal provinces became marginal while central Canada (Quebec and Ontario) prospered. This situation started off the emigration process in three directions. The first one drew people from rural areas to urban centres. The second migratory shift was directed towards the central Canadian provinces and the west, while the third one saw people leaving the Maritimes for the United States.[22]

For the period before the 1940s no official statistics exist on migration to and from the Maritimes, but some data can be collected from census records. The immigration office of the United States had enumerated the flow of emigrants from Canada. This information plus demographic calculations gives us the following figures for the number of emigrants leaving the maritimes:

Total Emigration from the Maritime Provinces, 1881-1941[23]

Census periods	Total emigration (minimum figures)
1881-1891	110,410
1891-1901	105,200
1901-1911	99,463
1911-1921	105,599
1921-1931	146,647
1931-1941	52,272
	619,591

A set of more accurate figures exists for the period 1941 to 1971:

Total Net Migration from the Maritime Provinces, 1941-71[24]

	1941-51	1951-56	1956-61	1961-71
Prince Edward Island	12,400	8,100	3,381	8,156
Nova Scotia	38,900	11,000	23,808	53,354
New Brunswick	41,600	20,900	16,200	60,875
Maritime Provinces	92,900	40,000	43,389	122,385

In the last half of the nineteenth century and until the Second World War, individuals of British stock were more inclined to emigrate than those of French origin. Starting with the depression this situation changed completely. The Acadians were then twice as likely to emigrate, feeling more acutely the disparity between their traditional economy and the industrial regions offering high salaries. A stagnant and, in certain cases, a decreased population is noticeable in counties having a majority of French-speaking people.[25]

During the 1970s we see a reversal of the out-migration in the three Maritime provinces; more people came than left.

Total Net Migration to the Maritime Provinces, 1971-76[26]

	1971-76
Prince Edward Island	3,963
Nova Scotia	14,919
New Brunswick	19,847
Maritime Provinces	38,729

Most of the influx of people to the region consisted of returning families who had migrated either to other provinces or the United States between 1945 and the early 1970s. As such, the region attracted few "new" immigrants. The bettering of economic conditions made the return easier for expatriates. Still a large percentage of young people left either because there were no jobs or because they were overqualified for available employment.[27]

Very few local emigration studies have been made. In one instance though, we can verify the accelerating process of loss of people in the small community of Pointe Sapin in the southeastern county of Kent, New Brunswick. From 1911 to 1941 the population grew from 420 to 770 but suffered a net emigration of 37 per cent; in the following three decades (1941-1971), the population decreased from 770 to 420 with a net emigration of 70 per cent.[28] Of those who left, 70 per cent did so before the age of twenty-five; and so the community lost those who were most likely to make a contribution.[29] This situation had serious consequences for the remaining francophones in New Brunswick as well as other provinces: future generations would be without the influence of those individuals who were directly involved in the Acadian survival process.

The marginal economy of the Maritimes resulted in a population exodus. This loss of population was detrimental to the natural growth of the Acadian community, which up until the Second World War had a relatively high birth rate and low level of emigration.

Relative Importance of the French Origin Population in the Maritime Provinces, 1871-1971[30]

Year	New Brunswick	Nova Scotia	Prince Edward Island	Maritime Provinces
	%	%	%	%
1871	15.7	8.5	—	—
1881	17.6	9.4	9.9	12.5
1891	—	—	—	—
1901	24.2	9.8	13.4	15.5
1911	28.0	10.5	14.0	17.5
1921	31.2	10.8	13.5	19.0
1931	33.6	11.0	14.7	20.5
1941	35.8	11.5	15.6	21.7
1951	38.3	11.5	15.7	22.8
1961	38.8	11.9	16.6	23.4
1971	37.0	10.2	13.7	21.5

Recent changes in demographic patterns seem to give a negative overtone to the future of francophones in Atlantic Canada. The Acadians seem to be losing ground. But figures do not tell the whole story. There is evidence of a cultural reawakening. An increased interest in economics and politics is creating a group sense of purpose among the Acadians. What the result will be is difficult to evaluate. In the past the Acadians were able to overcome their problems with resilience and fortitude. Why should it be any different today?

Notes

1. The best study on the Acadians is to be found in *Les Acadiens des Maritimes: études thématiques* (Moncton: Centre d'études acadiennes, 1980), 691 pages. The English edition *The Acadians of the Maritimes: Thematic Studies* will be available in late 1981.
2. See Jean Daigle, "L'Acadie, 1604-1763. Synthèse historique," in *Les Acadiens des Maritimes*, pp. 17-48.

3. Samuel Arsenault, Jean Daigle et al., *Atlas de l'Acadie. Petit Atlas des francophones des Maritimes* (Moncton: Editions d'Acadie, 1976), plate 15; and Jean-Claude Dupont, "Les Défricheurs d'eau," *Culture vivante* 27 (December 1972), pp. 6-9.

4. George Rawlyk, *Nova Scotia's Massachusetts. A Study of Massachusetts-Nova Scotia Relations, 1630 to 1784* (Montreal: McGill-Queen's University Press, 1973); Andrew Hill Clark, *Acadia: The Geography of Early Nova Scotia to 1760* (Madison: University of Wisconsin Press, 1968), pp. 178-85.

5. Naomi E.S. Griffiths, *The Acadians. Creation of A People* (Montreal: McGraw-Hill Ryerson, 1973), pp. 24-27.

6. W.S. MacNutt, "Why Halifax was founded," *Dalhousie Review* 12, no. 4 (1933), pp. 524-32.

7. Much has been published on the deportation. One would find it useful to consult the following bibliographies: *Bibliographie acadienne. Liste des volumes, brochures et thèses concernant l'Acadie et les Acadiens des débuts à 1975* (Moncton: Editions d'Acadie, 1976); *Bibliographie acadienne. Liste des articles de périodiques concernant l'Acadie et les Acadiens des débuts à 1976* (Moncton: Editions d'Acadie, 1977).

8. H. Bourde de la Rogerie, "Saint-Pierre-et-Miquelon des origines à 1778," *Le Bulletin de Granville*, 2nd series, no. 38, pp. 154-55.

9. Naomi E.S. Griffiths, "Acadians in Exile: The Experiences of the Acadians in the British Seaports," *Acadiensis* (Autumn 1974), pp. 67-84.

10. See Léon Thériault, "L'Acadie, 1763-1978. Synthèse historique," *Les Acadiens des Maritimes*, pp. 49-93.

11. Cited in W.S. MacNutt, *New Brunswick. A History: 1784-1867* (Toronto: MacMillan, 1963), p. 169.

12. Philippe Doucet, *Les Acadiens des Maritimes*, pp. 245-47.

13. This poem has been translated into twelve languages.

14. Edmé Rameau de Saint-Père, *La France aux Colonies: Acadiens et Canadiens* (Paris: A. Jouby, 1859).

15. Ferdinand J. Robidoux, *Recueil des travaux et délibérations des six premières conventions* (Shediac: Moniteur acadien, 1907).

16. *L'Impartial*, 10 July 1902, translation.

17. Ibid, 5 September 1911.

18. J. Goût and P. Mallet, "Les Acadiens entre l'assimilation et la pauvreté," *L'Evangéline*, 1, 2 and 3 March 1977.

19. Antoine Bernard, *Les Hospitalières de Saint-Joseph et leur oeuvre en Acadie* (Montreal: Les Hospitalières, 1958).

20. Euclide Daigle, *Petite histoire d'une grande idée* (Moncton: Assomption compagnie mutuelle, 1978).

21. Alan A. Brookes, "Out-migration from the Maritime Provinces, 1860-1900: Some Preliminary Considerations," *Acadiensis* (Spring 1976), p. 28.

22. See Chapter 4 on demography in *Les Acadiens d'aujourd'hui,* Report to the Royal Commission on Bilingualism and Biculturalism, 2 volumes (Ottawa, 1966).

23. Canada, Department of Trade and Commerce, *The Maritime Provinces in their Relation to the Economy of Canada* (Ottawa: King's Printer, 1948), p. 9.

24. Kari Levitt, *Population Movements in the Atlantic Provinces* (Halifax and Fredericton: Atlantic Provinces Research Board and Atlantic Provinces Economic Council, 1960), Table V; *1961 Census; International and Interprovincial Migrations in Canada* (Statistics Canada, 1977), pp. 107-08.

25. Levitt, *Population Movements,* Table XIII, p. 20; Table XIV, p. 21; and Table XIX, p. 31.

26. *International and Interprovincial Migrations in Canada,* pp. 107-08.

27. Muriel K. Roy, "Les Transferts linguistiques récents dans la population francophone du Nouveau-Brunswick," paper presented to the International Colloquium on Acadia, May 1978, Moncton, New Brunswick, p. 3.

28. Yvonne Robitaille, "L'Emigration de Pointe-Sapin, N.-B. (1945-1965). Caractéristiques des émigrants," paper presented to the 7th Meeting of Sociologists and Anthropologists of Atlantic Canada, Charlottetown, Prince Edward Island, March 1972, p. 6.

29. Ibid, p. 18.

30. Muriel K. Roy, "Peuplement et croissance démographique en Acadie," *Les Acadiens des Maritimes,* p. 180.

Emigration and Colonization: Twin Themes in Nineteenth-Century French Canadian Literature

David M. Hayne

Emigration was a fact of life and a continuing concern in Quebec throughout the nineteenth century. The socio-economic crises and adjustments of the period, so admirably documented in such studies as Fernand Ouellet's *Histoire économique et sociale du Québec, 1760-1850,* and Jean Hamelin and Yves Roby's *Histoire économique du Québec, 1851-1896,*[1] created situations from which an increasing number of French-speaking Canadians sought to escape by leaving their province of Lower Canada, or, after 1867, Quebec. Some few of these emigrants went west to Upper Canada or the prairies, but the vast majority of them crossed the border to the south, and the present paper will deal only with immigration to or through the United States.

This migration took many forms. Already in the first quarter of the century, the decline in agricultural prices after the Napoleonic Wars, the gradual exhaustion of arable land along the St. Lawrence, as a result of inefficient farming methods, and the endless subdividing of family farms held in seigneurial tenure served to aggravate the problems of large rural families in a population characterized by a high birth rate and a relatively low mortality rate. In the third decade of the century, the unsuccessful Rebellion of 1837-1838 resulted in banishments to Bermuda and Australia and in voluntary exile to the United States for many *patriotes* including the Lower-Canadian leader of the rebellion, Louis-Joseph Papineau. A decade later, the news of the discovery of gold at Sutter's Mill, California, in January 1848, spread like wildfire throughout North America, and young French Canadians were among the thousands who flocked to the region in the 1849 gold rush. In the 1860s, hundreds if not thousands of French-speaking Canadians fought for principle or for pay in the American armies clashing in the Civil War. A handful of French Canadians even joined Napoleon III's French expeditionary force in its ill-fated attempt to install Archduke Maximilian of Austria as France's puppet emperor in Mexico City. Some Quebec emigrants, attracted by offers of land grants, moved southwest to settle in the new states of Indiana (1816), Illinois (1818) and Michigan (1837). The largest number, however, sought work in the sawmills and textile factories of the New England states, particularly New Hampshire, Vermont, Massachusetts and Rhode Island.

Official recognition of immigration to the United States began in the 1830s. In his famous *Report* (1839), Lord Durham noted that, "From the French portion of Lower Canada there has, for a long time, been a large annual emigration of young men to the northern states of the American Union, in which they are highly valued as labourers, and gain good wages, with their savings, from which they generally return to their homes in a few months or years."[2] In 1849 a special committee of the Quebec Legislative Assembly (the Chauveau Committee) attempted to assess the extent of emigration by conducting an inquiry in the diocese of Montreal and in thirteen parishes of the diocese of Quebec. Eight years later (1857), the Dufresne Committee made a wider investigation, questioning the parish priests and notables of some sixty parishes. By this date it was estimated that about 100,000 Quebec residents had immigrated to the United States, but this figure was only approximate, based on incomplete investigation and distorted by the number of seasonal workers who re-entered the United States on several occasions. By the time the Chicoyne Committee reported in 1893, the estimates had reached several hundred thousand. Even today modern demographic research has not been able to provide an accurate total figure for the century. The studies made during the last decade by Albert Faucher, Jacques Henripin, Gilles Paquet and Yolande Lavoie included extremely sophisticated analyses based on United States Census figures and immigration records as well as Canadian statistics of various kinds, but were unable to resolve the question since the available records were so fragmentary, inconsistent or inaccurate. The most generally accepted estimates place the total number of Quebeckers immigrating to the United States during the nineteenth century at between 500,000 and 525,000, although some authorities would put the total at one million or more.

Private and public response to this haemorrhage of French Canadian society was chiefly of two kinds. In 1870 the provincial government launched a program of subsidized repatriation of emigrants wishing to return to Quebec, and the venture met with modest success. In the early 1870s an average of ten thousand persons a year took advantage of this opportunity, but by the 1880s the annual figure was a mere two or three thousand in a period when ten times that number were leaving the province each year.

A second and much more substantial response was the colonization movement, an immense but uncoordinated program carried out under both public and private auspices, the intention of which was to encourage and assist the clearing and settlement of unoccupied areas of the province. The first colonization societies were organized before the middle of the century, and soon government agents and subsidization programs were in place. The first colonization efforts were directed towards the more accessible regions: the Eastern Townships, the Saguenay and Saint Maurice valleys, and the Laurentian foothills north of Montreal. As these lands were taken up, the colonists moved further afield, up the Saguenay to Lac Saint Jean, north to Nominingue and even, in the twentieth century, into the wilderness of northwestern Quebec, to Temiscaming and Abitibi.

The colonization movement fitted in well with the clerico-nationalist ideology of Quebec in the second half of the nineteenth century. By keeping potential emigrants in the province, it assured the preservation of their French language and their Catholic faith. By exalting the simple agricultural life and the virtues of hard work and family solidarity, it perpetuated traditional moral standards and social values. Finally, by isolating the colonists in remote areas under the supervision of their missionary priests, colonization provided a bulwark against contact with Anglo-Saxon materialism and urban corruption. Thus colonization became not only the answer to emigration, but its opposite image: the positive values of colonization corresponded to the negative features of emigration.

It has been said that literature is the mirror a people holds up to itself, and this was never more true than in the case of the literature of nineteenth-century Quebec. From its first published works about 1830 to the end of the century, Quebec writing reflected the preoccupations of a linguistic community intent upon assuring its own survival in an often uncongenial environment. Since, as we have seen, emigration and colonization were dominant concerns of nineteenth-century Quebec society, they can be expected to have a prominent place in that society's literature.

Indeed, several of the more important Quebec writers of the period had some personal experience of emigration or exile. The author of one of Quebec's best novels of adventure, Georges Boucher de Boucherville, spent more than two years in voluntary exile in Louisiana after the rebellion. Antoine Gérin-Lajoie, whose novel *Jean Rivard* will be one of the principal documents for our study, tried his fortune in the United States as a young college graduate. So did French Canada's major nineteenth-century poet, Louis Fréchette; in fact, Fréchette subsequently moved to Chicago and lived there for five years, from 1866 to 1871, losing his manuscripts in the great Chicago fire of 1871. Another well-known poet of the century, the bookseller Octave Crémazie, was obliged to spend the last third of his life in exile in France after going bankrupt. Two widely-read secondary prose writers, Faucher de Saint-Maurice and Honoré Beaugrand, took part in the Mexican campaign: Beaugrand also lived for some years in both France and the United States.

Whether or not the author himself had experienced emigration or exile, he could not fail to have come in contact with the phenomenon, and the theme appears in French Canadian literature almost from its beginnings. Colonial literatures develop according to a pattern which seems almost invariable: the first writings are in verse, then prose fiction follows, and finally, often at a relatively late date, dramatic works are attempted. This is the sequence in nineteenth-century Quebec literature, and thus the emigration theme appears first in poetry.

The young French Canadians who tried to write verse in the 1830s did so under a double influence, that of French romantic literature and their own political environment. The French romantics were greatly concerned with the individual, and particularly the individual forced to flee society and country. Chateaubriand had described his own exile after the French Revolution, Balzac had written a novel about political outlaws (*Les Proscrits*, (1831), La Mennais wrote of the loneliness of exile in his *Paroles d'un croyant* (1834) and Théophile Gautier entitled one of his collections *Les Exilés* (c. 1835). In the midst of the political repression in Quebec in the 1830s, its youthful authors wrote dozens of poems on the theme of exile or banishment, as their titles reveal: "L'Expatrié dans l'infortune" (1835), "Aux exilés politiques" and "Les Exilés" (1838), "La Feuille au vent ou l'Exil" (1839), "Retour de l'exilé" (1842), "Rêve de l'exilé" (1844). One of these authors, Joseph-Guillaume Barthe, spent several months in prison for writing on this theme.

The most famous of the "exile" poems was composed in 1842 by a seventeen-year-old student, Antoine Gérin-Lajoie, to commemorate the banishment to Australia of fifty-eight *patriotes* in September 1839. First published under the title "Le Proscrit" (1844), it became popular under the opening line of its text, "Un Canadien errant." It was reprinted dozens of times and is still sung today as the best-known ballad from the rebellion period.

When the exiled rebels were exempted from further prosecution in 1843, the theme of political exile disappeared from poetry, but the wider concern over emigration replaced it. The first important poem on the twin subjects of emigration and colonization was Octave Crémazie's "Colonisation" (1853) in thirty six- and eight-line stanzas. In it Crémazie paid tribute to the half-dozen missionary priests who were already helping to settle the Eastern Townships, the Saguenay and the southern Lac Saint Jean region and deplored the indifference of the public and of the government of United Canada to the plight of the struggling colonists. Calling on his readers to give financial support to the colonization movement, "in order to keep young Canadians in this country" ("Pour garder au pays le jeune Canadien"), Crémazie stressed the fact that the future of the French race here would thus be assured. At the same time he urged the youth of Quebec to resist the gold rush and to cling to their native land. Ironically, this passage of the poem contains a moving stanza about the loneliness of the exile: when Crémazie wrote it, he little suspected that a decade later he would himself become a lonely exile. Crémazie's poem is an important text for the study of our theme, because it makes the reciprocal connection between emigration and colonization very clear, and it develops at some length the widely held conviction that emigration was an unpatriotic and disloyal act. Even at this early date the geographical basis of French Canadian nationalism is beyond dispute: being a Quebecker means living in Quebec.

The longest and most sentimental treatment of the emigration theme in poetry appeared in 1861. It was an 800-line narrative piece by Louis-Joseph-Cyprien Fiset entitled "Jude et Grazia, ou les Malheurs de l'émigration canadienne." (Note that in the nineteenth century, *canadien* means French Canadian, as opposed to *anglais* or Anglo-Saxon, English Canadian). Jude leaves the colonization district of the Saguenay to seek his fortune in Illinois; when he returns a year later, poorer and wiser, he finds his fiancée Grazia has died in the interval.

When Louis Fréchette immigrated to Chicago in 1866, he did so for both economic and political reasons. He had had little success either as a lawyer or as a journalist in Lévis, Quebec, and as an ardent Liberal he was disgusted by the Conservative party's manoeuvring to bring about Confederation. Thus, although one of his most sensational poetic works is entitled *La Voix d'un exilé* (1867-1869), it has little to do with exile or emigration; it is instead a scathing attack on Confederation and the "sordid band" of politicians who perpetrated it. Other poets of the 1870s and 1880s, however, dealt directly with the theme of emigration and/ or colonization in highly emotional verse. Benjamin Sulte included two such poems in his collection *Les Laurentiennes* (1870), one about French Canadian participation in the American Civil War ("Les Fils du Saint-Laurent") and the other about the wretchedness of the exile ("La Chanson de l'exilé"). William Chapman addressed poems to both Crémazie and Fréchette in their respective exiles in his collection *Les Québecquoises* (1876). Pamphile Le May included half a dozen poems on the themes of exile and emigration in *Une Gerbe* (1879); Adolphe Poisson (*Chants canadiens*, 1880), Adolphe Basile Routhier (*Les Echos,* 1882) and Napoléon Legendre (*Les Perce-neige,* 1886), among others, all considered the question deserving of poetic comment. The literary period in Quebec extending from 1860 to about 1890 had a number of common features, particularly a deep concern for patriotism, religion and the national past; emigration threatened all of these, and the poets used all their resources to dissuade their readers from it.

The poets had stressed the emotional wrench of leaving one's country; the novelists would attempt to propose alternatives to emigration. The first study of the question is found as early as the third novel written by a French Canadian, P.-J.-O. Chauveau's *Charles Guérin* (1846-1853). Chauveau was later to be the member of the legislature responsible for the 1857 special report on emigration, and after 1867 he was to become the first prime minister of the new Province of Quebec. The views expressed in his youthful novel are thus of particular interest. Chauveau cites two principal causes of emigration, the overcrowding of the four liberal professions (with priests, doctors, lawyers and notaries) and the shortage of arable land in the "old parishes," arising from the practice of bequeathing half the family farm to the eldest son, which left the other sons with inadequate holdings. Chauveau's response to the classical college graduate was to urge him to consider agriculture as a career, and to the younger sons of farmers he proposed the material and patriotic advantages of clearing new land with the help of colonization societies.

These matters are treated only incidentally in *Charles Guérin,* but a decade later Antoine Gérin-Lajoie made them the central concern of his two-volume novel *Jean Rivard* (1862-1864). Gérin-Lajoie also began by citing the overcrowding of the liberal professions and the lack of alternative opportunities for the educated youth of the time. His hero, Jean Rivard, leaves the classical college on his father's death and uses his modest inheritance to buy wooded land in the Eastern Townships, which he clears and develops as a prosperous farm. Before the end of the second volume, a new parish has sprung up around Jean Rivard's farm, and he is elected mayor of the village and eventually a member of the legislature for the new county soon to be created there. Although this "Horatio Alger" story is often naïve and contrived, Gérin-Lajoie, having already published two treatises on political economy, raised in his novel some serious questions: the unfair distribution of freehold lands, the unjust practices of speculators and absentee landholders, the inadequacy of the road system and the need for better government support, both financial and informational, for colonists. Gérin-Lajoie's novel was thus an effort to present in palatable form a colonization manual and a call for certain minimal reforms. *Jean Rivard* enjoyed wide popularity during the last quarter of the century, and thousands of copies were distributed as school prizes in the province. After the publication of *Jean Rivard,* the ideological pattern was clear: emigration was financially risky, a threat to religion and morality, unpatriotic and anti-national ("La pensée d'émigrer, de s'expatrier, lui venait bien quelquefois, mais il la repoussait aussitôt comme anti-patriotique, anti-nationale"[3]). Agriculture and colonization, on the other hand, were divinely ordained, healthy, profitable, satisfying, patriotic and in the national interest.

These same attitudes are apparent in dozens of novels and short stories written throughout the second half of the nineteenth century. In them we can trace the stages of emigration year by year. The first examples appear about 1860 and are concerned with the California gold rush: in Paul Steven's "L'Emigration ou Pierre Souci" (1860), the young hero leaves for California but has one mishap after another and returns to Quebec vowing to devote himself to farming. In Pamphile Le May's "L'Epreuve" (1863), a Lotbinière farmer goes off in search of gold, leaving his young wife and children in poverty during his years of absence. Only one minor author, Charles-Alfred-Napoléon Leclère, allows his main characters to return wealthy from California, and both are reformed alcoholics whose virtue must be rewarded ("Tic-Toc ou le Doigt de Dieu," 1866; "Pas une goutte de plus, Bruno," 1869). The more typical outcome is that of Ernest Gagnon's "Boisvert" (1892): five young French Canadians leave for the gold-fields, but three perish on the way and the other two come back as poor as before. Similarly in Le May's *Fantôme* (1895), the returning gold-seeker, despite some success, has a tragic tale to tell.

After the gold rush, the next American event to figure in novels and short stories was the Civil War, but it only became a fictional setting in the 1870s and 1880s when it had acquired a certain nostalgic perspective. Vinceslas-Eugène Dick used it incidentally in his tangled adventure novel *Le Roi des étudiants* in 1876. Eight years later, Rémi Tremblay, who had spent eighteen months in the Northern armies from 1863 to 1865, six of them as a prisoner of the Confederates, published a disguised autobiographical novel, *Un Revenant,* to recount his adventures. That same year Napoléon Legendre published a story entitled "Paul et Julien" in which a French Canadian volunteer returns from the Civil War wounded and disillusioned, and in 1888 Louis Fréchette used the same motif of wounding in his short tale "Entre nous."

France's campaign in Mexico was treated more positively by the two major French Canadian participants. Faucher de Saint-Maurice's two-volume autobiographical account, *De Québec à Mexico* (1866-1867), although not fiction, was as readable as a novel and was republished five times before the end of the century. Honoré Beaugrand's story "Anita" (1878) was a thinly disguised version of one of his own experiences in Mexico; and here again the author, although not sympathetic to the Mexicans, does not appear to have regretted his service in their country.

The gold rush, the American Civil War and the Mexican campaign all had a certain exotic appeal for writers, but the more realistic form of emigration used in fiction writing was the exodus to industrial New England. Frequently the migration separated lovers, either because of parental opposition to their marriage (Eugène L'Ecuyer, "Une Lingère de Montréal," 1849), the indifference of the young lady (C.-A.-N. Leclère, "Le Vieux Berlot bleu," 1869), or the young swain's desire to make his fortune (P.

Le May, "Mariette," 1890; Régis Roy, "Le P'tit Maxime," 1893).
On more than one occasion the disillusioned emigrant returned to
find his beloved dead, dying or married to another; he thus
suffered a double penalty for his defection. The case of Antoine
Bouet in V.-E. Dick's *L'Enfant mystérieux* (1890) is typical of
many others: "... pendant quatre années, Antoine végéta dans
les manufactures de la Nouvelle-Angleterre, travaillant dur, gag-
nant peu et dépensant tout. ... la désillusion étant complète, il
songea au retour."[4]

In the midst of this chorus of denunciation, only one novelist
dared to defend the emigrants. Although not encouraging expa-
triation, Honoré Beaugrand tried in *Jeanne la fileuse* (1875) to
show that emigration was primarily a socio-economic phenomenon, not a betrayal, and he loaded his text with statistics and
documents to demonstrate that in many cases emigration made
economic sense for the migrant unable to find comparable employment in Quebec. But Beaugrand's was a voice crying in the
wilderness; no other French Canadian writer of fiction in the
century achieved such objectivity.

The evidence from the theatre serves only to confirm the unan-
imity of voices raised against emigration. As might be expected,
the dramatic texts come later in the century, beginning in 1880
with two plays by Louis Fréchette dealing with the rebellion and
post-rebellion years. His *Papineau* is an attempt to rehabilitate the
patriote leader discredited after his flight to the United States; the
second play, *Le Retour de l'exilé,* is an adaptation—Fréchette's
contemporaries said a plagiarism—of a French novel dealing with
the experiences of a returning exile whose property has been
wrested from him. Incidental references to emigration are found
also in two comedies by Pamphile Le May and by Régis Roy. Le
May's *Sous les bois* (1891) depicts a French Canadian family
settling in Minnesota and finding there a long-lost emigrant son,
and his *En livrée* ends happily when a farm worker receives news
of an inheritance left by his uncle in California. And in Régis
Roy's one-act farce *L'Auberge du no 3* (1899), an Americanized
French Canadian returns to Quebec after working in the factories
of Massachusetts.

But at least two plays of this period, both written by priests,
deal extensively with the emigration question or with its opposite
pole, colonization. The first, by a French Jesuit, Father Edouard
Hamon, is significantly entitled *Exil et patrie* (1882). In its five
acts a Quebec family emigrating to Boston suffers one crushing
disaster after another: the mother dies, a son abandons his reli-

gion and his family, a daughter contracts tuberculosis in her factory and the father loses his savings in a railway speculation. As the last straw, a son is injured in a strike at his plant, and the family, having no further resources, returns to Quebec. In the last act the family's fortunes are miraculously transformed as they settle in a colonization area at Nominingue (about sixty-five miles north of Montebello), and all ends happily for the new colonists. Abbé Jean-Baptiste Proulx's play *Les Pionniers du lac Nominingue* (1883) is a similarly didactic piece in favour of colonization in the Nominingue district. A farmer from Sainte-Thérèse and his eldest son clear a farm there and prosper, while his two younger sons, who had immigrated to New England and Colorado, spend four fruitless years before admitting failure and joining their father at Nominingue. The subtitle of the play, "Les Avantages de la colonisation," is thus justified by the turn of events. In a curious early example of intertextuality, the author incorporates into his play references to characters of Gérin-Lajoie's novel *Jean Rivard* and allusions to Crémazie's poem "Colonisation."

Quite apart from this extensive use of the emigration/colonization theme in creative writings of the century, there are the many essays and pamphlets on the subject—too abundant, indeed, to be treated in a short paper, but a few names must be mentioned.

The first notable writer on colonization was the printer and journalist Stanislas Drapeau, who founded the Société de colonisation de Québec in 1856. In a pamphlet published two years later, he proclaimed the national importance of the cause of colonization, and in 1863 he compiled a detailed history of the progress of colonization during the decade of the 1850s (*Etudes sur les développements de la colonisation du Bas-Canada depuis dix ans, 1851-1861*) and began a new career as a government colonization agent. In later life he wrote a colonization manual for European immigrants (*Canada. Le Guide du colon français, belge, suisse, etc.,* 1887), which for many francophone immigrants was their first introduction to Canada.

The chief figure in the colonization movement wrote very little, although much was written for him and about him. He was the giant priest François-Xavier-Antoine Labelle, the "King of the North" who, as curé of Saint Jérôme, north of Montreal, from 1868 to his death in 1891, was responsible for founding some sixty new settlements and for the building of two railroads into the north. So effective were his efforts that Prime Minister Honoré Mercier of Quebec named him deputy minister for colonization in

1888. Labelle made two extended trips to France to attract immigrants, and the huge priest with his stirring eloquence became a legend wherever he went. His travels and achievements were reported on by his companion, Abbé Jean-Baptiste Proulx (*Le Curé Labelle et la colonisation*, 1885; *Cinq mois en Europe, ou Voyage du curé Labelle en France en faveur de la colonisation*, 1888; etc.), and were written up by his publicist and admirer, Arthur Buies, who produced a dozen books in the fifteen years between 1880 and 1895. Buies's guide-books and descriptive accounts of the Laurentians, the Ottawa Valley, the Saguenay and Lac Saint Jean regions, and the Matapedia Valley are classics of nineteenth-century travel literature and are still among the most readable accounts that we have of the geographical areas of Quebec.

Even more popular than the works of Buies, at least in rural areas, were the agricultural manuals published by the Oblate Father Zacharie Lacasse. Inexpensively printed and widely distributed throughout the province, Lacasse's five little books, all of which promised a mine of information in their titles (*Une mine produisant l'or et l'argent*, 1880; etc.), presented the advantages of the agricultural life. "If by my writings I could prevent a single one of my compatriots from leaving for the States," Lacasse wrote, "I should be satisfied." His wish may well have been granted because his first book was reprinted seven times in one year, and all five sold thousands of copies.

The last two books that require mention appeared in the 1890s and dealt specifically with emigration. Father Edouard Hamon, author of the play *Exil et patrie*, who had published two articles on the topic in the French Jesuit magazine *Etudes*, was invited by Cardinal Elzéar-Alexandre Taschereau to expand his account into a book, which he did in 1891 under the title *Les Canadiens français de la Nouvelle-Angleterre*. Although deploring the migration of French Canadians to New England, Hamon sympathetically described the emigrants' continued efforts to preserve their language and their Catholic faith in the New England setting, where 120 churches and chapels were by that time being served by French Canadian clergy. The other work was a study by the ex-papal-Zouave Charles-Edouard Rouleau entitled *L'Emigration: ses principales causes* (1896), which called for greater efforts of will on the part of Quebec farmers. Like others before him, Rouleau saw emigration primarily as a moral and patriotic problem rather than an economic one.

This rapid survey of nineteenth-century French Canadian liter-

ature concerned with the theme of immigration to or through the
United States suggests several conclusions: (i) that the theme is
mentioned or treated at length in a considerable number of literary texts from 1835 on, with the greatest number falling between
1860 and 1890, the period usually referred to as the Quebec
Movement or Movement of 1860; (ii) that the theme occurs in all
genres: poetry, fiction, drama and essays, with particular frequency in fiction; (iii) that, with the sole exception of Beaugrand's novel *Jeanne la fileuse,* the literary allusions to emigration
are invariably unfavourable on ideological grounds; (iv) that the
only solution consistently proposed is colonization, which is invariably presented in ideologically positive terms; (v) that these
themes are frequently linked in reciprocal fashion, the negative
aspects of emigration being compensated for by the positive values of colonization; (vi) that the emigration/colonization theme
offers further confirmation of the essentially didactic character of
much nineteenth-century Quebec literature.

Notes

1. Fernand Ouellet, *Histoire économique et social du Québec, 1760-1850*
   (Montreal: Fides, 1966); Jean Hamelin and Yves Roby, *Histoire
   économique du Québec, 1851-1896* (Montreal: Fides, 1971). Further
   bibliographical information about the titles cited in the paper may
   be found in the following reference works:

   Boivin, Aurélien. *Le Conte littéraire québécois au XIXe siècle: essai
   de bibliographie critique et analytique.* Montreal: Fides, 1975.

   Dictionnaire des oeuvres littéraires du Québec, I; des origines à 1900.
   Sous la direction de Maurice Lemire. . . . Montreal: Fides, 1978.

   Lortie, Jeanne d'Arc. *La Poésie nationaliste au Canada français
   (1606-1867).* Vie des lettres québécoises 13. Quebec City: Les Presses
   de l'Université Laval, 1975.

2. G.M. Craig, ed., *Lord Durham's Report* (Toronto: McClelland and
   Stewart, c. 1963), p. 136.

3. Gérin-Lajoie, *Jean Rivard le défricheur,* pp. 13-14.

4. Dick, *L'Enfant mystérieux* I, p. 65.

The Acadiens and Quebecois in the United States

The Rise and Fall of Félix Albert: Some Reflections on the Aspirations of Habitant Immigrants to Lowell, Massachusetts in the Late Nineteenth Century*

Frances H. Early

John Higham, the noted American scholar of immigrant history, once remarked, "The immigrant is not ... a colonist or settler who creates a new society and lays down the terms of admission for others. He is rather the bearer of a foreign culture."[1] The implication of this remark is, of course, that the historian must understand the immigrant's society of origin before he or she can understand the immigrant. Unfortunately, American historians have often failed in this task. Instead, they have generally erroneously assumed that most nineteenth-century immigrants to America came from fairly static, pre-industrial, self-sufficient agricultural societies and were, therefore, imbued with pre-capitalist "traditional" behaviour patterns and beliefs. Historians of the Irish, the Italians and the French Canadians have all fallen into this trap.[2]

The current generation of social-immigrant historians rejects this uni-dimensional view of immigrant origins. Scholars now argue that most immigrants came from societies, which although predominantly rural and agrarian, were hardly pre-capitalist and traditional.[3] Quebec provides a case in point.

In the course of the nineteenth century, Quebec society underwent a tremendous amount of socio-economic change.[4] Its populace experienced a demographic-agricultural crisis of enormous

---

*Author's note: Thanks are extended to Jack Little for his helpful comments on an earlier draft of this paper.

proportions as well as the beginnings of significant industrialization. These developments modified older rural-based economic and social structures and values and helped to create a land of large contrasts. In such circumstances habitant life must have varied greatly throughout the province. Unlike its economic history, however, the social history of Quebec is still largely unwritten. We know very little about the "plain people" of this century. For this reason it is difficult to generalize about the life experiences and values the average French Canadian habitant carried with him or her from Quebec to a city like Lowell, Massachusetts in the latter decades of the nineteenth century.

Fortunately during one of my research trips to Lowell I came across an autobiography of an habitant who immigrated to the city in 1880. *Histoire d'un enfant pauvre* allows us an intimate look at the shape and texture of one man's life, Félix Albert, first in Quebec and later in New England. His story is important because it provides crucial insights into the habitant way of life in a period of extreme economic crisis in Quebec (1830s-1870s). In addition to describing material existence at the time, it reveals much about habitant culture. This autobiography, then, helps the historian to understand the "cultural baggage" which French Canadian immigrants took with them to the United States. As this paper will demonstrate, Félix Albert arrived in Massachusetts with a well-developed work ethic and a petty-bourgeois consciousness which was rooted in the Quebec habitant experience and helped him to survive, even to prosper briefly, in a new and very different setting, urban-industrial Lowell.

Félix Albert was born in 1843 of habitant parents (Fermin and Céleste) in the old seigneury of Ile Verte,* situated along the St. Lawrence about twenty miles north of Rivière du Loup in what was at that time Rimouski County (it became Témiscouata County in 1854).[5] Twelve years before Félix's birth, Joseph Bouchette, the surveyor general of Lower Canada, described Ile Verte and neighbouring parishes as thriving farm communities peopled with prosperous habitant families.[6] This government official also noted, however, that in Ile Verte a certain proportion of habitants held more land than they could cultivate which deprived "young labourers of the power to obtain lands."[7] In this same year information collected for the 1831 Census modified this picture. The census enumerator reported that in Ile Verte parish roughly 4 in 10 of the 152 habitant families owned more

---

* Now Isle Verte.

than 100 arpents of land (one arpent equals approximately five-sixths of an acre). However, almost 6 in 10 families, and this includes the Albert family, owned less than 100 arpents of land.[8] Many of these latter farms did not yield enough to support families adequately. Fermin Albert, Félix's father, reported that on his eighty-four-arpent farm only sixteen arpents had been under cultivation in the previous year, and the poor soil resulted in a small harvest: 42 minots of potatoes, 36 minots of rye, 16 minots of wheat, 11 minots of barley, and 9 minots of peas (a minot equals approximately 1.10 bushels). Although they also raised livestock— 9 sheep, 5 horned cattle and 6 pigs—this added food source was probably not enough to provide an adequate living for a family of eleven.[9]

Félix's reminiscences reveal that the Alberts, like other families in the area, survived on their exhausted land only because of the supplementary income the children could earn from time to time by working as day labourers for better-off farmers or as woodsmen in the lumber industry.[10] Félix was the youngest of sixteen children. In 1842 one year before Félix's birth, Fermin reported to the census enumerator that he had managed to cultivate only three acres that year;[11] farm yields could hardly provide adequate sustenance for the Albert household. During the 1840s as Fermin and Céleste's older children grew up and moved off the family farm to establish their own households, the Alberts found it increasingly difficult to keep the farm going. In the early 1850s Fermin sold the farm, and he, Céleste, two daughters and young Félix moved to a small plot of land which an older son owned in Ile Verte. Félix and his father worked the land as well as a rented piece of property for a few years. Félix, already a budding entrepreneur at age ten, augmented the family income by selling apples which the local blacksmith procured for him in Quebec City.[12] In 1857 when Félix was fourteen, he, his father and one other brother decided, on the advice of the parish priest, to take up colonization land in St. Eloi, a newly established parish six miles from Ile Verte.

Félix's memoirs for this period portray the life of a colonization family quite graphically: unremitting back-breaking work, material and social deprivations and months of anxiety each year over the threat of early frost and ruined crops. Nevertheless, the Alberts succeeded on this land after a fashion. By selling the timber they felled they survived the first arduous years.[13] Eight years after the Alberts had first taken up their colonization land, Félix, by this time in his early twenties, was able to state proudly that that autumn they had harvested 300 minots of grain and their barn sheltered 4 dairy cattle, 2 horses, 12 sheep and several pigs.[14]

In the following years Félix established himself as the head of the Albert farm. His brother left the land to work in the lumber mills. In February 1866 Félix, at twenty-three, married seventeen-year-old Desneiges Michaud of St. Arsène, Rivière du Loup County. They soon began to raise a family—one child arrived on average every eighteen months.[15] Fermin, and later Céleste, died. The Alberts generally enjoyed good harvests, although some years early frosts wreaked their vengeance. They built up a stock of animals and accumulated some savings.[16] By the 1870s Félix was even hiring workers—he commented tellingly at one point that there were "beaucoup de pauvres gens qui avaient besoin de travailler."[17] At this time the Alberts went into the dairy business; Félix noted that one year their fourteen milch cows provided 800 pounds of butter which sold at twenty-five cents a pound.[18] Félix then confidently hired more workers to help in the construction of a bigger house for his growing family.[19]

At this point catastrophe—in the form of an early frost—hit. Two-thirds of the wheat crop was destroyed—a crop which, if successfully harvested, would have sold on the market for between $1,200 and $1,500, according to Félix.[20] The situation was grim. Félix had workers to pay, and the price of butter was abnormally low that year. Nevertheless, he found a way out. By working "dans le bois," he pulled his family through the winter months.[21] The next hay harvest, which Félix sold to nearby sawmills, saved the Alberts. Two good years followed, and Félix decided he was ready to try his fortune "encore une fois."[22]

At this juncture in the late 1870s, Félix bought for a pittance two lots of forest land, located two miles from his farm. He, along with some hired hands, cleared twenty-four arpents which they seeded with wheat. Here Félix was following the example of one of his brothers who had also recently cleared new land in the vicinity; this brother had harvested 700 minots of wheat which he sold at two dollars per minot. Félix was not so furtunate. Lack of rain ruined the crop.[23] Even though Félix did not realise it, this was his next-to-last attempt at farming for many years. He became quite depressed and demoralized, a state of mind he shared with other struggling habitant neighbours. The forced exodus of habitants, from the settled parishes surrounding St. Eloi into backwoods colonization lands or into areas where work in the timber industry could be procured, is a strong theme in *Enfant pauvre.*[24]

One day, after consulting with a neighbour who was on his way to Ottawa to work in the sawmills, Félix, too, decided to leave St. Eloi. Since his wife, Desneiges, had a relative in Caribou, Maine, Félix elected to seek winter employment there for himself and for one of his young farm-hands. He outfitted himself as a pedlar and sold houseware goods along the way to Caribou. Once in Caribou Félix placed the lad he had brought with him in a sawmill. Next he bought some land with the help of his wife's relative. Then Félix, not having found work for himself, returned home with needed provisions for his family and $200 cash (profits from the sale of his goods). This trip was undertaken in January. In March Félix returned to Caribou to pick up his hired boy (and collect his wages, which he pocketed). Félix managed to sell the land he had purchased two months before at a profit and returned to St. Eloi for the approaching growing season. This time wheat rust rather than frost or lack of rain ruined the crop.[25]

Finally Félix threw up his hands in despair, and after securing a lukewarm blessing from his parish priest to resettle in New England, he, his wife and children boarded a train headed south. After a brief stopover in Sherbrooke to visit a relative, the Alberts found themselves in the bustling textile city of Lowell, Massachusetts.[26]

What kind of person was Félix Albert in 1880, the year he and his family found themselves on a train headed for Lowell? Félix was thirty-seven years old. From his early youth his character and outlook on life had been shaped primarily by his existence as a capitalist-minded habitant. Though forced by sheer necessity, even as a child, to seek secondary employment from time to time as a hired farm-hand, a woodsman, or a pedlar, Félix had always clung tenaciously to the land and saw his future in farming. He willingly helped with his father's colonization effort in St. Eloi. And when the farmland, which he inherited from his father, was exhausted, he tried to begin a new farm on nearby colonization land.[27]

Besides wishing to stay on the land, Félix wanted to remain in the region where he had been born and raised.[28] For a while he succeeded. Like many of his fellow habitants, Félix availed himself of the way of life necessary for those who wished to stay: colonization of the surrounding wilderness in conjunction with part-time employment in the woods. However, as the years went by, good colonization land in the region became scarce; work in the woods could not support a large family year round. Thus, Félix, like many others, had to uproot himself and seek his livelihood elsewhere.

Félix had grown up knowing that inequalities in wealth, status and opportunities existed. In Ile Verte a small minority of habitants owned many acres of land and doubtless prospered, while another small minority owned very little land and surely just scraped along.[29] Félix's family situation resembled that of the struggling small-scale semi-subsistence families in Ile Verte. But because success models did exist, Félix felt he had a chance to "make it" as a commercial farmer in St. Eloi.

Certain character traits helped the habitant endure and even prevail: a sense of independence, a willingness to work hard, tenacity, frugality and patience. Félix appears to possess these necessary "virtues." Nevertheless, a careful reading of *Enfant pauvre* reveals a person whose frugality shaded into parsimony (perhaps necessarily so) and whose patience could occasionally be tried to the breaking point. Further, Félix had a driving will to succeed and by the time he was thirty-seven this ambitiousness had acquired a hard, calculative edge. His character reflected the imperatives of a market economy reinforced by the embattled quality of his life. It is important to keep these observations in mind as we follow Félix through the next stage of his life in Lowell.

In the census year 1870, Lowell, Massachusetts had a population of 41,000 and was the second-largest textile manufacturing city in the United States. Three in every four working people earned their living in manufacturing establishments or as common labourers. Sixty-five per cent of the population was American, 22 per cent was Irish, 4 per cent was English and 3 per cent was from Scotland, Nova Scotia, New Brunswick, Newfoundland, Prince Edward Island, and elsewhere. In addition in 1870, 6 per cent of Lowell's citizenry was Canadian (from Lower and Upper Canada), in large measure French Canadian. In the next years French Canadians would come in increasing numbers; by 1881 approximately 11,000 French Canadians lived in Lowell, 18 per cent of the total population of 60,000.[30]

In 1880, when the Albert family journeyed to Lowell, the French Canadian community there was small but thriving. It already had a parish church (established in 1868) with a French-speaking Oblate father. Various church-related benefit associations and social circles existed. French Canadians had also established two neighbourhoods in Lowell, and a Petit Canada was developing on what had once been marshland.[31]

The way French Canadians earned their living at this time was largely determined by age and sex. Women and children laboured in the textile mills near their tenement homes six days a week, while men found employment as common labourers, or less frequently as skilled craftsmen. A small minority of men worked in the mills; an even smaller group owned small stores or craft shops or followed a profession.[32]

When Félix Albert and his wife and nine children stepped off the train in Lowell in 1880, no one they knew was there to meet them. To their knowledge none of their acquaintances or relatives resided in Lowell. Félix's brother in Sherbrooke had recommended Lowell over Fall River, another Massachusetts textile town where the Alberts had first intended to go, because there were fewer labour strikes in Lowell than in Fall River, and so they could be assured steadier employment.[33]

Although the Alberts arrived in Lowell friendless, Félix wasted no time in making acquaintances. In fact upon arrival at the train depot, he engaged in a conversation with a fellow countryman, Jules Tremblay, who offered to assist the Alberts. To quote Félix, "[Mr. Tremblay] offered to let me stay with him for a few days while I looked for accommodations. He, like me, had a large family, and we made a jolly group in one lodging. We spent a few days with Mr. Tremblay. Then we found a home.... "[34]

Once established in a small rented flat, Félix found factory employment for four of his children. Since the oldest child was fourteen, the youngest employed Albert child must have been nine or ten. Félix had been engaged in heavy farm and lumbering work at this young age himself and doubtless felt it proper that his children contribute their labour towards the sustenance of the family. This was certainly the attitude of most French Canadian immigrant parents at this time: seven in every ten children between the ages of ten and sixteen laboured full-time in the textile factories.[35]

Félix, like many other immigrant men, initially found it difficult to secure employment for himself. But he did manage to procure temporary work, first as a woodcutter, then as a construction worker.[36] Old patterns of survival, learned in Quebec, soon came to his rescue. With money earned from his construction job and, presumably, from his children's wages, Félix purchased a six-acre wood lot which was located four miles from Lowell; he also bought an old horse and a broken-down wagon. By working long, gruelling days—chopping wood and carting it to Lowell—Félix earned four to five dollars a day (as a construction worker he made $1.50 or $1.75 a day).[37] By the end of the year his earnings and those of his children allowed Félix to return to St. Eloi briefly with $375 in gold coins, which he used to clear up his debts and to secure his land there.[38]

The next few years brought a large measure of success to Félix. After woodcutting and carting, he moved into building tenements and rented them to newly arrived French Canadian immigrants. He also opened a second-hand furniture business on the ground floor of one of his tenement buildings as well as a grocery store. He built his own stables to shelter his hack and horses.[39] These projects Félix accomplished gradually. As the years passed, Félix and his family became comfortable in their new home. A momentous decision was reached: the Alberts decided to reside permanently in the United States, and Félix sold the farm in St. Eloi, now worth very little, for next to nothing. By this time—the late 1880s and early 1890s—many young people and whole families, like the Alberts, had left St. Eloi.[40]

During this period Félix became known in the French Canadian community as *l'habitant*. When French Canadians first arrived in Lowell at the train station they heard about Félix. According to *l'habitant* himself:

> Several people with whom I had done business returned home, and when some of their acquaintances came to Lowell, these people told them, if you go to Lowell ask for l'habitant. He is a man with whom one can do business; it is very easy to arrange things with him.[41]

Eventually Félix went in person to the railroad station to meet his "clients"; he was not one to underestimate his importance for French Canadian newcomers:

> When people arrived from Canada I went to meet them at the train station. I sold them furniture and I lodged them in my tenements. When I did not have any vacancies, I knew where there were some and I directed people there. In this way, the name of l'habitant became well known.[42]

Félix's ascendancy to status and power in the French Canadian community was abruptly curtailed during the Panic of 1893. Once again he had overreached himself. As was the custom among shopkeepers and small businessmen in New England as well as in Quebec, Félix had extended credit liberally to many regular store customers; he also had debts of his own which he had contracted in the course of his business dealings. Félix was cash poor. The depression which followed in the wake of the 1893 panic all but ruined Félix. His French Canadian customers were unemployed and could not pay their bills. Félix, who had fixed mortgage payments to make, was forced to liquidate his assets in order to pay off his creditors. In what Félix considered to be the final indignity, he watched many of his goods sold at public auction. At the time of the auction, Félix was convinced people were laughing at him; he was mortified by what he perceived to be a complete loss of face.[43]

Nonetheless, Félix, doggedly tenacious as always, managed to pull through this trial. He recovered enough money to buy a farm on the outskirts of town.[44] Hence in 1894, at the age of fifty-one, *l'habitant* had apparently come full circle: he was back on the land. From 1894 to 1909 (the year *Enfant pauvre* was published) the Albert family earned a modest living from the soil. Significantly, Félix insisted upon maintaining a wood business, as a sideline, on his farm.[45] In a sense, then, he continued the Quebec tradition of working *dans le bois* as an insurance policy against calamity.

As he approached old age Félix became ever more suspicious of others and miserly. He probably cheated one of his hired hands out of his rightful wages, and he refused to entrust his eldest son with increasing responsibility for running the farm.[46] The upshot of this was that his son left home for a number of years. When he eventually returned, Félix dithered around over the inheritance question until the son issued an ultimatum: transfer the farm to his name immediately, or he would leave again, this time for good. Félix's reaction reveals much about what kind of person he had become. He recounted in his autobiography the following conversation with Desneiges (one of the few glimpses we have of Mrs. Albert and obviously coloured here by Félix's thinking):

"What do you think?" I asked my wife.
"If you're a fool, give him [the son] everything."
"I'm no fool."
"Alors, garde ton bien."[47]

The oft celebrated French Canadian family solidarity was, in this case, a shambles. Although Félix had been parsimonious and calculating in St. Eloi, the life he had led in Lowell and the experiences he had had as a struggling petty-bourgeois businessman seem to have heightened or exacerbated the negative qualities of his character.

Félix's life was in many ways a tragedy. Born into grinding poverty, he struggled against difficult odds, often quite courageously, to make his way in the world. But in the end he was defeated if we consider the manner of man he became in his old age: mistrustful, even of his own family, stingy and embittered. His tragic flaw was that he allowed his understandable desire for economic security for himself and his family to become a rather ruthless drive for material wealth.

It is important to see Félix's tragedy in terms of the kind of society and culture which first formed him. Félix inherited a work ethic—ambition, tenacity and hard work—from his Quebec rural culture. This work ethic went hand in hand with a profit-minded approach to farming, a consciousness which in Félix's lifetime was tied intimately to the realities of Quebec's agro-forest market economy. When Félix moved to Lowell, he was already an "expectant capitalist" who had experienced hardship and disappointment but was nonetheless ready to plunge into the hurly-burly world of getting-and-spending.[48]

Most French Canadians who came to Lowell and to other New England mill towns in these years did not experience the petty-bourgeois career which Félix had. Opportunities in this respect were limited. Instead, most French Canadians were proletarianized: women and children as well as some men became mill workers, while most men became common labourers. Nevertheless a few, like Félix, became businessmen (or professionals). Research on Lowell French Canadians indicates that businessmen were generally self-made; that is, they often came to the City of Spindles as disinherited, penniless habitants. They achieved a certain material success and social status within a limited opportunity structure because they possessed a capitalist work ethic like Félix. Indeed, to be more accurate, we need to say a capitalist *family* work ethic because it was the labour and wages of children as well as the boarding services and fees of home-based mothers, which generally supplied the needed capital for the business ventures of fathers.[49]

We cannot, of course, assume that Félix's character, values and aspirations reflect those of all other French Canadian immigrants in this era. Nevertheless, when placed in the context of nineteenth-century rural Quebec society and culture, the autobiography of *un enfant pauvre* goes far to dispel the still-lingering image of the French Canadian as a "traditional peasant" with "low horizons of expectations."[50]

Notes

1. John Higham, quoted in Thomas Kessner, *The Golden Door: Italian and Jewish Immigrant Mobility in New York City, 1880-1915* (New York, 1977), p. 24.

2. See for instance the two well-known works by Oscar Handlin, *Boston's Immigrants* (Cambridge, 1941), and *The Uprooted* (Boston, 1951). On French Canadians see Jacques Ducharme, *The Shadows of the Trees* (New York, 1943).

3. See Rudolph J. Vecoli, "*Contadini* in Chicago: A Critique of the Uprooted," *Journal of American History* 51 (December 1964), pp. 404-17; Virginia Yans McLaughlin, "Patterns of Work and Family Organization: Buffalo's Italians," *Journal of Interdisciplinary History* 2 (Autumn 1971), pp. 299-314; and Kessner, *Golden Door*.

4. Fernand Ouellet, *Histoire économique et social du Québec, 1760-1850* (Montreal, 1966), and Jean Hamelin and Yves Roby, *Histoire économique du Québec, 1851-1896* (Montreal, 1971).

5. Félix's year of birth is given incorrectly as 1833 in his autobiography. Birth records (ANQ-Q, CE 3-2/3, Etat civil Saint-Jean-Baptiste-de-l'île-Verte, 1843, f. 20) reveal that he was born 1 June 1843.

6. Joseph Bouchette, *The British Dominions in North America* 1 (London, 1832; reprint New York, 1968), pp. 316 and 318.

7. Ibid., vol. 2, Appendix, not paginated.

8. Manuscript census returns for the parish of Ile Verte, Lower Canada, 1831.

9. Ibid. It was estimated at the time that subsistence living for one person was 16 minots of wheat annually. See Fernand Ouellet, "Répartition de la propriété foncière et types d'exploitation agricole dans le seigneurie de Laprairie durant les années 1830," *Eléments d'histoire sociale du Bas Canada* (Montreal, 1972), pp. 113-49, esp. 138. Thus, the Alberts would have required 176 minots of grain (16 minots × 11 people), or the equivalent in other food sources. Their harvest of 63 minots of grain, even with the addition of peas and potatoes and livestock, was probably inadequate. See also Gauldrée-Boilleau, in *Paysans et ouvriers québécois d'autrefois*, ed. Pierre Savard (Quebec, 1968), pp. 48-51. Gauldrée-Boilleau found that a habitant family of nine, living in St. Irénée, Charlevoix in the 1850s, survived adequately on an annual wheat harvest of 165 minots.

10. Félix Albert, *Histoire d'un enfant pauvre* (Nashua, New Hampshire, 1909), pp. 8, 12-13, 19. On the importance of the timber industry to the habitant colonizer see Normand Séguin, *La Conquête du sol au XIX siècle* (Sillery, Quebec, 1977), and Gérard Bouchard, "Introduction a l'étude de la société saguenayenne aux XIX et XX siècles," *Revue d'histoire de l'Amérique française* 31 (June 1977), pp. 3-27.

11. Manuscript census returns for the parish of Ile Verte, Lower Canada, 1842.

12. Albert, *Enfant pauvre,* p. 8.

13. Ibid., pp. 13-14. They also purchased a sugar refinery.

14. Ibid., p. 32.

15. The story of Félix's courting years makes fascinating reading; the process by which he makes his final decision regarding a life mate resembles that of pragmatic Euchariste Moisan in Ringuet's novel, *Thirty Acres;* Albert, *Enfant pauvre,* pp. 21-23, 26-36. After his marriage Félix mentions his wife only occasionally which is regrettable. He never gives her Christian name. For Félix, she is always "ma femme." Marriage records fortunately supply Mrs. Albert's maiden name, Desneiges Michaud. See Le tableau généalogique des mariages célébrés dans le diocès du Rimouski pour les années 1701 à 1902 (on file at the Cour Supérieure, Palais de Justice, Rimouski, Quebec).

16. Albert, *Enfant pauvre,* p. 41.

17. Ibid., p. 42.

18. It is quite possible that Félix was selling his dairy and grain products beyond the local market in the 1870s. In 1860 the Grand Trunk rail line between Montreal and Rivière du Loup was completed. Hamelin and Roby, *Histoire économique,* p. 124.

19. Albert, *Enfant pauvre,* pp. 42-43.

20. Ibid., p. 43.

21. Ibid., p. 44.

22. Ibid.

23. Ibid.

24. Ibid., see for instance pp. 44-45.

25. Ibid., pp. 45-55.

26. Ibid., pp. 56-58.

27. Gérard Bouchard provides useful information on inheritance patterns and family survival strategies among habitants who settled on colonization land in the Saguenay region. Gérard Bouchard, "Family Structures and Geographic Mobility at Laterrière, 1851-1935," *Journal of Family History* 2 (Winter 1977), pp. 350-69.

28. J.I. Little develops the theme of habitant loyalty to the land in his article "The Social and Economic Development of Settlers in Two Quebec Townships, 1851-1870," in *Canadian Papers in Rural History* 1, ed. Donald H. Akenson (Gananoque, Ontario, 1978), pp. 89-113.

29. Manuscript census returns for the parish of Ile Verte, Lower Canada, 1831.

30. Frances H. Early, "Mobility Potential and the Quality of Life in Working-Class Lowell, Massachusetts: The French Canadians ca. 1870," *Labour/Le Travailleur* 2 (1977), pp. 215-16, and Massachusetts, Bureau of Statistics of Labor, *Thirteenth Annual Report, 1882,* pp. 43-44. The 11,000 population figure for 1881 came from a private French Canadian community census taken in 1881 and cited in the *Thirteenth Annual Report.*

31. Frances H. Early, "French-Canadian Beginnings in an American Community: Lowell, Massachusetts, 1868-1886" (Ph.D. dissertation, Concordia University, 1980), pp. 150-66 and 208-14.

32. Ibid., pp. 93-128.

33. Albert, *Enfant pauvre*, p. 58.

34. Ibid., my translation.

35. Frances H. Early, "The French-Canadian Family Economy and Standard of Living: Lowell, Massachusetts, 1870," *Journal of Family History* 7 (June 1982), forthcoming.

36. Albert, *Enfant pauvre*, pp. 59-61.

37. Ibid., pp. 63-64.

38. Ibid., pp. 64-66.

39. Ibid., pp. 68-73.

40. Ibid., p. 68. Between 1881 and 1891 the population of St. Eloi decreased by 23 per cent, from 1,193 to 913; the number of families decreased even more by 29 per cent, from 185 to 132. *Census of Canada, 1880-81* I, pp. 26-27, and *Census of Canada, 1890-1891* I, p. 110.

41. Albert, *Enfant pauvre*, p. 70, my translation.

42. Ibid., p. 71, my translation. Although Felix never worked as a labour recruiting agent his business activities in other respects bear close resemblance to the padrone system of Italian immigrant communities. See for example, Kessner, *Golden Door*, pp. 40, 50, 58, 70, 167; and Robert F. Harney, "Montreal's King of Italian Labour: A Case Study of Padronism," *Labour/Le Travailleur* 4 (1979), pp. 57-84.

43. Albert, *Enfant pauvre*, pp. 74-82.

44. Ibid., p. 77.

45. Ibid., p. 95.

46. Ibid., p. 83 passim.

47. Ibid., p. 92, my translation.

48. An important article which demonstrates the success of French Canadian habitants who settled on farm land in the American midwest and also illustrates their commercial work ethic values is D. Aidan McQuillan, "Farm Size and Work Ethic: Measuring the Success of Immigrant Farmers on the American Grasslands, 1875-1925," *Journal of Historical Geography* 4 (1978), pp. 57-76.

49. Early, "French-Canadian Beginnings," pp. 217 and 224-27. On the ability of French Canadians to adapt the French Canadian family farm economy to an urban-industrial way of life, see my article, "French-Canadian Family Economy"; Bettina Bradbury, "The Family Economy and Work in an Industrializing City: Montreal in the 1870s," Canadian Historical Association, *Historical Papers, 1979* (Ottawa, 1979), pp. 71-96; Tamara K. Hareven, "Family Time and Industrial Time: Family and Work in a Planned Corporation Town, 1900-1924," *Journal of Urban History* 1 (May 1975), pp. 365-89, and "The Laborers of Manchester, New Hampshire, 1912-1924: The Role of Family and Ethnicity in Adjustment to Industrial Life," *Labor History* 16 (Spring 1975), pp. 249-65. On the practice of boarding and its importance to working-class family economies, in addition to the above-cited works, see John Modell and Tamara K. Hareven, "Urbanization and the Malleable Household: An Examination of Boarding and Lodging in American Families," in *Family and Kin in Urban Communities, 1700-1930,* ed. Tamara Hareven (New York, 1977), pp. 164-86.

50. Stephan Thernstrom made this comment (without a shred of evidence) about Lowell French Canadians. See his article, "Urbanization, Migration, and Social Mobility in Late Nineteenth-Century America," in *Towards a New Past: Dissenting Essays in American History,* ed. Barton J. Bernstein (New York, 1967, Vintage paper, 1969), pp. 161-62.

Language and Ethnic Identity in South Louisiana: Implications of Data from Mamou Prairie

Gerald L. Gold

It is difficult to speak of a national ethnic ideology in the French-speaking regions of Louisiana, or of any national institution, including the Catholic church, that has consistently represented the Louisiana French. An incipient French movement has only recently encouraged a unified cultural and linguistic revival of a francophone population that is dispersed in several regions of south and central Louisiana. These territorial blocks of Cajuns and Creoles—the southwestern prairie, the Têche country, the southeastern bayous and the river parishes—are cross-cut by a heterogeneity of national origins, racial and ethnic identification, and occupational sub-groups. The variety of south Louisiana can mask an important linguistic common bond. The 1970 US Census accounts for 572,162 Louisianans who reported French as their mother tongue, though within Louisiana some have questioned this figure as being too low or too high in terms of the actual number of French-speakers. The regional studies of Projet Louisiane suggest that about 200,000 Louisianans use French on a daily basis, even as their language of work.[1]

The identification of a large population of French-speakers in Louisiana does not justify Canadianizing Louisiana into francophone and anglophone segments. With the weak development of national ideologies, the French language does not have the same political importance as it does in New Brunswick (with an apparently smaller French-speaking population!), or even as it does in Manitoba. The territorial dispersion of French Louisiana favours a regional approach in a serious study of the Louisiana French. Regional studies, such as the nine territorially-defined studies that Projet Louisiane undertook from 1976 to 1980 are, in the Louisiana context, an alternative to the kind of demographic research and census work that has been carried out elsewhere.

There have been several attempts to map Louisiana from a socio-linguistic perspective.[2] But these studies are based either on the single 1970 Census question on mother tongue, or on sketchy secondary sources. An alternative methodology is a combination of a field study, conducted largely in French, and structured interviews that permit the identification of the more subtle factors that aid the survival of the French language and culture. Until 1969 the State of Louisiana has offered very little public support for French. Since this survival of French is a local-level phenomenon, regional history acquires the importance that national history has in the Canadian context. The present analysis demonstrates the utility of regional studies with an account of changing patterns of French language use in a single sub-region—Mamou Prairie, Louisiana—an area that was selected for the pilot research of Projet Louisiane.[3]

A basic finding of this pilot research is that language and ethnic identity in Mamou Prairie are more closely tied to regional changes in economy and occupational structure than they are to state-wide or national change within a "French Louisiana." However, neither local nor national influences have affected the French language in Mamou Prairie in a manner that could be described as uniform or linear. Technological change, unilingual English-language public education and television have all had negative effects upon the generational transmission of French. But simple census-based generalizations on assimilation rates and exogamy do not account for the tenacity of French within some sectors of the population, or for the shifts that are made in language use within the life cycles of individuals. And though it may be too early to measure the general impact of the Louisiana French movement on language retention, the specific impact of the movement is selectively visible.

French language use, as the discussion that follows demonstrates, varies significantly by generation, occupation, neighbourhood and sex of the speaker. Men involved in blue-collar and primary resource occupations (farming and fishing) tend to use French as a language of work; while many women, especially those who remain at home, reserve their French for family suppers and contacts with older people. Outside the household, occupationally-based networks develop their own ideologies with regard to the meaning of their Cajun identities. Thus language is not equally significant as an element of ethnic identity for every segment of the population of Mamou Prairie.

Little Communities of the Prairie: Cotton Cultivation and Cajun Identity

After the Civil War, French, Irish, Acadian, Anglo-American, German and Black migrants left the more restrictive plantation society of the Mississippi Delta and travelled overland from Opelousas to settle on the higher ground of the flat grassy expanses of the southwestern prairie.[4] In a reversal of the metaphor of the melting pot, the prairie frontier rapidly became a French-speaking Catholic enclave in a region of the Unites States that is primarily English-speaking and Baptist.[5]

Although the prairie residents were less subject to the elitism of planter rule, they were nonetheless quickly absorbed into the cotton system that dominated post-Reconstruction agriculture in the South.[6] The economic realities of intensive cotton production led to the rapid sub-division of the sections and quarter sections of recently homesteaded land. By the turn of the century, sharecropping was displacing land ownership in many communities. By 1930 sharecroppers were the largest single occupational group in the region.[7]

Mamou Prairie is one of several dozen settlements on the northern fringe of the triangle of French settlement that stretches toward the Texas border. Its social history is similar to that of most communities that were isolated from major communication networks. Like other towns and villages of southwestern Louisiana, the settlement of Mamou Prairie preceded its industrial development. When the Rock Island railroad depot, several cotton mills and stores created the nucleus of the small incorporated village of Mamou in 1910, the merchants and gin-operators of the new village were latecomers to a densely-settled prairie.[8] More than a dozen farming hamlets ringed the new service centre. Most of these communities already had a social charter, a regional identity invoked even by their names: Duralde, la Pointe de Grand Louis, l'Anse Johnson, John Reed, l'Anse des Cazans, la Pinière, la Pointe aux Pins, 'Tit Mamou, l'Anse Bleu, l'Anse Maigre, etc.

The 1900 manuscript census reports 3,821 people living along

"Mamou Road," 3,199 whites (84 per cent of the local population) and 622 blacks (16 per cent), roughly the present-day ratio.
The majority of the population were young, mostly under forty,
born in Louisiana and predominantly uneducated. Three-quarters
of the prairie dwellers could not speak English, even though
many had names like Tate, Reed and McGee. Patronymics mat-
tered little to those who had built a common identity *in situ.*
Therefore, it is not surprising to find that in 1900 there was no
strong correlation between land ownership and bilingualism.
Aside from a few wealthy local landowners, 55 per cent of farmers owned their own land, and the economic status of most farmers was often not very much different from that of a sharecropper. Both were considered to be fellow habitants,[9] part of the
same community.

There were substantial tracts of prairie land owned by outsiders from Opelousas and Ville Platte. Those landowners who
were not French-speaking relied on intermediaries to contract
their "bargains" with tenant farmers and collect their share of the
cotton harvest.[10] To many residents of the cove communities, the
largest outside landowners, such as the descendants of Colonel
Samuel Haas, a Jewish entrepreneur from Opelousas, represented
the socially-distant world of the *Américains.* To the Cajun habitant, these outsiders were an important part of the boundary
between the self-subsistence and mutual aid of the cove community and the external cash economy. Their presence reinforced the
frontier enclave within which the cove was the centre of a relatively closed social universe.

Within the coves, sharecroppers moved frequently. Sometimes
a habitant moved to get a better verbal bargain from a landlord
(bourgeois or "boss") for his harvest; but often a farmer was
seeking a change, and his new home was likely to be near his
kinsmen and not far from where he used to live. The only alternative for some Mamou cotton farmers was to move to nearby
Texas,[11] where land and work were considered to be more plentiful.

It must be emphasized that the opportunities presented by the
petroleum industry and by rapid urbanization were not yet sufficient to dismantle the farming communities. Agricultural settlements were dispersed, egalitarian and strongly French speaking.
The towns, however, were market oriented, tied to state government and relatively more open to the influences of English-speaking American society. This situation was probably prolonged by
the depression, an assessment that is supported by the work of

Benjamin Kaplan on the economic alternatives of tenant farmers in nearby Lafayette Parish.[12]

Ethnic identity in Mamou Prairie was inseparable from the rural-urban dialectic of the cotton system.[13] The criteria of exclusion or inclusion were not derived from genealogical credentials, but they emerged from the regimen of cotton production and the modes of cooperation that were established to make life easier for the producers. The prairie communities developed an idiosyncratic Cajun identity that was nurtured at the micro-level, rather than through the promotion of ethnic elites. Within the local community, French was the language of work and of most social relations. Moreover, newcomers rapidly adapted to French as a universal means of communication. A retired sharecropper from la Pointe aux Pins highlights this point in his account of his grandfather's entry into the cove community:

> Mon grandpère était un O'Connor. Il est venu de Irish. Lui, il parlait l'anglais. Mais quand ils ont deménagé ici, à la Pointe aux Pins, le monde connaissait pas parler en anglais. Puis il a montré à ses petits de parler en français. Il n'a jamais envoyé à l'école, parce que ça voulait pas que ça apprend à parler en anglais. Sa femme parlait pas en anglais aux enfants. Eux autres parlait anglais entre eux.

> My grandfather was an O'Connor. He came from 'Irish' (stock). Him, he spoke English. But when he moved here to Pointe aux Pins, no one could speak English. So he taught his kids to speak French. He never sent them to school, because he did not want them to speak in English. His wife did not speak English to the children. They spoke English to each other.
>
> (female, age 67)

O'Connor, Tate, Reed, McGee, and Israel became "good Cajun names," as authentic as Soileau, Guillory, Fontenot, Cormier, Ardoin, or Aucoin. In this process of group creation or "ethnogenesis,"[14] even those genealogies that could be easily traced to the eighteenth century (e.g., Fuselier) were compressed by a population that grouped all the country Cajuns (*les Cadiens de la campagne*) within a single inclusive identity. This Cajun identity, however, was not shared by all who lived on the prairie.

To the village dwellers, Cajun was an inferior status, a referent to uneducated rural people with a distinctive way of talking and doing things. Villagers expressed this status difference through such actions as restricting contacts between their children and the rural Cajun children. Many respondents recall that the introduction, in the mid-1930s, of bussing from the coves to the village school permitted children from the rural communities to visit each other more frequently, but bussing did not increase contacts between the village children and their rural classmates. In some cases, the barrier between the two was a linguistic one.

French was the dominant language of the prairie, and even the wealthiest village parents could not stop their children who remained in Mamou from having frequent contacts with Cajun life. For many villagers, however, such as the daughter of a large landowner, that exposure to French came later in life:

Well, quand on était petit, ça nous parlait tout le temps, juste en anglais parce que quand on allait à l'école on pouvait pas parler en français ... quand les enfants parlaient français à l'école, ça les fouettait. Ca fait ... moi j'ai pas parlé en français quand j'étais grande.	When we were small, they spoke to us all the time in English only, because when we went to school we were not to speak in French. They would whip us. So, I could not speak French when I grew up.

This woman later married a merchant who currently speaks with her only in French. Other villagers of her generation never became as conversant as she in Cajun French (she was interviewed in French). After the Second World War, when cotton collapsed and the small farmers began to stream into the village, some of the pre-war villagers failed to participate in the increased public visibility of Cajun French in business, politics and social relations in general. Paradoxically, this rise in the public use of French came at the same time as a decline in its private use, as families began to teach their children English at home.

Mamou Prairie after the Collapse of Cotton Cultivation

The most significant postwar development in Mamou Prairie was the collapse of cotton cultivation after 1952 and the resulting displacement of hundreds of sharecropping families into the village and into unskilled urban employment in nearby cities in southwestern Louisiana and in eastern Texas.[15] Except on the few remaining large family rice farms, the family ceased to be a viable economic unit in primary agricultural production. As a direct consequence of this occupational shift, the sexual division of labour in Mamou Prairie changed dramatically. Although men and women had worked together in cotton production, such cooperation was possible in the village only in the context of a family business. This does not mean that cooperation between kinsmen broke down. For example, the Cajun respect for the elderly was maintained, and this furthered opportunities for intra-familial and inter-generational communication.[16]

In Mamou Prairie the sudden and massive resettlement led to the opening of numerous groceries, mechanical shops and other small enterprises, many of which represented the only employment alternative at the time. These new merchants and other migrants relied heavily on mutual aid from their kinship networks in the village. An intensive round of suppers and the exchange of home-grown food and of cooperative labour kept these networks from disintegrating in an urban context (although there is considerable variation in how these networks function).[17] In many cases family cooperation is reflected in residential proximity as blocks of kin regroup in rough approximation to their rural origins.

Family business in Mamou Prairie has been extremely stable because of this support from friends and relations. Moreover, Cajun French, formerly the language of cotton production has become the preferred mode of communication in small business. With these cultural constraints on the marketplace, no outside chain stores can effectively establish supermarkets or fast food outlets in Mamou, despite the fact that Mamou village (now a town) has over 4,000 inhabitants in 1981. As this kind of entrenched local control suggests, the new merchants and the landowners are important within local politics, and local politics are carried out virtually entirely in French.

With politics and small business as French-language spheres of activity, French has remained essential to the males of Mamou Prairie, and relatively fewer women are involved in the labour force. Moreover, with many men now employed in offshore oil work, they are not with their families on a consistent basis. It follows that in the town context, women take the largest responsibility for home life and for the socialization of the children. Most of these children are raised speaking English. Their major contacts with their parents' cultural past is through their grandparents, and some have managed to learn French in this manner. Mamou youth are thus separated from adult networks until they enter the local labour market. Many depart and never return: over half of the children of household heads in our sample have left the prairie to seek work and higher education in the cities. Those who do return are reintegrated into family networks and into male work groups.

These are only general tendencies in the linguistic and cultural consequences of the break-up of the cotton system in Mamou Prairie. They are sufficient to suggest that linguistic assimilation in rural Louisiana may not be a linear phenomenon, and that, while the view from a distance of French language use may indicate considerable generational language loss, actual patterns of language use are more complicated. For this reason, an approach to patterns of language use in Louisiana should not be predicated on a linguistic "numbers game," such as the one that is all too familiar to the student of Canadian francophone minorities.[18] Without denying that there has been language loss, our objective is to shed some light upon the process of linguistic accommodation in Louisiana and the meaning of language as part of the construction of a Cajun ethnic identity.

Language and Socialization in Mamou Prairie

Even with the limitations to Louisiana language statistics, a sampling of linguistic data from a random sample of Mamou households, interviewed in 1976,[19] provides some of the dimensions of the problem in understanding language shifts in Louisiana. Field observations of the daily routine of Mamou households serve to confirm the accuracy of interview responses and their meaning in terms of other matters that are relevant to Cajuns. Quite early in the course of this research, the language question emerged very much as an issue that is of greater concern to Canadians and Quebecois than it is to some Louisiana Cajuns. For example, some respondents who speak French on a daily basis, expressed more apprehension over the survival of Cajun music than over Cajun French. Others who were concerned about Cajun French did not necessarily speak it with their own families.

Four out of every five household heads visited use French in their daily conversations at home, and one-third of the sample speak French with their spouses "all of the time." Many of these are functional unilinguals who can communicate only a few perfunctory sentences in English. A little less than half of the householders listen to the French-language news on the radio, and this group of listeners includes some of the respondents who do *not* use French at home. Other situational uses of French that are covered by the study, though not fully reported here, include speaking French with friends, neighbours, servicemen, merchants, the police, postal clerks and court-house employees.

Evidence of Anglicization is not difficult to find, if that is what

Table 1: Language Most Frequently Used at Home and Language Most Frequently Used at Work, Compared by Age of the Male Head of Household in Mamou Prairie, Louisiana[1]

AGE	20-25		26-30		31-35		36-40		41-45		46-50	
	Work	Home	Work	Home	Work	Home	Work	Home	Work	Home	Work	Home
Mostly French	7 64%	0	4 50%	0	7 58%	1 8%	10 59%	7 35%	5 50%	3 23%	13 87%	13 57%
Mostly English	4 36%	10 100%	4 50%	12 100%	5 42%	12 92%	7 41%	13 65%	5 50%	10 77%	2 13%	10 43%
Total	11	10	8	12	12	13	17	20	10	13	15	23

AGE	51-55		56-60		61-65		66-70		Over 70		Total	
	Work	Home	Work	Home	Work	Home	Work	Home	Work	Home	Work	Home
Mostly French	7 64%	10 62%	6 50%	11 69%	12 80%	18 100%	9 90%	13 81%	5 100%	13 100%	85 66%	81 48%
Mostly English	4 36%	6 37%	6 50%	5 31%	3 20%	0	1 10%	3 19%	0	0	41 33%	89 52%
Total	11	16	12	16	15	18	10	16	5	13	126	170

1. This data is based on two interview questions:
"What language do you speak at work?" (and how often), and "What language do you use with your wife (or husband)?" (and how often).
"Mostly French" includes "all French," "mostly French" and "half and half."
"Mostly English" includes "all English" and "mostly English."

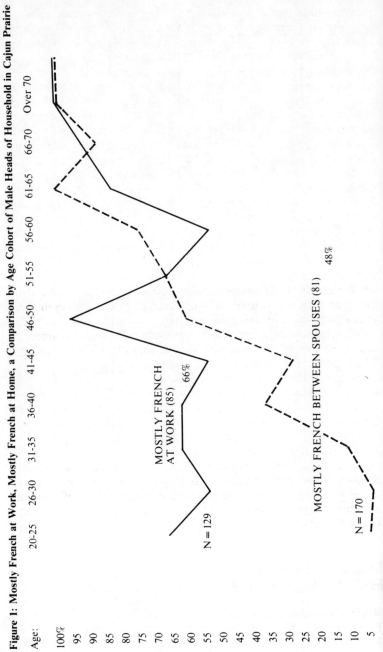

Figure 1: Mostly French at Work, Mostly French at Home, a Comparison by Age Cohort of Male Heads of Household in Cajun Prairie

one is seeking. Age is correlated in almost linear manner with the language used between spouses (French speakers are older), and no more than 10 per cent of the parents with young children at home speak French with their children. Closer examination of this data and a discussion of the situational dynamics of language use demonstrate a more complex reality that returns our attention to the socio-historical factors summarized in the introduction.

A few more statistics are needed to underscore this complexity. Of particular interest is the relationship between language used at home and language of work. Table 1 and Figure 1 graphically demonstrate what our field workers knew from the first day of the research: many of those Mamou Cajuns, who work in French, speak English in their home environment. The greater strength of French as a working language is most visible among men and women under fifty. These are the tradesmen, artisans, merchants and offshore oil workers whose attachment to French will be treated later in a discussion of language of work. As for men over fifty, they tend to manifest roughly the same linguistic behaviour at work as they do with their spouses (and children). These are predominantly ex-sharecroppers, living on welfare or social security, and farming couples in their second career as small merchants or manual labourers in the town.

What causes the relationship to remain somewhat unequal between the ages of fifty and sixty-five is that older residents of the village, merchants or professionals and white-collar workers have often never worked in French. When these variables are controlled for the socio-economic status of neighbourhoods (the town of Mamou only), there are few differences that can be found between neighbourhoods. There is also no significant relationship between either male or female language of work and neighbourhood status. But women who work primarily in French are over-represented in high and medium status neighbourhoods. The differences between home and work language only begin to make sense when we return to the problem of socialization of children and the intrusion of school and wider societal pressures within the Cajun household.

Multiple Registers: French Usage after the Collapse of Cotton

When compulsory education began in the rural areas of Mamou Prairie in the 1930s, thousands of schoolchildren, speaking only French when they arrived for their first day of class, were forced by both Cajun and *Américain* teachers to speak nothing but English in the classroom. The lesson of English dominance in public life was etched in the minds of both schoolchildren and their parents through psychological pressure and the lash of the teacher's whip. As the son of one L'Anse Johnson sharecropper recalls:

Ma génération à mon et à elle, ils nous ont fait commencer l'école. On pouvait pas parler en anglais, et ça m'a retardé un an d'école. Tu pouvais pas montrer les deux langages!

Ceux qui a eu des petits après ça, ils ont commencé à leur montrer à leur parler en anglais qui ça serait pas en arrière.

In my generation and hers, they made us start school. We could not speak English, and that lost me a year of school. You could not teach two languages!

Those who had their children after that, began to teach them to speak in English so that they would not be behind.

(policeman, age 51)

It was almost an insult if you made your little ones speak French. It had to be English, nothing else. But my mother and her mother spoke no English, and it would have been a sin to have taught her children to speak French!

(retired bar owner, age 60)

The massive move to the village that followed the Second World War reinforced the definitive switch to English as the language of socialization. There were no ethnic leaders in Mamou or elsewhere in Louisiana who could resist forced anglicization in the 1950s. An organized French movement would not appear until the late sixties.

In many families, the new rules of the game led to a widening gap between the social universe of parents and the peer groups of their children. Speaking English to children, however strained, became what many parents call "notre mauvaise habitude." This placed considerable stress on mothers who, with the move into town, were no longer equal partners in a domestic unit of production. Their new role, legitimately American, was that of a housewife, and much of the preparation of children for school fell on their shoulders. There was no precedent in Mamou Prairie for women to take the role of outsiders in the socialization of their children. Nevertheless, the three schools in Mamou grew as enclaves within an enclave; their curriculum having little direct relation to life on the prairie.

Men were able to continue working in French in occupations that were not radically separated from skills that they had learned as farm and wage labourers, but many women became more concerned with the legitimizing value of English and the stigma of Cajun French. As their own children became their points of entry to the wider society, they became immigrants in the very territory where their identity had been created. This ambivalence is reflected in the words of the sixty-nine-year-old wife of a retired small farmer:

I'll tell you how it is. I'll *try* to tell you. I don't know if you'll understand us, (or) our children.

We can't say we are well-educated people, that we speak very good English and all that, but we had our children, we sent them to school. We talked what we knew of English with them, and then we also kept the French. As long as they were with us, they understood, and talked with us like that. But when they left and went to college, went away, they mixed more with people who speak only English.

Sometimes they come and there's a few things we would tell them. They stop and think before they understand what we are saying, but they don't dare say it. . . . Sometimes, even if they wanted to tell us something in French, they have to think about if they are going to say it right or not.

They didn't *need* that French. So you find some of these people who—*ça connait pas parler en français ou ça veut pas en français. . . . Il y avait un tas du monde qui connait juste français, ça voulait montrer aux enfants de lire et parler en anglais.*

(they don't know how to speak French or they don't want to speak French. . . . There are a lot of people who can only speak French. They want to teach their children to read and to speak English.)

In many families the oldest children under thirty, particularly males, have learned to speak French, but the youngest, in serial progression, have not. In those families where a business such as a small grocery store or even a farm is operated in French on a daily basis with family labour, some children may refuse to speak French. The children brush aside attempts by their parents to keep them bilingual, being faced with peer group pressure and the English curriculum in school. Such attempts are sometimes reduced to simple commands, counting, greetings or cursing. Yet the refusal to learn may be a dramatic experience for the parents, leading to bewilderment or disillusionment:

Celui qui a 14 ans dit: "Don't speak to me in French. I don't understand."

(father (disabled), age 50)

Nos enfants, quand ça vient chez nous, nous autres on va parler en
anglais. . . . On parlait anglais pour eux autres, tu connais, pour eux
autres.
(When our children visit us we will speak in English. We spoke
English for their sake, for them).
(couple in early sixties, husband is an ex-sharecropper
working as a manual labourer for the town)

On leur parle en français. Ca dit: "what you said?"
(oilfield worker, age 49, wife is 41, with three teenage
daughters)

Elle voulait rien faire avec le français. Elle va à l'école à Eunice, et
ses petites amies à Eunice, ça parle pas le français.
(She wants nothing to do with French. Going to school in Eunice,
her little friends do not even speak French.)
(insurance agent, 41 – active in the popular revival of
Cajun culture)

Je crèle ma fille. Je lui dis: "t'es créole et tu montres pas à tes
petits à parler en Créole."
(I argue with my girl: "You are a Creole, and you do not teach
your little ones to speak Creole.")
(black female, 63, retired sharecropper)

J'ai essayé. J'ai tout le temps parlé en français. Mais il n'a pas
appris.
(I tried . . . but he did not learn.)
(mechanic, 39, who works in French)

In the majority of families, close contact with grandparents,
who visit on an almost daily basis, assures linguistic continuity. In
several cases, grandparents have taught both a father and his
children how to speak French. Some grandparents insist on
speaking French to their grandchildren, though this does not
always imply that the grandchildren will speak French unless they
see each other on a very frequent basis. As one seventy-year-old
grandmother recounts:

C'est moi et lui, on leur a montré, les autres [her children] ça leur
parle tous en anglais.
(It is the two of us who taught them [to speak French]. The others,
they talk to them only in English.)

In this manner many grandparents have assured linguistic continuity in families where parents are under strong pressure to
teach English to their children. Those grandparents or parents

who are successful have usually also been able to inculcate a sense of importance in their grandchildren for the preparation of Cajun foods, gardening, husbandry, hunting, fishing and domestic arts. Those children who retain French, also become interested in the popular revival of Cajun culture, listening to Cajun music in dance-halls or learning to play it themselves. Most, though not all, of these music-oriented youths are males, and the interest in Cajun culture among Mamou adolescents has a *macho* tinge to it, supported by the use of French in offshore oil work and rough primary resource-related jobs. These are attractive alternatives in a relatively impoverished area with few other outlets for mobility.

A single case serves to illustrate these inter-generational pressures that lead to selective linguistic socialization:

> Elaine and Buford Leblanc both in their late forties, are children of sharecroppers. They live in a modern air-conditioned bungalow in a nearby city. Buford is a supervisor in a regional oilfield construction firm where he works mainly in French. His father continues to farm on a part-time basis in a nearby community. Elaine remains at home with her three children with whom, she and her husband, usually speak English. Elaine's parents live in a Mamou rural neighbourhood where her father, Charles, a unilingual French speaker, and a lifetime sharecropper, now works for the parish road crews. Her brother works in Lake Charles, fifty miles away. Elaine's mother, Hazel speaks English, and works during the day by minding small children [in English] for working mothers.

> Elaine and Buford's oldest child Sam [age 18] learned French from Grandfather Charles and has worked, bilingually, for his father's company before becoming a tradesman himself. His younger sister, Cheryl, who will go into nursing and who spends a great deal of time with *pépère* Charles and *mémère* Hazel, understands only a little French and rarely tries to speak it. His youngest sister, Susan, does not speak or understand French and has had much less contact with her grandparents.

The linguistic behaviour of men in Sam's generation who continue to work in French is important for an understanding of the recent culture change in southwestern Louisiana. Many of these men work on offshore oil platforms earning incomes that are substantially higher than anything they could earn in their home towns. On their return to Mamou Prairie after three weeks "on the water," the oil workers take jobs in the building trades or in local commerce. This dual life with three weeks away from the prairie, working with other Cajuns from other towns and from other regions, leads many oil workers to attach a new importance to the uniqueness of their identities and the absence of the stigma many had assumed would be their penalty for being Cajun.

As a result of their outside experiences, most of the offshore oil workers who were interviewed claimed to be anxious to raise their children bilingually. Also in almost every case, the oil workers' wives were much less committed to using French in their households. Some workers turned to grandparents to solve the problem of their own frequent absence and inability to teach French to their children (see the discussion of the role of grandparents below), while others attempted the linguistic socialization themselves, usually only with their sons.

Before turning to the question of French at work, some final comments should be made about grandparents and their sociolinguistic significance in Cajun culture. In numerous cases grandparents did *not* continue to speak French with their grandchildren after socializing their first grandchild or first few grandchildren in French. Many learned English from their own children or from their grandchildren, while others found that with the out-migration mentioned earlier, fewer of their grandchildren were able to visit them on a regular basis. However, contact with grandparents is no guarantee that French will be transmitted to grandchildren. Being bilingual is often reason enough not to speak French. In the words of an offshore worker in his early forties, who had himself learned French from his grandparents: "Now the grandparents speak English. They are bilingual today, so I guess that's why they don't speak French."

Several parents comment that their pre-adolescent children who do speak French choose to talk to the old people because they have nobody of their own age with whom to talk. This observation is so frequent, both in the interviews and in casual conversation, that we believe it to be related to a lack of structured opportunities for non-adults to speak French with each other. When these occasions do arise, for instance during the annual Mardi Gras, or on private occasions such as within an athletic team, or with older siblings who will not chide them for speaking *croche* (crooked or poorly), many more adolescents in Mamou speak French together than interviews with their parents would reveal.

The generational break in linguistic continuity makes it difficult for children to use the French, which they have learned elsewhere, with their parents. In other instances we have recorded that adolescents who learned French at school, in work activities, from neighbours, or even from their grandparents are unable to reintegrate that skill into a household context. Perhaps the most important of these instances are the dozen or more Mamou youth who have perfected their French through contacts with teachers and frequent visitors from Quebec, France and Belgium (ties that have even led to foreign visits). As will be shown in the next section, work and social contexts for using French are available outside of the household.

Language and the Work World

To an outsider, Mamou may appear to be an English-speaking town. There are few French signs, and the masthead of the bilingual newspaper would be easy to miss if one were not looking for bilingualism. But Mamou is also a place where an individual can conduct most, if not all, of his daily business in French. This becomes even more apparent when French as the predominant language of work is cross-tabulated with occupation (Table 2— *Language of Work (Males) by Occupation*). The use of French at work is then found to be highest in services, small retail businesses and trades; whereas, English is more evident in those areas which demand technological specialization (medicine, law, pharmacy), though it is not exclusively used in these fields. The enigma that became apparent in our discussion of language use within families now complicates any simple statements about language as a sorting mechanism within the community and within French-speaking south Louisiana.

It may be useful to regard this work world as a field of language conflict, though the conflict is covert. In Mamou Prairie business and politics are the last defences of the French language, and not the household. In most types of work, there is not yet any serious competition from public institutions or from the computerization of the retail distribution system. Working in French does not interfere with the English-language socialization of children.[20] It is paradoxical, however, that some of those who complete high school may be expected to enter a French-speaking world which was marginal to their everyday lives during their school years.[21] Those who cannot make that entry may use this new incompatibility as a pretext for migrating out of the region.

Those who remain in the region find their friendships within their occupational sub-groups. Moreover, linguistic patterns within these sub-groups, at least for the males, reflect the pattern of language use at work. One such occupational group are the

Table 2: Language Used by Male Heads of Households at Work and Current Occupation of Male Household Heads, Mamou Prairie, Louisiana (1976)

Current Occupation	French Only or Mostly French	Mostly or Only English	Total	
Modern farmer and other farm work	11	1	12	(9.5%)
Skilled tradesman (traditional occupations)	13	2	15	(12%)
Unskilled blue-collar	1	4	5	(4%)
Unskilled oilfield worker	8	0	8	(6.3%)
Other unskilled labour (including services)	11	2	13	(10.3%)
Supervisory (mostly oilfield work)	7	3	10	(8%)
Skilled services	0	3	3	(2.3%)
Uniformed, low rank	4	0	4	(3.2%)
Unskilled clerical	2	0	2	(1.6%)
Professionals (including teachers)	2	2	4	(3.2%)
Merchants (small business)	6	1	7	(5.6%)
Merchants (medium and large)	9	0	9	(7.1%)

Table 2: (continued)

Current Occupation	French Only or Mostly French	Mostly or Only English	Total	
Pensioner*	4	1	5	(4%)
Disabled (occupationally)*	2	2	4	(3.2%)
Disabled (medically)*	19	4	23	(18.3%)
Other	2	0	2	(1.6%)
Total	101 (80.2%)	25 (19.8%)	126	(100%)

* Language of use applies to last occupation held.

rice and soy bean farmers. Once the largest occupational group of
the region, farmers now represent a select group of large landowners who have made significant capital investments to remain
solvent in commercial agriculture.

The nine farmers in the Mamou interview sample are organized, with one exception, in family corporations each of which
shares labour and machinery. The language of work on the farms
is always French, even among teenagers who are assisting their
parents with a harvest. French is also the prime means of communication in the country stores which are the setting for information exchanges, local politics, card games and barbecues.

One large farmer (who plants 800 acres of rice) notes that
those who cannot initially speak French in this work environment
will do so within a short period of time:

J'ai deux hommes qui parle français et j'en ai un qui parle pas, mais il est après apprendre parce que on parle assez entre nous autres que s'il veut comprendre quelque chose, il faut qu'il parle français.	I have two men who speak French and one who does not, but he is learning because we talk a lot among ourselves and if he wishes to understand anything he will have to talk French.

Because his farm is a family enterprise, the extensive use of
French at work has implications for the amount of French used
in his home environment.

Construction and country road crews are two other occupations
where all of the workers speak or understand French. These job
networks are frequently followed through in inter-personal networks. One construction company owner explains the necessity
for speaking French in his work crews:

Mes hommes à moi parle tous français et là ben tout les contracteurs alentours d'ici parle tout français. Et quand on se rejoint, c'est tout français. . . . Ca parle de l'anglais du tout.	My men all speak French. And all the contractors around here speak French. And when we get together, its all French. They don't speak English at all.

The same exclusiveness applies to independent truckers who
will only speak English when a stranger forces the issue, that is,
when they meet someone "they do not know." Repairmen are
also expected to speak French, even in the case of those who use
English predominantly at home. A twenty-five year-old gas pump
repairman explains the situation quite well:

Je travaille à des boutiques eyou y'a du vieux monde, et aux magasins (I work in shops where there are old people and in stores) and ça me demande de 'speak French.' Sometimes you have to, you know! I practise it, and sometimes with people I try to lead, in practice. We do speak French. All of the workers, we do speak French. Where I work its all young people, but its all people for raising speaking French. And we practise.

The same French dominance prevails in the retail trade where one hardware merchant (age forty-five) estimates that 90 per cent of his sales are in French and almost always to people whom he has seen or already knows. In a day of interviewing and observation with an auto dealer, virtually every sale observed, all telephone calls and all inter-employee communications were carried out in French!

It is at the large community hospital that French tends to be spoken to patients rather than between staff members; and the same relation between the public and the staff exists in federal government offices such as the post office. At city and county offices, the situation is more complex, perhaps because these offices are closely tied to the local political system, which in turn is controlled by the small local businessmen, whose personal networks almost always include local politicians. In this category are the parish offices in nearby Ville Platte, the local police and parish sheriff's office and all local employees who use French extensively as an informal though not exclusive language of work. Perhaps the most surprising use of French in the public sector is between school teachers when they are in common rooms or at social events.

When these occupationally-defined networks are compared, the offshore oil workers emerge as a group with career interests that are similar if not linked to those of the merchants and tradesmen. In practice, many small merchants obtained their working capital through offshore labour. And most men who are now working offshore are already spending their weeks "off" (i.e., onshore) operating a small business either alone or with a kinsman.

The local networks of oil workers are reinforced offshore. In virtually every case, the Mamou men work on platforms and on supply boats with others from the prairie region, while their wives visit and stay with each other during their absences. Many live in the same brick bungalow neighbourhoods, such as "Estropiéville," a suburban-styled housing area for offshore workers, many of whom have paid for their homes after an injury on the job.

On the rig inter-regional communication poses special problems. For example, Mamou offshore workers do not usually attempt to communicate in French with workers from other regions. Treating each other as fellow Cajuns, but with their own networks, they speak English together. When they have to communicate with non-Cajuns, the conversation is always in English. Though they do not necessarily keep French conversations out of the hearing range of non-Cajuns. The same uncertainty that surrounds inter-regional communications also prevails for salesmen, drivers and repairmen when they must work outside of the southwestern prairie. All are aware, for example, that workers from the Têche region speak a creole dialect, what Mamou Cajuns call *Vini Couri* or "Nigger French," but few will even attempt to understand it, or take the time to think about why other Cajuns do not speak the way they do. That is taken for granted.

The relationship between language, group affiliation and identity in Mamou Prairie has been shown to be more than a simple linear relationship. The development of local groups, closely tied to cotton production in a peripheral, frontier region, has led to the emergence of an indigenous or autochthonous identity, for which language is one of many components. When linguistic socialization is examined in both the home and work contexts, the differential effects of modernization become saliently visible. Within the family, the role of alternate generations in Cajun social structure has been an important buffer as families adjusted to redefined division of labour and to externally-validated ideologies. Within the work context, oilfield labour has not had any negative effects on local economies because of the flexibility of work schedules and the transference of wages into local commercial capital. In the same way Mamou Cajun merchants have utilized French in a public environment to protect their status, a success that they cannot replicate in their private interactions, even within their own families.

Perhaps the most divisive element of family life is the differential response to modernization by men and women. Whereas the former accentuate Cajun ethnicity as an efficient means of adapting to their new situation, the latter emphasize their "Americanness" and de-emphasize their "Cajun-ness," particularly in the socialization of their children.

When the various forces that influence language use are considered, some attention should be given to the French movement itself. Mamou merchants, together with school teachers, lawyers and policemen, have been instrumental in making Mamou a centre for the revival of Cajun folk culture—the music and oral traditions of the coves. Elsewhere, I have discussed this revival in considerable detail and argue that it has been an essential component of the movement to revive French language and culture in Louisiana that began, in an official way, in 1968. In this paper the merchant leaders of "popular revival" in Mamou Prairie are placed into a wider demographic context.[22] This context probably places an undue emphasis on the economic and structural factors that have favoured the selective survival of the French language. However, this does not negate the presence of the ideological aspects of the French movement that have given Mamou several French radio broadcasts, a bilingual newspaper and at least three explicitly Cajun festivals (Mardi Gras, Cajun Day and November 11). But it does serve to put the popular revival into the perspective of the small everyday dramas within the family and the workplace.

Notes

1. Projet Louisiane began in 1975 and continued through the summer of 1980. Funding was provided by the Wenner-Grenn Foundation for Anthropological Research, the SSHRCC and the Ford Foundation. The major participants are G.L. Gold of York University, Eric Waddell, Louis-Jacques Dorais and Dean Louder of Laval, and David Haas of Louisiana State University, Baton Rouge (external associate). Alain Larouche, Jean-Claude St. Hilaire, Louis-Jacques Dorais, Louis Assier and Paul Leventhal assisted in the Mamou interviewing and data analysis.

2. Roland Breton, *Géographie du français et de la francité en Louisiane* (Quebec: Centre international de recherche sur le bilinguisme, Université Laval, 1979); Roland Breton and Dean Louder, "La géographie linguistique de l'Acadiana," *Cahiers de Géographie du Québec* 23, no. 59 (1979), pp. 217-38; and, Larbi Oukada, "The Territory and Population of French-Speaking Louisiana," *Revue de Louisiane/ Louisiana Review* 7, no. 1 (1978), pp. 5-34.

3. The Mamou Prairie research was used to develop an interview schedule that was adapted for use in eight other Louisiana regions and cities plus Port Arthur in eastern Texas. The present discussion does not deal with the study of the leaders of Cajun popular revival that was initiated during the Mamou research. Mamou is not a pseudonym. Our respondents urged us to disguise their names, but not their identities, and this wish has been respected. A full report on the research in Mamou Prairie will appear in a forthcoming research monograph.

4. A readily available account of the settlement of the southwestern prairie is Lauren C. Post's collection of geographic sketches, Lauren C. Post, *Cajun Sketches from the Prairies of Southwest Louisiana* (Baton Rouge: Louisiana State University Press, 1974 (1962)). Also of interest is a book by Mamou Prairie broadcaster Revon Reed, *Lache pas la patate! Portrait des Acadiens du Sud de la Louisiane* (Montreal: Les Editions Parti Pris, 1976), which contains many anecdotal accounts, in a standardized Cajun French, of the settlement of Mamou Prairie. See also, Gerald L. Gold, "The French Frontier of Settlement in Louisiana: Some Observations on Cultural Change in Mamou Prairie," *Cahiers de géographie du Québec* 23, no. 59 (1979), p. 265ff.

5. This notion of a Catholic enclave is mentioned by Malcom Comeaux, "Louisiana Acadians: the Environmental Impact," in *The Cajuns: Essays in Their History and Culture*, ed. Glen Conrad, USL History Series No. 11 (Lafayette: Center for Louisiana Studies, University of Southwestern Louisiana, 1978). It is the subject of a dissertation research project by Cécyle Trépanier, an associate of Projet Louisiane currently at Pennsylvania State University. Cécyle Trépanier, "French Louisiana Culture Region: a Geographic Interpretation," (Ph.D. dissertation, Pennsylvania State University, 1981).

6. Rupert C. Vance, *The Human Factor in Cotton Culture: a Study in the Social Geography of the American South* (Chapel Hill: University of North Carolina Press, 1929). Vance provides a dated but very readable description of the cotton system in the southern states. His account of sharecropper-landlord relations could well apply to Mamou Prairie.

7. Gold, "The French Frontier of Settlement in Louisiana," p. 275.

8. Robert Gahn, Sr., in a biographical history of Mamou and Evangeline Parishes, devotes about a page to the status of Mamou before C.C. Duson, a Franco-American railroad entrepreneur laid out the plan for the town and after considerable land speculation, promoted the first settlement. Robert Gahn, Sr., *The Opelousas Country, with a History of Evangeline Parish. Its Land, its Men and its Women Who Made it a Beautiful Place to Live* (Baton Rouge: Claitor's Publishing, 1972), p. 51. See also Mary Alice Fontenot and Paul B. Freeland, *Acadia Parish Louisiana, A History to 1900* (Baton Rouge: Claitor's Publishing, 1976), pp. 212-29 for superb biographical data on Duson and his role in opening various communities in the southwestern prairies.

9. This is a considerable simplification of a very complex situation in which Cajun landlords lived in both town and countryside, although most lived on their farms. There were also a few Anglo-American and other non-Cajun landlords who lived in the countryside.

10. Shares were usually taken in either "halves" or "thirds." Under an arrangement of halves, the farmer provided little more than his labour and the landlord decided what was to be grown and what was to be worked, taking half of the crop at harvest time. When the habitant paid a third to the landlord, he was also responsible for supplying the seed and the team, and occasionally, his home. Halves were usually more exploitative in the sense that the landlord could have a greater control over the tenant farmer's labour. Often such an arrangement included care of the landlord's rice fields. Gold, "The French Frontier of Settlement in Louisiana," p. 271; and Post, *Cajun Sketches,* pp. 141-45.

11. The move to Texas began in the 1930s when it was already a favourite theme of Cajun folk music in some of the first Cajun recordings made before and during the depression. Research by Michael Leblanc, in Port Arthur, Texas, confirms reports by Mamou Prairie old-timers that land tenancy was thought to be less severe in Texas. Migrants hoped to acquire land of their own or regular employment. Dean Louder and Michael Leblanc, "The Cajuns of East Texas," *Cahiers de géographie du Québec* 23, no. 59 (1979), pp. 317-30.

12. Benjamin Kaplan, *Under All ... the Land* (Lafayette: Southwestern Institute, 1942). The irony of Kaplan's analysis is that fifteen years later Lafayette Parish entered a sustained oil boom.

13. The economic isolation of sharecropping communities was not confined to Louisiana. Most of the pre-industrial old South was characterized by highly localized sub-cultures. What was distinctive of south Louisiana was the triple-enclave created by the combination of linguistic and religious isolation with a shortage of land and an absence of other economic alternatives.

14. John W. Bennett, *The New Ethnicity: Perspective from Ethnology* (St. Paul, Minnesota: West Publishing, 1975).

15. There is a significant difference in migration destinations between younger and older children of household heads in Mamou. The first children migrated towards Lake Charles and further west to various destinations in Texas. The younger generations have followed the expansion of oil fields towards the city of Lafayette and its environs. There has been virtually no migration to New Orleans from our sample households.

16. In most households interviewed, grandparents are visited very frequently and often live in close proximity to their grandchildren. There are no old age homes in Mamou, but there are many elderly people in the town's two public housing projects, and many more living in poverty in small wooden migrant homes.

17. Gerald L. Gold, "The Changing Criteria of Social Networks in a Cajun Community," *Ethnos* 1-2 (1980), pp. 60-81.

18. Richard Joy, *Languages in Conflict* (Toronto: Carleton Library, McClelland and Stewart, 1972).

19. There were 207 households interviewed in a stratified random sample based on an evaluation of neighbourhoods and by externally-visible social characteristics. Thirty-five interviews were done in black households, and about eighty interviews were done in a "checkerboard" sample of white and black rural neighbourhoods.

20. Cajun parents teach their children "Cajun English," making it difficult to find cues in the speech of adolescents that would unquestionably indicate their ability to speak French. English-speaking families from other parts of Louisiana who move to Mamou also tend to acquire Cajun accents.

21. CODOFIL teachers from France and from Belgium have been stationed in Mamou schools since 1972 as French specialists associated with Mamou's participation in the Evangeline Parish Title VII Bilingual Education Program. As recently as 1980, French classes were no longer than thirty minutes a day. There has been a lack of continuity in terms of which students take the Bilingual Program, and foreign associate teachers have never been able to remain in Mamou for more than several years. The result has been that the Bilingual Program has had little measurable impact on the use of the French language in Mamou homes. See Gerald L. Gold, *The Role of France, Quebec and Belgium in the Revival of French in Louisiana Schools* (Quebec City: Centre international de recherche sur le bilinguisme, Université Laval, 1980), and an appendix to Gold's monograph by Pierre Thibaud, "1972-1974: Deux années de coopération en Louisiane."

22. Gerald L. Gold, "The French Movement in Louisiana," paper presented at the annual meeting of the American Anthropological Association, Houston, Texas, 1977; Gerald L. Gold and Eric Waddell, "Le mouvement: analyse critique du renouveau ethnique en Louisiane," paper presented at the annual meeting of the Canadian Ethnology Society, Montreal, 1980; and, Gerald L. Gold, "*Cousin* and the *gros chiens*, the Limits of Cajun Political Rhetoric," in *Politically Speaking, Cross-Cultural Studies of Rhetoric*, ed. Robert Paine (St. John's, New Brunswick: The Institute of Social and Economic Research (ISER), Memorial University, 1981).

The Franco-Americans: Occupational Profiles

Madeleine Giguère

Franco-Americans are Americans who believe they share a common French Canadian or Acadian descent. Typically, they live in New England, although traditionally they have lived in New York, Michigan, Illinois, Missouri, Louisiana, and today we find substantial numbers in Florida, California and Texas. This analysis restricts itself to the Franco-Americans of New England. As a demographic study of contemporary occupational patterns among Franco-Americans this paper examines three questions:

(1)　What are the occupational patterns of French persons in New England?

(2)　How do these patterns compare with those of English mother tongue in these states?

(3)　How may these comparative patterns be explained?

The primary source of data reported on here is the 1970 Census which asked a sample of the total population, "What language was spoken in this person's home when he was a child?" It is a language background question, and whatever its defects as an indicator of language ability, in 1970 it was still a good delineator of the size and distribution of the Franco-American population with its high rate of ancestral language maintenance lasting well into the second quarter of this century. Like many social science indicators, the French mother tongue category may be a distorted mirror of the reality we want to study, but it is the best mirror we have at the moment.

There were nine hundred thousand persons of French mother tongue in New England in 1970. *The Public Use Samples of Basic Records from the 1970 Census* on tape[1] made it possible to create tables not found in the census itself. With the use of the Statistical Package for the Social Sciences' (SPSS) subprogram CROSSTABS,[2] I created social and economic profiles for the population of each of the New England states and Louisiana by French and English mother tongue. It is the occupational data from these cross-tabulations that I will now describe, compare and attempt to explain.

The occupational description of the French in the New England states (Table 1) in 1970 can best be summarized by their proportion of blue-collar workers. Table 1 documents just over one-half of New England workers of French mother tongue in blue-collar occupations, with a greater proportion of them male (63 per cent as compared to 38 per cent for women). A greater proportion of the women are found in white-collar occupations (42 per cent) than in blue-collar occupations. One can conclude that the traditional image of the Franco-American as a blue-collar worker no longer applies to the contemporary Franco-American women, but still holds true for the male population. (More than twice the proportion of males are blue-collar workers as are white-collar workers.)

Table 1: Occupational Distribution of Persons of French Mother Tongue, by Sex: New England, 1970

	Male and Female %	Male %	Female %
White Collar[1]	34	26	42
Blue Collar[2]	51	63	38
Farming[3]	1	2	—
Service[4]	14	9	20
(Numerical Total)	(4,876) 100	(2,625) 100	(2,251) 100

1. Professional, technical, managerial, sales and clerical
2. Craftsmen, operatives, labourers
3. Farmers, managers, labourers
4. Including private household workers

An inspection of occupations of persons of French mother tongue in the separate states (Table 2) indicates that in every New

England state less than one-third of the males are engaged in white-collar occupations. Over 60 per cent of the male labour force are blue-collar workers in every New England state except Vermont (which retains the agricultural-service profile of a more rural state). If the males of French mother tongue are, in the majority, blue-collar workers in the individual New England states, the women, on the whole, are not. Only in Rhode Island do they approach majority participation in blue-collar work. If we combine the proportion in lower level white-collar jobs and blue-collar work, we find approximately two-thirds of the women of French mother tongue in these occupations in each state, except Vermont.

Percentage of Women of French Mother Tongue
in Sales and Clerical Work and Blue Collar Occupations

Maine	64	Massachusetts	68
New Hampshire	67	Connecticut	69
Vermont	58	Rhode Island	76

In fact, a striking feature of the distribution of occupations among French women (Table 2) is the proportion in semi-skilled work, ranging from 30 per cent in Connecticut and Maine to 39 per cent in New Hampshire and 45 per cent in Rhode Island.

If we compare the occupational distribution of persons of French and English mother tongue in each state (Table 3), we find that a consistently smaller proportion of French males have white-collar occupations than their English counterparts. The difference is particularly noticeable in Massachusetts, Connecticut and Rhode Island. Alternatively, these three southernmost states have a substantially greater proportion of French than English male blue-collar workers. Among French women, the pattern is similar, substantial under-representation in white-collar occupations in Massachusetts, Connecticut, Rhode Island and New Hampshire (especially noticeable in Massachusetts, due to little participation in sales and clerical work).

Could we hypothesize then that mother tongue is associated with occupational patterns in New England? To test this, we measured the extent of association between mother tongue and occupation in each state (Table 3). It is to be noted that what is compared here is the occupational distribution of those of French mother tongue and the people in each state who answered "English only" to the question, "What language other than English

Table 2: Occupational Distribution of Persons of French Mother Tongue, by Sex: New England States, 1970 (by percentage)

Male

	Maine	New Hampshire	Vermont	Massachusetts	Connecticut	Rhode Island
WHITE COLLAR	25	27	30	26	26	26
Upper[1]	14	15	18	16	15	14
Lower[2]	11	11	12	10	11	11
BLUE COLLAR	62	63	45	64	67	64
Skilled[3]	28	27	16	30	35	27
Semi-skilled[4]	27	28	20	26	27	29
Unskilled[5]	7	8	8	7	4	8
FARMING	3	1	13	1	0	—
SERVICE	10	10	14	9	7	10
(Numerical Total)	(455)	(404)	(167)	(708)	(558)	(333)

Female

WHITE COLLAR	40	36	48	43	49	38
Upper[1]	10	8	12	12	12	8
Lower[2]	30	27	37	31	37	29
BLUE COLLAR	35	42	20	38	33	49
Skilled[3]	4	1	3	3	2	2
Semi-skilled[4]	30	39	18	34	30	45
FARMING	2	–	–	–	–	–
SERVICE	23	23	31	19	16	13
(Numerical Total)	(415)	(399)	(118)	(586)	(444)	(294)

1. Professional, technical, managerial and administrative
2. Sales and clerical
3. Craftsmen
4. Operative, manufacturing and transportation
5. Labourers

Table 3: Major Occupation Groups for those of French or English Mother Tongue, by Sex: New England States, 1970 (by percentage)

Male

	Maine		New Hampshire		Vermont		Massachusetts		Connecticut		Rhode Island	
	Fr.	Eng.	Fr.	Eng.	Fr.	Eng.	Fr.	Eng.	Fr.	Eng.	Fr.	Eng.
WHITE COLLAR[1]	25	32	27	37	30	36	26	44	26	47	26	42
Clerical & Sales	11	11	11	12	12	12	10	18	11	16	11	16
BLUE COLLAR[2]	62	54	63	56	44	46	64	43	67	43	64	45
Semi-skilled	27	22	28	19	20	16	26	17	27	16	29	19
SERVICE WORKERS[3]	10	8	10	10	14	10	9	12	7	9	10	12
FARM WORKERS[4]	3	6	1	2	13	9	1	1	–	1	–	1
(Numerical Total)	(455)	(2230)	(404)	(1557)	(167)	(1223)	(708)	(5635)	(558)	(5546)	(333)	(1454)
Cramer's V	0.13		0.13		0.13		0.16		0.16		0.16	
P	0.0		0.001		0.02		0.0		0.0		0.0	

Female

WHITE COLLAR[1]	40	48	36	55	48	56	43	67	49	69	38	67
Clerical & Sales	30	32	27	38	37	37	31	48	37	47	29	42
BLUE COLLAR[2] Semi-skilled	35	26	42	22	20	15	38	15	33	15	49	24
	30	22	39	20	18	12	34	13	30	13	45	20
SERVICE WORKERS[3]	24	23	23	20	31	27	19	18	16	15	13	17
FARM WORKERS[4]	2	3	–	0.7	–	1	–	–	–	1	–	–
(Numerical Total)	(415)	(1950)	(399)	(1342)	(118)	(882)	(586)	(5056)	(444)	(4887)	(294)	(1410)
Cramer's V	0.11		0.21		0.12		0.16		0.16		0.24	
P	0.001		0.0		0.23		0.0		0.0		0.0	

1. Professional, technical, managers, administrators, sales, clerical, etc.
2. Craftsmen, foremen, operatives, non-farm labourers
3. Service, including private household workers
4. Farmers, farm managers and farm labourers

was spoken in this person's home when he was a child?" The measure of association is Cramer's V, which varies from zero to plus or minus one. The degree of association between French and English mother tongue and occupation varies from 0.11 to 0.24. The results can only be characterized as indicating a *low degree of association* between mother tongue and occupation.[3] The highest degree of association, as found among the women of New Hampshire and Rhode Island, is still in the low range (Cramer's V = 0.24 and 0.21). Therefore, our hypothesis is not well supported.

Explanations of ethnic attitudes and behaviour in the United States are many.[4] To illustrate: there are explanations in terms of achievement orientation;[5] immigrant culture;[6] emphases on the context of the social structure of the ethnic experience in the United States;[7] and a combination of cultural and structural characteristics of both the ethnic group and the receiving society.[8] Cross-cutting these are the assimilationist[9] and the pluralist schools.[10] How do Franco-Americans fit into this theoretical spectrum? The following discussion should be taken as a first or tentative explanation.

The major reasons for the overall low levels of association of mother tongue and occupation are structural. Economic conditions in the Saint Lawrence homeland led to the great immigration of Quebecois to the United States in the latter part of the nineteenth and the beginning of the twentieth century.[11] The French came to New England because of the demand for their labour.[12] They had many of the qualities of ideal "hands": they were docile, quick to learn, deft and contented with low wages.[13] James Allen has shown that in 1908 textile employment explained 84 per cent of the residential distribution of the French in Maine.[14] Their high job mobility in the United States[15] probably contributed to the demand for their labour.

The key to getting out of the mills was English language proficiency as well as education. The use made of public schools by French immigrants has been little studied; but they were there, and an undetermined portion of the French did attend. With the beginning of the French parochial school system in New England in the 1880s, English was taught as a second language.[16] Later, the parochial schools taught a half day of English. Today the instructional language of the remaining Franco-American schools is English. Contrary to the popular image, schools were important to the Franco-Americans—almost as important as the church.

The great engine of change for the Franco-Americans was the Second World War. Men were drafted out of their community into the armed services; others, both men and women, volunteered. Others still were attracted by employment opportunities in defense industries in other parts of the country. Many of these never returned to their Franco-American communities. But many who did had acquired new English-language skill and new occupational skills (both technical and managerial), which would give them a larger range of employment opportunities than their parents had had. Some made use of the GI Bill to go to college and graduate school, or had acquired educational aspirations for their children, so that by 1970 young Franco-Americans had substantially more education than their elders[17] and had achieved, educationally at least, "rough parity" with the rest of the American population.[18] They said, "My children won't be laughed at for their accent," and they taught them only little French. Associated with these postwar phenomena was the decline in the use of parochial and private religious schools in the 1960s and the decline of bilingual instruction in these schools.

After the Second World War, the assimilation of the French into the occupational structures of their respective states became a fact. Yet, there is still an over-representation of them in blue-collar occupations. It has been pointed out that the initial employment for an ethnic group seemed to mark its future occupational patterns.[19] For Franco-Americans this was semi-skilled factory work.[20]

There also may be a blocked mobility factor to consider. The French are not chosen for managerial positions. This can be seen among the diocesan clergy where, with few exceptions, Franco-Americans are not recruited into the hierarchy. Has the same blockage occurred in other bureaucratic structures, both private and public? Has this also been the case with regard to lower level white-collar occupations? The substantial under-representation of French women in lower level white-collar occupations in Massachusetts is suggestive of this (Table 2). Family and home, however, may play a greater role in Franco-American life than career aspirations. One works to support a family and a life style and not for occupational prestige. The egalitarianism[21] bred in the *rang* (country road) and the effect of the devaluation of individual success preached from the pulpits of Quebec[22] may still be seen in the French workers' attitudes.

The specialization of French women in operative work in Rhode Island and New Hampshire was to a large extent a product of the structural and cultural factors just mentioned. But in addition, it may be that these women were trapped by their limited English-language ability. The high concentration of the French in Rhode Island and New Hampshire and the well-developed ethnic community institutions there may have made it possible to live out one's life in French and not learn much English. The consequence is that many are constrained, by their poor command of the English language, to work in semi-skilled occupations.

In summary: the structural factors of employment, schools and the Second World War explain the low level of association of French mother tongue and occupation. With regard to the small over-representation of Franco-Americans in blue-collar occupations in general, and semi-skilled occupations of the women in some states, historical experience, family-oriented values, blocked mobility and limited English-language ability must be considered among the major independent variables. Despite some survival of an earlier occupational specialization or pluralism, overall these data support an assimilation thesis with regard to the occupational profiles of Franco-Americans. In 1970 in New England, the occupational patterns of those of French mother tongue were only marginally different from those of English mother tongue. The hypothesis that ethnicity is related to occupations must be reformulated. A promising hypothesis is that those Franco-Americans who are French-dominant are more likely to retain their blue-collar occupations than those who are English-dominant. The 1980 United States Census micro-data should permit the testing of this reformulated hypothesis.

Notes

1. U.S. Bureau of the Census, *Public Use Samples of Basic Records from the 1970 Census,* Files 101, 102 (Washington, D.C., 1972).

2. Norman H. Nie, C. Hadlai Hull, and Dale H. Bent, *Statistical Package for the Social Sciences* (New York: McGraw Hill, 1970).

3. The X^2 test of significance indicates that all of the measures are statistically significant at the $p \leq 0.02$ level except for Vermont women ($p = 0.23$). Had we included the other non-English mother-tongue persons, fragmentary evidence indicates that the measures of association of occupation and mother tongue would be even lower.

4. William L. Yancey, Eugene P. Erikson, and Richard N. Juliani, "Emergent Ethnicity—A Review and Reformulation," *ASR* 41 (1976), pp. 391-403.

5. B.C. Rosen, "Race, Ethnicity, and the Achievement Syndrome," *ASR* 24 (1959), pp. 47-60, rpt., in *A Franco-American Overview: New England*, no. 4, ed. Madeleine Giguère (Cambridge, Mass.: National Assessment and Dissemination Center for Bilingual/Bicultural Education, 1981), pp. 85-101.

6. Harold J. Abramson, *Ethnic Diversity in Catholic America* (New York: Wiley, 1973); Carmi Schooler, "Serfdom's Legacy: An Ethnic Continuum," *AJS* 81 (1976), pp. 1265-86.

7. Yancey et al., "Emergent Ethnicity," pp. 391-403; Freida Schoenberg Rozen, "Employment and Ethnicity," *Civil Rights Issues of Euro-Ethnic Americans in the United States: Opportunities and Challenges* (Washington, D.C.: U.S. Commission on Civil Rights, 1980), pp. 466-88.

8. Milton N. Gordon, *Assimilation in American Life* (New York: Oxford University Press, 1964); Andrew M. Greeley, *Why Can't They Be Like Us?* (New York: Dutton, 1971); Rudolph Vecoli, "The Italian Americans," *The Center Magazine* (July/August 1974), pp. 31-43.

9. Gordon, *Assimilation in American Life*, pp. 60-83.

10. Nathan Glazer and Daniel Patrick Moynihan, *Beyond the Melting Pot* (Cambridge: MIT Press, 1963).

11. Yves Roby speaking at the Second Annual Conference of the French Institute, Assumption College, March 1981.

12. Pierre Anctil, "La Franco-Américanie ou le Québec d'en bas," *Cahiers de géographie du Québec* 23 (1979), pp. 39-52.

13. William MacDonald, "The French Canadians in New England," *The Quarterly Journal of Economics* (1898), rpt. in *A Franco-American Overview*, no. 3, pp. 1-21; Iris Saunders Podea, "Quebec to 'Little Canada': The Coming of the French Canadians to New England in the Nineteenth Century," *New England Quarterly* 23 (1950), pp. 365-80, rpt. in *A Franco-American Overview*, no. 3, pp. 113-23.

14. James P. Allen, "Franco-Americans in Maine: A Geographical Perspective," *Acadiensis* 43 (1974), rpt. in *A Franco-American Overview*, no. 3, pp. 83-111.

15. Tamara K. Hareven, "The Laborers of Manchester, New Hampshire, 1912-1922: The Role of the Family and Ethnicity in Adjustment to Industrial Life," *Labor History* (Spring 1975), rpt. in *A Franco-American Overview*, no. 3, pp. 157-70.

16. Antonin Plourde, "Cent ans de viè paroissale," *Le Rosaire* (April-September 1970), p. 15.

17. Madeleine D. Giguère, "Social and Economic Profiles of French and English Mother Tongue Persons: Maine, 1970," in *A Franco-American Overview*, no. 4, p. 149.

18. Andrew M. Greeley, "Educational and Economic Differences Among Religio-Ethnic Groups," in *Ethnicity in the United States: A Preliminary Reconnaissance*, ed. Andrew M. Greeley (New York: John Wiley and Sons, 1974), p. 69.

19. Rozen, "Race, Ethnicity, and the Achievement Syndrome," p. 481, rpt. in *A Franco-American Overview*, no. 4, p. 110.

20. W. Lloyd Warner, T.O. Low, Paul S. Hunt, and Leo Srole, *Yankee City* (New Haven: Yale, 1963), p. 389, rpt. in *A Franco-American Overview*, no. 4, p. 110; Podea, "Quebec to 'Little Canada'," rpt. in *A Franco-American Overview*, no. 3, pp. 113-23; Allen, "Franco-Americans in Maine," rpt. in *A Franco-American Overview*, no. 3, pp. 89-90.

21. Peter Woolfson, "Traditional French Canadian Value Orientations and Their Persistence Among the Franco-Americans of Northeastern Vermont," in *A Franco-American Overview*, no. 3, pp. 193-98.

22. Christian Morissonneau, *La Terre promise: le mythe du Nord québécois* (Quebec: Hurtubise HMH, 1978), p. 53.

Franco-Americans and Ethnic Studies: Notes on a Mill Town

Robert F. Harney

Seventy-two per cent of the French Canadians in the United States in 1912 lived in New England. There must then be dozens of French communities in the United States which deserve separate enclave study in the way that we are now studying ghettoes, Little Italies, Chinatowns and Slavic neighbourhoods. Except for the work of Pierre Anctil on Woonsocket, Frances Early on Lowell, the earlier work of Theriault on Nashua and studies of Biddeford and Holyoke, few such social scientific studies of Little Canadas exist or, at least, have reached a larger academic public.[1]

The contrast between the scant attention given to the "French fact" in current historical scholarship and the importance of the French Canadian presence in my home town intrigued me. Could Salem, Massachusetts really be atypical of New England and America? For the Salem of my childhood was, along with witches, Yankees, Irish and all the immigrant peoples of Europe, above all a French Canadian mill town. I have spent most of my time as an historian of immigration and ethnicity studying Italians and Little Italies. But if you will indulge me in my late act of filio-piety toward Salem, I will reminisce with the aid of a few random sources about Mill Hill and Castle Hill—Salem's two Little Canadas—and their relationship to the larger city. To do this, I have simply applied some of the ways of looking at Little Italies as ethnic enclaves to the mill neighbourhoods that I grew up near.

I have used the Salem city documents, assessment rolls, several municipal annual reports from the turn of the century and the

statistics of the United States Senate's great inquest into the new
migration (the Dillingham Commission of 1911) to complement
my nostalgia.[2] Salem in 1900 had 35,000 people, 23,000 of them
foreign-born. Of those, 9,000 were Irish and 7,000 were French
Canadian. If one accepts the Dillingham Commission's own ex-
trapolations on births among the foreign-born, there were probably another 2,000 French Canadian children of American birth so
that close to 9,000 people, or one-quarter of Salem's population
was French Canadian. The French community had the highest
birth rates in the city during the first decade of the century and
the most new marriages contracted in Salem per ethnic group
were between French Canadians. That statistic is the more remarkable if we assume that a certain number of young people
returned to Quebec or the Maritimes for their weddings. French
Canadians in Salem had a densely settled neighbourhood with
well-defined boundaries that only in the last decade has begun to
fade at the edges with the arrival of large numbers of new Hispanic immigrants. The decline of neighbourhood has more to do
with the partitioning of the mill buildings to create small, modern
plastics and textile sweat-shops than it does with any deliberate
decision by the French Canadians to leave the ethnocultural ambiance around the mill and the church.

The German clergy, in their struggle against Irish domination
of the church, justified their national parishes by declaring that
"language saves faith." For the French in Salem, the reverse
seemed equally true. In a town which once had a Polish grammar
school and daily masses in Italian, Polish, Ukrainian and Portuguese, only the French on Mill Hill with the new, modern St.
Joseph's Church and its surrounding schools seemed to be avoid-
ing the slide into homogeneity. (Of course, that was more form
than reality. The grammar school now has many Hispanic children; the girls' high school is gone; the parish, in the outlying
town of Beverly, was burnt down and rebuilt in the farther suburbs; Ste. Chretienne's Academy long ago became a finishing
school for the Irish American bourgeoisie rather than a centre of
French culture.) One can still walk up Mill Hill, though, and feel
the power of the alliance of the holy faith with French Canadian
ethnoculture. The new church faces down the hill toward Salem's
centre and the other ethnic neighbourhoods below. It does not
dominate the tenements and mills behind it in quite the way the
old red-brick church did, but the very decision to raze that old
church after a fire and build just as big a new one on the site, at a
time when the last of the cotton and sheet mills were closing,

could be seen as an assertion that the church and the ethnic group—not the mills—defined the neighbourhood. That has proven only partially true and streets between the church and the mills that were once almost totally inhabited by Quebecois immigrants and their descendants now harbour pockets of more recent Latin immigrants, drawn to new unskilled jobs in the mill buildings.

Farther out from Mill Hill, in what was long an unincorporated part of Salem, separated from the Quebecois by the Boston and Maine freight yards, lies Castle Hill with its "shingle-town" housing and its own parish church, a wooden one, Ste. Anne's. Most of the parishioners are Acadian; they or their parents arrived in Salem later than the Quebecois, and one could notice, at least into the 1950s, the sub-ethnic differences between the two parishes. The Acadian one was visibly more rural and poorer. Between the two neighbourhoods, next to the tracks on Canal Street, there stood, when I was a boy, a pretty white, wooden and spired church which my grandmother called, rather primly, the French Baptist church. That church, now covered with ghastly yellow siding, the spire reduced to a turret, has become a Kingdom Hall of the Jehovah's Witnesses. I do not know how many of its members are of French Canadian descent. The disappearance of such a Protestant French subculture on the margins of the ethnic group may be a harbinger of the decline of the larger immigrant culture. Or perhaps the transition simply parallels changing religious vogues in Quebec.

I have not seen any studies by social scientists of Salem's Little Canadas; few of the local Franco-Americans go to graduate school in history and fewer yet would waste their French language skills on anything less than Napoleonic or Balzacean studies.[3] (The valedictorian of my Catholic high school class came from Mill Hill. I believe he teaches Aramaic and biblical archaeology somewhere in the Ivy League.) In the face of a tendency in the neighbourhoods for primordial ethnicity—that is, the Quebec and quaint ways of the old folks and the legends about the migration and first years in the mills—to be taken for granted or undervalued, something should be done now to preserve oral testimony banks of the Quebec and Acadian diaspora. The sources, especially in the form of the oldest settlers, are terribly fragile. No amount of demographic study or Canadian and New England government sources will compensate for the loss of knowledge—about the migration chains, the recruiters, the attitudes of family toward migration, the encounter with the mills, with the other ethnic groups, and the use of religion and language as a way of rallying the community—that will ensue if the memory culture of the old people is not systematically recorded and preserved.

In the first decades of the twentieth century, St. Joseph's on Mill Hill was the centre of the ethnoculture. Its shadow and penumbra loomed over the parochial schools, self-help associations, ethnic institutions and even much of the business life of the Salem French. To varying degrees, all institutional life and aspects of the socio-economy, not controlled by the mills, depended on the parish. The Salem French in the 1900s had an active male youth organization, the Cercle Veuillot, named significantly after a rabid ultramontane. The Caisse St. Jean Baptiste, bank and credit union for most of the community, perfectly mirrored the alliance of faith, ethnic trust and enterprise on the Hill. Less clearly tied to the church were a newspaper, the *Courrier de Salem,* and the French Naturalization Society which, despite its name, seemed more a badge of the ethnic neighbourhood's structure of notability and respectability than an agent of its subversion.

From the municipal tax books for the neighbourhood in 1912, we can see that French Canadian immigrants or their sons and daughters owned at least sixty businesses that were substantial enough to require payment of over $200 annually in taxes on their stock and property. Successful provisioners and businesses could be found at the corners of most of the streets running back from the church and school toward the mills. Many have since been converted from storefronts to residences; so the city archaeologist walking through the Little Canada on Mill Hill has a reduced sense of the entrepreneurial life of the neighbourhood in the 1900s. I remember those stores even though they were not memorable. They recall for me the faint suggestion of prejudice in my childhood perspective. My grandfather would say "go to the little French store," no matter what the size of the store in question. The diminutive hid something that was vaguely derisive. He would not have believed that the "little French shopkeepers" who ran the "little stores" appeared to some later historians as the petty-bourgeois base of a middle-class hegemony which advocated ethnic *survivance* so that they could, with their allies in the church and school, control more easily the economy and ideology of their mill worker clientele.

In that same neighbourhood now, a remnant of such corner stores, usually under new ethnic management, struggle to survive, give credit to Hispanic neighbours and tolerate loitering children of the new ethnoculture; they seem to be as unlikely *noyaux* (nuclei) of ethnic persistence for Puerto Rican and Dominican immigrants, as their French Canadian predecessors were.

Mill Hill was a neighbourhood conceived and constructed during the era of the "three-decker madness" when local investors, not content with the profits to be made exploiting immigrants in the work place, built tenements specifically to house mill workers. At first these landlords were mostly Yankee, but some multi-family investment dwellings on Mill Hill did have a French Canadian investor's surname proudly chiselled upon them. Wise adjustment to Salem's economic possibility, individual good fortune, occasional proceeds from a farm inheritance in Quebec, along with the traditional structure of notability produced a discernible social ladder within the ethnic group, understood, in a way that is often lost upon a younger generation of anthropologists and labour historians, by all who tried to climb it.

The concentration of crowded worker housing near the mills did leave an impression of universal poverty or proletarianization at the core of the ethnic ambiance. The apartment houses of Ward Street and behind the mills seem to have been built almost to predict the tiny urban ghetto they have become in the last ten years. From the city records of 1912, it is clear that much of Salem's poverty and contagious disease was concentrated on Mill and Castle Hills. Of the 106 victims of smallpox in Salem in 1911, 102 were French Canadians who lived in the mill neighbourhoods. (Nuns from Quebec ran a floating hospital for the contagiously ill on one of the islands in Salem harbour for a number of years.) Yet the city nurse described the Mill Hill homes she visited as the cleanest and best run households she had encountered; the problem was crowding and poverty, not social pathology. Officials were far more apt to find fault with the family life and health habits of Greek, Italian and Polish immigrants, even of shanty Irish.

Without good social history studies, it is difficult to see beyond the perception of the French Canadians, held by public officials, to the reality of their daily lives. The best fictional glimpses of French Canadian life in New England, if one leaves aside the moments of genius in Ti-Jean Kerouac's fictionalized memories, are in the writings of Jacques Ducharme, especially his *The Shadows of the Trees* (1943). Ducharme describes a Franco-American community in the Connecticut River valley. He calls his co-nationals "the small people of New England," not just mill workers, but shopkeepers, lady clerks in the downtown stores, artisans and white-collar employees, niched throughout the lower levels of the socio-economy of small industrial cities. The jury lists from Salem in 1912—a source that is a bit skewed because only citizens appear on the lists—give some insight into the variety and range of French Canadian insertion into New England's economy. Twenty-one different occupations were represented by the Franco-Americans picked for jury duty, and only one of them had any connection with the mills. The jurors included an undertaker, an insurance man from the St. Jean Baptiste Society, tailors, carters and drivers, contractors, bookkeepers and a dinker (a man who, like my grandfather, cut out the patterns for the uppers and soles of shoes as piece-work in the shoe and leather shops). From this distance, I cannot say whether leaving the mills for the shoe and leather factories represented a victory of upward mobility.

It is striking how little the writing of modern labour history does to inform us about the aspirations, *mentalités* and workscape of the immigrant worker in this regard. What does emerge from a cursory look at Salem's records is a profile of a city in which one-third of the populace—immigrants or the children of immigrants from Quebec or l'Acadie—found work and sustenance without seeming to arouse the fierce hostility among the English-speaking population that the European immigrants did. Yankees and their Irish Catholic junior allies and competitors seemed to accept the French quickly as part of the New England landscape. One reason, in Salem at least, why the coming of the French Canadians did not arouse a nativist reaction seems to be related to their slowness to compete for jobs with Salem's chief employer—not the mills but the municipal government. While other ethnic groups, especially the Irish, were, at the very time the municipal employment rolls were expanding, wresting city jobs from the Yankees, the French Canadians, as one-third of the city's populace, remained vastly under-represented among those feeding at the public trough. Salem in 1912 had no public school teachers of French Canadian descent. Indeed there was only one Franco-American school janitor. Jobs in the school system, like many other city jobs, were sinecures, especially when compared with work in the mills and leather factories. The jobs were secured by finding one's place in the city's political "pork-barrel." French Canadians did not have the clout to demand their share of city jobs in the first days of the century. One can attribute their limited participation to the "cost of community" itself. Undiminished vocations, an excess of nuns, too many children in the parochial schools and a confidence that not just the schools but all the ethnocultural institutions of the group formed an "institutional completeness" to shelter them from the larger community deluded French Canadians into accepting a form of double taxation without representation. They lacked a say in Salem's public institutions, and at the same time, they failed to receive their just share of the city's spoils system.

For example, in the fire department, only four out of ninety-eight men were French in 1912. Thus, while they constituted more than 25 per cent of the city's population, they made up only 5 per cent of the fire-fighters. Only four of the sixty policemen were French. (Among them, however, was the chief inspector whose name was Gidéon Pelletier. That gentleman was the best paid policeman and certainly the highest city official with a French surname.) In the other city departments, the same low representation of the ethnic group prevailed. Only one out of forty-one full-time workers in the Water Department was French. A certain number of the casual workers and 10 per cent of the Public Works Department also came from the ethnic group. There were no Franco-Americans, except as casual and day labourers working for the city Parks Department, the most politicized of all municipal appointments. Sometimes service in this department carried with it the right to reside in a pleasant little cottage in the middle of a park. In my boyhood, all such "plums" belonged to the Irish, even at Forest River Park in the heart of the Franco-American neighbourhoods. (I should add that Salem's mayor today is named Levesque and that the wards where the two parishes are located have usually had Franco-American aldermanic representation; but I do not think that even now the municipal pay-roll has proportionate French Canadian representation.)

Ducharme has written that the part Franco-Americans have played in New England is not a showy one, and the historian Barbara Solomon makes the striking statement in her *Ancestors and Immigrants* that by 1900 old stock New Englanders displayed little interest in the French Canadians.[5] One is left to conclude that if ethnic stereotypes existed about Franco-Americans, they were so muted as to be inconsequential. Surely French Canadians in New England had to settle into some relationship of respect or prejudice with their Yankee, Irish, Italian, Greek, Polish, Portuguese, Jewish, Armenian and Lebanese neighbours—all peoples with whom they jostled for jobs, housing, political and educational advantage. Or did they? Why do we know so little about the subject beyond a few pioneer works like Kenneth Underwood's study of Holyoke and Lloyd Warner's studies of Newburyport?[6]

The revival of ethnic identity through the new ethnicism, the spilling over of some of Quebec's anger towards anglophone Canada and a justified irritation at being ignored in American history leads, I think, to a need to emphasize conflict and injustice, to deny docility and peaceful adjustment. One can catalogue the nasty resistance of the Irish clergy to the cultural rights of the French Canadian Catholics. One can concentrate on the instances of aggravated ethnic rivalries in the labour movement, such as during the great Lawrence textile strikes.[7] No doubt thousands of Quebec and Acadian immigrants were exploited in the work place and taunted and derided for their alien ways by other New Englanders. However, if concentrating on the rhetoric of nativist labour leaders and restrictionist politicians and seeing a racialist and consistent hostility to the francophone immigrants in such slogans as the "Chinese of the East" is politically expedient, it is also retrospective falsification. When authentic Chinese were brought into North Adams, Massachusetts in 1867 to break a strike in the shoe industry, they were met by angry Irish mobs at the railway station.[8] According to the Dillingham Commission, that same town of North Adams had about five thousand French Canadians working in it—probably some as scabs—by 1905. There were no riots against them, no violence save the small personal inter-ethnic skirmishes.

So it seemed to be in Salem. The danger in being French Canadian was less one of being assaulted and insulted and more one of being ignored in poverty and exploitation. In turn-of-the-century Salem, the public night-schools taught courses on Abraham Lincoln, personal hygiene and the history of the United States in Greek, Polish and Italian. None were taught in French. Was it because Franco-Americans were not seen as immigrants? Was it assumed that priests and nuns taught them American civics in parochial schools? The immigrants from Europe were besieged by public health nurses, school teachers, do-gooders and evangelists who tried to Americanize, christianize, sanitize and improve them. Why didn't this happen to the immigrants from Quebec and l'Acadie? If it did, where are the studies about acculturation, language retention, ethnic persistence and the power of the church?

By the decade before the First World War, French Canadians formed part of the mental landscape of other New Englanders.

They were everywhere, and their presence was not a surprise or
an alien intrusion like that of newly arrived Armenian and Jewish
leather workers or Italian street labourers. It helped that their
presence was not exclusively, or even typically, a big city phenomenon. (In fact, Franco-Americans made up less than one per
cent of Boston's population.) Although many of them journeyed
back and forth to Quebec farms and retained the *mentalité* of
sojourners, they did not appear as "birds of passage"—suspicious-
looking foreign migrants—to the natives. The French Canadian
presence in all types of New England environments is borne out
in the statistics of ethnic distribution for those years. There were
almost as many French Canadians per thousand inhabitants in
cities under 25,000 people and in rural areas as there were in the
cities over 25,000. (That fact may very well be a statistical artifact
caused by the drift of Quebecois and Acadians into agriculture
and lumbering in northern New England. Nonetheless one encountered some French Canadians in almost every city and town
of the six states.) Only the Yankees themselves have a more
balanced distribution between cities, small towns and rural areas.

Such statistics help to explain the lurking stereotypes, the sense
of the socio-economic order of Yankee Salem in my childhood.
The French Canadians were not like the Greeks, Italians, Poles,
east European Jews or Armenians with whom I grew up. On the
other hand, they were not quite as settled, as grafted onto the
official power structure in Salem, one might even say as native, as
the English-speaking Irish. Yet one always sensed that the Yankees, especially employers and politicos, saw French Canadians as
acceptable allies, not competitors like the Irish and not foreigners
like the others.[9] The Irish in turn, despite the remaining mutual
incomprehensions of disparity of culture and a tendency to make
fun of the "Frenglish" often spoken at work sites, lost their hostility for the Franco-Americans once they no longer needed to
protect mill and factory positions from them. I believe, in Salem,
that records of intermarriage between the two groups during and
after the depression would confirm this.

Moreover, some of the Irish and French clergy discovered a
Jansenist and ultramontane bond between the two communities.
(It was an Irish nun who taught me to say "merci, mon père" to
the French Canadian priest umpire every time a boy named
Jalbert struck me out playing baseball against St. Joseph's in the
Salem parochial school league. That I was encouraged to answer
courteously in French was not an acknowledgement of a living
alternative ethnoculture but, as with the Latin mass a few years
later, a farewell to a folkway.) Most of the clergy, I suspect,

would have agreed with the priest in Ducharme's novel of the 1940s:

> For my part I will always preach in French, and I prefer to read in French. On parish business however, I often have to speak English. So do my parishioners. They cannot escape assimilation where the clergy can. In time I suppose we will all be assimilated, and apart from a few societies, and a nucleus interested in the problem as a cultural one, there will be no Franco-Americans.[10]

As early as 1911, the Immigration Commission's statistics on language use in mill towns like Salem showed French Canadians leading all other foreign-born in their ability to get by in the English language. At the same time, the Commission's figures suggested that Franco-Americans continued to use the French language at home, in the ethnocommunity itself and for their ritual life. Over a few generations this functional bilingualism of the Little Canadas has effectively disappeared. The ethnolinguist Joshua Fishman has described the process precisely. "What begins as the language of social and economic mobility ends, with three generations or so, as the language of the crib as well."[11]

At the 1980 Worcester conference entitled "Situation de la Recherche sur la Franco-Américanie," a participant insisted that a Franco-American reality was "alive and well" in New England, and that there was a "future for Franco-American studies." A walk through Mill Hill and Castle Hill, the fossils of Salem's Little Canadas, leads me to be more certain of the latter than the former. It also leads me to believe that, if local studies are not undertaken systematically and soon, it will be too late to recapture the richness of the ethnoculture, the complexity of the socioeconomy and the variety of *mentalités* that characterized the French Canadian neighbourhoods of New England.

Notes

1. The best introduction to the bibliography of Franco-American studies is Gérard J. Brault, "Etat présent des études sur les centres franco-américains de la Nouvelle-Angleterre" in *Situation de la Recherche sur la Franco-Américanie,* eds. C. Quintal and A. Vachon (Quebec, 1980), pp. 9-25.

2. See City of Salem, *Valuation and Assessments for the Year 1911* (Salem, 1911); City of Salem, *City Documents for 1912* (Salem, 1913); and, Senate of the United States, *Reports of the Immigration Commission presented by Mr. Dillingham, Dec. 5, 1910* (Doc. #61) (Washington, 1911), especially volume III "Statistical Review of Immigration, 1820-1910" and vol. X "Immigrants in Industries on Cotton Manufacturing."

3. Salem's puritan, colonial and clipper ship past dominates local history writing even though, as Jacques Ducharme observed of another mill town in *The Shadows of the Trees* (New York, 1943), p. 8, in demographic terms, "the tables had been turned," since the 1880s, "in the land of the Puritans, to whom Frenchmen and Papists [Irish, Italians and Poles] were an abomination"; and the history of modern Salem is properly that of a polyglot industrial Catholic city.

4. Two recent studies that seem to see the French Canadian mill workers as permanent subspecies of an American proletariat rather than as possible sojourners or entrepreneurs in a stratified ethnic enclave are: D. Walkowitz, *Worker City, Company Town, Iron and Cotton Workers Protest in Troy and Cohoes, New York 1855-84* (Urbana, 1978) and Tamara Hareven and R. Langenbach, *Amoskeag: Life and Work in an American Factory City* (New York, 1978). A more complex view of social and ethnocultural stratification can be found in Pierre Anctil, "Aspects of Class Ideology in a New England Ethnic Minority: the Franco-Americans of Woonsocket, Rhode Island (1865-1929)" (Ph.D. dissertation, New School for Social Research, New York City, 1980).

5. Barbara Solomon, *Ancestors and Immigrants: a Changing New England Tradition* (New York, 1965), p. 163.

6. W. Lloyd Warner and Leo Srole, *The Social System of American Ethnic Groups,* volume III of the Yankee City Series (New Haven, 1945) and Kenneth Underwood, *Protestant and Catholic. Religious and Social Interaction in an Industrial Community* (Boston, 1957).

7. See, for example, the image of French Canadians in Daniel Cole, *Immigrant City: Lawrence, Massachusetts 1845-1921* (Chapel Hill, North Carolina, 1963).

8. Ronald Takaki, *Iron Cages. Race and Culture in Nineteenth Century America* (New York, 1979), pp. 232-34.

9. I am not sure how much conviction there was in Senator Lodge's description of the French Canadians as fellow Normans—about as much perhaps as when the late Premier LeSage of Quebec attributed his ability to best anglophone political opponents to his Norman blood lines. More to the point was the non-threatening quality of the French Canadian presence, especially in terms of political competition and labour unrest. Nathaniel Shaler of the Immigration Restric-

tion League saw them as a good alternative to the Irish, who had "threatened to overwhelm us [Yankees] for so long," quoted in B. Solomon, *Ancestors and Immigrants*, p. 161.

10. J. Ducharme, *The Shadows of the Trees: the Story of French Canadians in New England* (New York, 1943), p. 212.

11. Joshua Fishman, "Language Maintenance and Ethnicity," *Canadian Review of Studies in Nationalism* VIII, no. 2 (Fall 1981), pp. 233-34.

French in the Canadian West

The Decline of French as Home Language in the Quebec and Acadian Diaspora of Canada and the United States

Charles Castonguay

During the past decade, research in the demography of language groups has been able to establish, fairly precisely, to what extent French is spoken as main language in the homes of the Quebec and Acadian minorities in North America. We will attempt to summarize the research, based mainly on the 1971 and 1976 Canadian censuses and the 1976 Survey of Income and Education in the United States. The results will not only shed some light on the demographic future of French-speaking people outside Quebec and their various efforts to better their chances of survival; but they may also lead to a better understanding of the recent measures taken by several governments to render the French language secure at least within the Province of Quebec.

Measuring Language Loss among French Minorities in Canada

The principal home-language question of the 1971 Census ("What language do you most often speak at home now?") is the only major source of information on the use of French in Canadian homes. The 1971 Census also included the more frequently asked mother-tongue question ("Language first spoken and still understood?"), which amounts to asking what language was most often spoken by the respondent at home in early childhood. By comparing the responses to these two questions, we can determine to what extent members of various language minorities have ceased to use their mother tongue as principal home language. Outside Quebec, when a mother tongue is abandoned as the main home language, English almost always becomes the adopted home language; so such language loss is commonly referred to as Anglicisation.

Anglicisation usually occurs during the processes of growing up and establishing a home of one's own. It can be generally assumed that, by the age of thirty-five, if a person of French mother tongue still uses French as principal home language, then he or she will continue to do so. As a result, the current rate of loss of French as home language, or rate of Anglicisation, is usually determined through the comparison of mother tongue and current home language among mature adults between thirty-five and forty-five years of age. The Anglicisation of this age group, which is at the height of the child-rearing years, is also demographically important for minority language groups, since the home language spoken by the parents normally determines their children's mother tongue.

Table 1 gives the Anglicisation figures for Canada's eight major provincial French-language minorities. The data in Table 1 can be read in several ways. For example, the Anglicisation rate given for Ontario's French mother-tongue population between thirty-five and forty-five years of age is 38 per cent. That means the French home-language population in that age group in Ontario represents only 62 per cent of the French mother-tongue population of the same age. In the same way, the Anglicisation rate of 45 per cent given for the same age group in Manitoba indicates that, of the total French home-language population expected on the basis of mother-tongue strength, there is a representation of only 55 per cent.

The 1971 Census is the only one which yields information on current Anglicisation. The data collected then among older age groups can, however, be used as reference to gain some insight into the Anglicisation rate that was current when former generations first reached mature adulthood. For instance, the Anglicisation rate of persons from forty-five to fifty-five years of age in 1971 tells us the approximate rate of Anglicisation of the thirty-five to forty-five years of age group of ten years previous, and so on. Read in this way, the data on the older age groups (Table 1) reveal a general increase in the Anglicisation rate of French minorities in Canada over the past three or four decades.

Table 1: Anglicisation Rate of French Mother-Tongue Minorities by Age Groups, Canada, 1971 (percentage)

Age Group

	35-44	45-54	55-64	65 and older
Prince Edward Island	50	48	42	43
Nova Scotia	42	40	37	30
New Brunswick	12	12	9	6
Ontario	38	36	32	26
Manitoba	45	41	34	22
Saskatchewan	60	58	47	37
Alberta	64	59	53	42
British Columbia	77	79	75	66

Source: *1971 Census of Canada: Language by Age Groups* (Statistics Canada, 1974).

Such an intergenerational reading of Table 1 shows, for example, that over the past thirty or forty years, the rate of Anglicisation of the French minority in New Brunswick has increased approximately from 6 per cent to 12 per cent, while that of the French minority in Saskatchewan has risen from about 37 per cent to 60 per cent. Generally, the higher Anglicisation rate among the younger mature adults (Table 1) shows a decline over recent decades in the use of French as home language among all the French-speaking minorities outside Quebec.

Objections have been raised to interpreting the 1971 data over several generations in this way.[1] However, the socio-linguistic model underlying this method of analysis was laid out some years ago[2] and has received considerable acceptance.[3] Furthermore, the data in the 1976 Census (which contained only the mother-tongue question) confirm the general rise in the Anglicisation rate among the younger adults. Maheu (1968) first pointed out, at the time of the Royal Commission on Bilingualism and Biculturalism, that the mother tongue declared for children under five years of age can be used as an approximate indicator for the home language of their parents.[4] Applying this indirect method of determining language loss to the 1976 mother-tongue data, Lachapelle and Henripin (1980) confirmed that the Anglicisation rate of the younger French mother-tongue adults continued to increase beyond 1971.

Mixed Marriages: a Parallel Increase

Exogamy, or intermarriage with members of other language groups, is a well-known cause of language loss and demographic decline of language minorities. Insight into the accelerating Anglicisation rate of French minorities can therefore be gained by studying the frequency and linguistic outcome of mixed marriages. The 1971 data show that, among French mother-tongue spouses in linguistically mixed marriages outside Quebec, over 90 per cent spoke English most often at home. The exception was the French minority in New Brunswick, where the Anglicisation rate was 80 per cent.

As for the frequency of intermarriage, the 1971 data show that, outside Quebec, the rate of exogamy of French mother-tongue youths has risen rapidly over the past five decades or so.[5] This can be inferred from the higher exogamy rate among younger age groups as compared to those of older age groups. Marriage generally occurs in early adulthood; therefore, the marriage partners in the various adult age groups can be used, much as in the case of language loss, to obtain an approximate comparison between the past and present exogamy rates.

Unlike language loss, which cannot be measured directly from the results of the 1976 Census (for lack of information on the respondents' current home language), our knowledge of linguistic intermarriage can be updated using the 1976 mother-tongue data alone. Comparison with the 1971 observations confirms that exogamy is on the rise among the French minorities, with the possible exception of New Brunswick. The trend towards increasing intermarriage on the part of the younger adults is evident from the 1976 statistics given in Table 2.

The increasing frequency with which French mother-tongue youths tend to marry outside their language group explains, to a large extent, the recent rise in the Anglicisation rate of Canada's French minorities. It also paves the way for further increases in Anglicisation through the late 1970s and 1980s. As can be seen from Table 2, the exogamy rate of the younger adults, between fifteen and thirty-five years of age, is generally higher than that of the thirty-five to forty-five year age group; this difference can serve as a reference for measuring language loss. As a consequence, if the marriage choices of the younger adults not yet married in 1976 follow the trend shown by those already married at that time, and if language loss continues to be as closely related

---

Table 2: Exogamy Rate of French Mother-Tongue Minorities by Age Groups, Canada, 1976 (percentage)

Age Group

	15-24	25-34	35-44	45-54	55-64	65 and older
Prince Edward Island	44	46	37	27	20	15
Nova Scotia	47	45	41	34	26	17
New Brunswick	12	13	12	10	8	6
Ontario	37	37	34	30	27	20
Manitoba	46	45	38	31	27	20
Saskatchewan	66	63	53	43	38	27
Alberta	60	60	55	48	41	32
British Columbia	71	67	64	60	60	51

Source: *1976 Census of Canada*, special tabulation.

---

to exogamy, it is to be expected that the Anglicisation rate of the 1981 and 1991 Census reference groups will, generally, be higher than those observed in 1971.

Aside from external contemporary causes of increasing exogamy and Anglicisation, such as urbanization, the mass media explosion, greater religious tolerance, or greater geographic and professional mobility, further study shows that the increasing proportion of already Anglicised persons of French ancestry provides a growingly efficient internal mechanism of ever higher assimilation. Indeed, the English mother-tongue youths of French descent (on their father's or mother's side, or both) show a marked facility to marry back into the French minorities; and Anglicisation of the French mother-tongue spouse is, once again, the usual linguistic outcome of such marriages.[6] The processes of exogamy and Anglicisation thus bear the seed for their own regeneration.

The rate of exogamy and Anglicisation of the younger French mother-tongue adults has reached such a level that almost all of Canada's French-speaking minorities, save again that of New Brunswick, have been dwindling noticeably in relative numerical importance throughout the past three or four decades. Table 3 shows in particular the effects of exogamy and Anglicisation of young parents, combined with the normalization of birth rates, on the relative statistical strength of French mother-tongue children outside Quebec.

Table 3: Relative Importance of French Mother-Tongue Minorities among Total Provincial Population by Age Groups, Canada, 1976 (percentage)

Age Group

	0-4	5-9	10-14	15-19	20-44	45 and older
Prince Edward Island	3.5	4.1	4.9	5.6	5.4	7.1
Nova Scotia	2.6	2.9	3.2	3.6	4.7	6.1
New Brunswick	32.5	32.9	34.8	36.0	34.7	31.2
Ontario	4.7	4.8	5.6	5.9	6.0	5.8
Manitoba	3.6	3.9	5.1	5.4	5.8	6.2
Saskatchewan	1.2	1.6	2.0	2.4	3.1	4.1
Alberta	1.3	1.4	1.8	2.0	2.8	3.2
British Columbia	0.6	0.6	0.8	1.0	1.9	2.1

Source: *1976 Census of Canada: Mother Tongue by Age Groups* (Statistics Canada, 1978).

As far as can be seen, exceptionally high birth rates and waves of immigration from Quebec are things of the past, while the rate of exogamy and Anglicisation will continue to rise in the future. It is not surprising, then, that the French mother-tongue minorities have shown a general drop in absolute numbers between 1971 and 1976.[7] While this is the first time in Canada's history that such a decline has been observed between two censuses, it is certainly not the last.

Language Loss among French Minorities in the United States

Until quite recently, very little information was available on language use in the United States. In 1976, however, several language items were included in the Survey of Income and Education carried out by the United States Census Bureau. The geographically stratified sample of some 440,000 respondents was representative enough to admit a regional breakdown of the United States' French-language population into three major groups. They are northern New England (Maine, New Hampshire and Vermont), southern New England (Massachusetts, Rhode Island and Connecticut, excluding the metropolitan areas of

Bridgeport and New Haven) and Louisiana (all non-metropolitan regions of that state together with the metropolitan regions of Baton Rouge and New Orleans, and that of Beaumont, Texas).

The questions in the survey included a mother-tongue question ("What language was usually spoken in this person's home when he was a child?") and a current principal-language question ("What language does this person usually speak?"), which correspond roughly to the language questions in the Canadian census. Analysing this data by age groups, as was done for Canada's French-language minorities, Veltman (1980, cited in note 3) found that the Anglicisation rate of various language minorities is on the increase in the United States as well.

More significantly, the principal-language question was accompanied by a second ("Does this person often speak another language?"). As a result, answers to the principal- and second-language questions taken together should record all cases where French is spoken often by a French mother-tongue respondent, be it in the context of the home or not. Combining the data in this way, Veltman has shown that, of the native-born French mother-tongue adults of child-rearing age in northern New England and Louisiana, over 40 per cent do not speak French frequently at home, neither as first nor as second language.[8] The frequency of this kind of Anglicisation, which is more definitive than that which the Canadian data allow us to determine, rises above 60 per cent for the native-born French mother-tongue reference group in southern New England.

The demographic implications of this type of Anglicisation for the Quebec and Acadian diaspora in the United States can be grasped by looking at the age pyramids of its three major components (Table 4). There, the French-language population consists of persons of French mother tongue, together with persons of other mother tongues who speak French often, either as principal or second language.

The age pyramids of Table 4 cover what could therefore be termed the "active" French-language population of the three regions. The picture is clear: there are few children who are of French mother tongue (or who speak French often at home) in any of the regions. And in each region, at least two-thirds of the French-language population is over forty years of age and unlikely to procreate.

Research in the demography of language groups shows that, among the Quebec and Acadian diaspora in both Canada and the United States, the use of French as home language is declining

**Table 4: Age Distribution of Major French-Language Populations,
United States, 1976 (percentage)**

Age Group	Northern New England	Southern New England	Louisiana
0-9	2.3	1.8	1.4
10-19	8.4	4.0	4.1
20-29	9.4	8.0	8.1
30-39	15.0	10.1	14.5
40-49	17.2	18.6	22.8
50-59	18.8	22.0	20.7
60-69	14.4	17.7	16.5
70 and more	14.4	17.7	12.0
Total	100.0	100.0	100.0
N (weighted)	181,000	286,000	377,000

Source: Veltman, "Le Sort de la francophonie aux Etats-Unis," pp. 43-57.

rapidly. Analysis of exogamy rate and age pyramid structure
strongly suggests that, outside Quebec and New Brunswick, future
Anglicisation rate will be even higher than that observed in the
1970s. If, in the twenty-first century, the French language continues to be learned and practised as a distinguishing trait of the
diaspora, it will be more as a language of culture or of international and scientific communication acquired outside the home
than, as in the past, a mother tongue and home language.

Notes

1. John De Vries and Frank Vallee, *Language Use in Canada*, Catalogue No. 99-762E (Ottawa: Statistics Canada, 1980).

2. Charles Castonguay, "Dimensions des transferts linguistiques entre
   groupes anglophone, francophone et autre d'après le recensement de
   1971," *Annales de l'Association canadienne-française pour l'avance-
   ment des sciences* 41, no. 2 (1974), pp. 125-31; and, "Les Transferts
   linguistiques au foyer," *Recherches sociographiques* 17, no. 3 (1976),
   pp. 341-51.

3. Réjean Lachapelle and Jacques Henripin, *La Situation démolinguistique au Canada: évolution passée et prospective* (Montreal: Institute
   for Research on Public Policy, 1980); Commissioner of Official Lan-

guages, *Annual Report 1979* (Ottawa: Supply and Services Canada, 1980); and, Calvin Veltman, *The Assimilation of American Language Minorities: Structure, Pace, and Extent* (Washington: National Center for Education Statistics, Office of Education, Department of Health, Education, and Welfare, 1980).

4. Robert Maheu, "Les Francophones au Canada, 1941-1991" (Masters thesis, Département de Démographie, Université de Montréal). Reprinted as *Les Francophones du Canada, 1941-1991* (Montreal: Partipris, 1968).

5. Charles Castonguay, "Exogamie et anglicisation chez les minorités canadiennes-françaises," *Canadian Review of Sociology and Anthropology* 16, no. 1 (1979), pp. 21-31.

6. Charles Castonguay, *Exogamie et anglicisation dans les régions de Montréal, Hull, Ottawa et Sudbury,* Publication B-97 (Quebec: International Centre for Research on Bilingualism, Presses de l'Université Laval, 1981).

7. Lachapelle and Henripin, *Situation démolinguistique au Canada,* Tables B40 and B41.

8. Calvin Veltman, "Le Sort de la francophonie aux Etats-Unis," *Cahiers québécois de démographie* 9, no. 1 (1980), pp. 43-57.

'L'Affaire Forest': Franco-Manitobans in Search of Cultural and Linguistic Duality*

Gilbert-L. Comeault

On December 13, 1979 the Supreme Court of Canada ruled that the Province of Manitoba went beyond its legislative powers in 1890 when it passed the Official Language Act abrogating the French-language rights defined in Section 23 of the Manitoba Act of 1870. The ruling restored official status to the French language in the debates of the legislature and in the courts of Manitoba. It also reinstated the mandatory use of French in the printing and publication of legislative journals, records and acts.[1]

The Government of Manitoba responded by stating that "with good will and ... a reasoned approach," the judgment "could be applied in sound practical terms."[2] Both Premier Sterling Lyon, and the province's Attorney General Gerry Mercier promised to use as a guideline the decision of the chief justice of the Manitoba Court of Appeal in the case of the *attorney general* versus *Forest*.[3] The chief justice concluded that "Constitutions can be made to work only if the spirit of them is observed as well as the

---

*This paper is not a criticism of a particular government. In 1890 a Liberal government under Thomas Greenway abolished French as an official language. It ignored a court ruling in 1892 which declared Manitoba's Official Language Act unconstitutional. The Conservative government of R.P. Roblin dismissed a similar court decision in 1909. T.C. Norris' Liberal government abolished French as a language of instruction in public schools in 1916. In 1976 the NDP government of Edward Schreyer refused to accept the unconstitutionality of the 1890 legislation. The Conservative government of Sterling Lyon appealed a Manitoba Court of Appeal ruling in 1979 making the province's Official Language Act inoperative.

black letter they contain, and if there is a disposition on the part of all concerned to make them work in a practical and reasonable way without, on the one hand, intransigent assertion of abstract rights and without, on the other hand, a cutting down and chipping of those rights."[4] In what was described as "a major first step to meet both the spirit and the legal requirements of the Supreme Court ruling," the Manitoba government, on January 25, 1980, announced that it would expand its translation services substantially to make statutes, bills and legislative documents available in both French and English.[5]

The final Supreme Court ruling on the *Georges Forest* case represented a moral and legal victory and offered the Franco-Manitoban community[6] a psychological lift.[7] It remains to be seen, however, whether this court decision will turn out to be a watershed in the history of the community. The Société franco-manitobaine (SFM),[8] formed in 1968 to lobby for linguistic and cultural rights, interpreted the ruling as only a partial victory in terms of meeting the needs of the province's official minority. According to the society's vice-president, the judges failed to recommend changes to provincial government delivery of services which should have been redesigned to make them more sensitive to the community's needs. There was serious doubt about the practical effects the ruling would have on the everyday life of the Franco-Manitoban community.[9]

In the months that followed, critics maintained that the Government of Manitoba was merely following the letter of the law. Its stated commitment to a spirit of fair play and to a reasoned approach were only empty words at a time when Canada was seriously divided over the Quebec referendum.[10] The Supreme Court decision, it had been argued, was but a ruling in favour of national unity. René Lévesque's statement that it took ninety years to successfully challenge Manitoba's Official Language Act but only two years to overrule that of Quebec,[11] certainly lent credence to that belief.

As the referendum debate heated up, the ruling had a major impact on the national unity campaign in Manitoba. Politicians who had previously fought the reinstatement of French as an official language because they claimed it would be too expensive, came to accept the ruling because "there had been considerable changes in Canada in regards to the unity issue."[12] Thus Manitoba came to be perceived as "the king-maker of national unity": the people of Quebec could now be told that their province rightfully belonged with the rest of Canada. The francophone minority, by having a ninety-year injustice corrected, had once again become pawns in the struggle against Quebec's sovereignty forces. However, their rights to bilingual traffic tickets depended on whether or not the Government of Quebec destroyed Canada.[13]

If, aside from the national unity issue, the ruling has had little impact on the Franco-Manitoban community, partial blame must rest with Canada's highest court which failed to rule on whether bilingualism should be extended to the services which emanate from Section 23 of the Manitoba Act as well as provincial statutes. For example, although either official language could be used in court proceedings, the ruling did not guarantee the right to be understood, nor did it state how the judiciary was expected to function in French when Manitoba has only four judges and some twenty lawyers whose mother tongue is that of the official minority, all of whom were trained in English.[14] In the words of Professor Joseph-Eliot Magnet, of the Faculty of Law of the University of Ottawa, "[n]ever has a judgment of the Supreme Court deliberately been more silent on such an important effect of its rulings; never has such silence boded more portentous in Canadian law."[15] The narrowness of the decision left the Manitoba government more concerned about doing the minimum required by the court ruling than with trying to accommodate the needs of its francophone community. Undue emphasis was given to the translation of statutes and regulations at the expense of making government services available in French.

The effects of the Supreme Court ruling may very well turn out to be slight. One might even be tempted to say that ninety years of constitutional or legal discussions were in the end futile. After all, the events which took place in Manitoba can be explained in demographic terms. Manitoba became an English-speaking province because Great Britain and Ontario sent more settlers than did Quebec, France, Belgium and Switzerland.[16] Today, simple constitutional, legislative or judicial measures could never hope to nullify the combined effects of demography and economic power. In the end, laws are responsive to economic, political, sociological and linguistic realities.[17] It would be a mistake to believe that a law, when translated into another language, could have the same effect, convey the same meaning, or retain the same interpretation. Laws are the product of the collective will and culture.[18]

Moreover, assuring the development of the Franco-Manitoban culture in an overwhelmingly English-speaking environment is agonizingly difficult when governments are hostile, indifferent, insensitive or unhelpful.[19] The re-implementation of an Official Languages Act will not make Franco-Manitobans cultural millionaires. It cannot restore the community to its 1870 prominence, nor can it give back the institutions and services which were lost during the past ninety years. As pointed out by the Société franco-manitobaine, the forces of assimilation have already had their effect and the court ruling will not enable the community to recover what a normal evolution would have given it.[20] As the member of the Legislative Assembly for St. Boniface said: "the Supreme Court... righted a historic wrong, but it is too late to make Manitoba truly bilingual."[21]

Doubt about the vitality of the Franco-Manitoban community will always exist. The circumstances, which in the past had helped maintain a way of life (as reported in *Le Devoir* after viewing a 1977 production of the National Film Board entitled *Le Manitoba ne répond plus*), have largely disappeared or are about to vanish as are the motivations which gave it unremitting determination. Who would dare insist, he added, that Franco-Manitobans sacrifice themselves to live a type of existence which requires nothing short of acts of heroism just to survive?[22]

Franco-Manitobans have not had an easy existence. Numerous outside observers, especially those from Quebec, have not hesitated to comment on their unpromising destiny. These impressions, or perhaps convictions, have been reinforced time and again by community leaders who are themselves caught up in a desperate struggle for existence. Franco-Manitobans are nevertheless experts in cultural survival. Their numbers may be depleted by law, birth rates, emigration, intermarriage and other such forces of assimilation, but their battle to survive will not be won or lost on the basis of sheer numbers. If the community's existence depended on statistics it would have withered long ago.

Conviction that its culture is worth preserving has kept the community alive. Its evolution, according to one newspaper editorial, will depend "on the skill of community leaders in identifying useful, achievable reforms that will increase the opportunities to live in French for those who wish to do so."[23]

Following passage of the 1890 Official Language Act, the community's leaders, despite repressive legislation, made the best of the situation by using the schools as their first line of defence. In the 1960s, realizing that the school could not remain forever the source of a community's vitality, a new leadership operating from a broader base began to stress a program which manifested itself at the political, economic, cultural and social levels. The 1970s witnessed the growth of institutions and services for which this leadership had lobbied.[24] Today there are signs of a cultural renewal.[25]

The francophone community remains, however, quite frail in spite of the fact that French is once again recognized as an official language in Manitoba. Although present laws, at least in principle, allow full participation in the life of the province, day-to-day government services which should have flowed from a practical and reasonable application of the Official Languages Act have to a large measure eluded Franco-Manitobans. This situation cannot be allowed to continue. To counter-balance the Franco-Manitoban's environment of English-language radio, television, kindergartens, sports programs, technology, American music and an English work setting, a greater commitment in terms of French-language services must be obtained from the Manitoba government. A favourable disposition would give the official minority a chance to thrive. An adverse inclination to comply with the spirit of the Manitoba Act can only be viewed as an attempt to check a community's legitimate aspirations.

The Government of Manitoba must remember that Article 23 of the Manitoba Act of 1870 gives credence to the concept of equality between two founding nations. In 1870 the Province of Manitoba was expected to reflect a duality which presupposed the recognition of basic language rights. The implications are enormous, and they cannot be described as theoretical, symbolic and folkloric. Manitoba must recognize the official status of its francophone minority and accept its responsibilities by being sensitive to the needs of the community. Assisting it through everyday services to achieve a normal growth, the government will have given back to the Franco-Manitobans their rightful constitutional status. "The real essentials for the survival of that community," editorialized the *Winnipeg Free Press,* "are not translations of government documents but government support on the economic, education and cultural fronts. . . . It should be imposed by the provincial government upon itself as a basic recognition of the rights and needs of its own citizens."[26]

In January 1980, the Manitoba government had been commended for having moved quickly on the translation of legal documents.[27] Three months later, however, it became apparent that the government did not have any "immediate plans to make the full range of . . . [its] services available in both languages."[28] At the 1980 annual meeting[29] of the Société franco-manitobaine, the attorney general of Manitoba intimated that the province had already gone beyond the letter of the law in deciding to provide, at cost, translation services for litigants to permit witnesses and counsels to speak in either official language.[30] The message was clear: an officially bilingual province amounted to translators, legislators, judges and litigants, not to mention criminals. Nothing was said about making French-language schools or immersion programs more widely available, about having drivers' licences or birth certificates in either official language, about providing social, cultural, recreational or agricultural services in French.[31]

Frustrated and angered by the attorney general's stand, the Société franco-manitobaine saw no other solution but to adopt radical measures in what was later described as "an effort to shock political leaders into making reforms."[32] On April 1 it announced its support for the YES vote in the Quebec referendum. The society stated that the Canadian constitution had not provided "even the minimum of what is required for the development of French Canadians in Manitoba. It is therefore necessary ... to negotiate a new agreement based on the equality of nations. ... To support a NO vote ... would indicate that the SFM was thoroughly satisfied with the experience of the Francophone community in Manitoba" and would be saying yes "to the linguistic and economic disparities that we have been subjected to. ... "[33]

Though splitting the francophone community apart and controversial as it was,[34] the decision served notice to Manitoba and Ottawa that Franco-Manitobans would no longer wait passively for governments to acknowledge French-language rights in keeping with the principle of the equality of nations.[35] It also had the effect of shock therapy. The decision made the Franco-Manitoban community realize that it had made little progress. While it suffered from a 50 per cent assimilation rate, the government was spending "millions on statute translation."[36] The controversial YES had once again left Franco-Manitobans with the painful realization that they had little control even over those institutions designed to meet their own needs. The Public School Act still did not grant parents the right to French schools,[37] and the establishment of such schools could still lead to friction, animosity and bitterness among parents and among school board members.[38] Premier Sterling Lyon's declarations that "services in French were a matter of simple courtesy"[39] and a "spirit of fair play and compromise ... rather than ... legal decree ... continues to motivate most Manitobans," could only be greeted with anger.[40] The controversial YES had fired the second cannon shot in the battle for linguistic rights.

While federalist supporters among Manitoba's francophone community expressed delight at the result of the Quebec referendum, their optimism was tempered by the rather disquieting realization that the May 20 vote would be interpreted as support for the status quo rather than for constitutional reform.[41] In the post-referendum euphoria, Winnipeg City Council passed a motion to have its traffic tickets printed in both official languages as a gesture of goodwill toward the people of Quebec.[42] One could only wonder if it would take another national crisis before there would be a bilingual policeman issuing the ticket.

Following the referendum debate, Manitoba's premier resisted, more than had other provincial leaders, major constitutional reforms. The post-referendum discussions held with federal Justice Minister Jean Chrétien had nevertheless led him to favour "entrenching language rights in the Canadian constitution...."[43] That they should be entrenched in a basic charter of freedoms and rights was, however, totally unacceptable. In the months that followed, the premier stood firm on this issue, claiming that "rights and freedoms are better protected in countries where a bill of rights is not part of the constitution"[44] and where better protection is offered by elected representatives[45] and tradition.[46] Calling Ottawa's proposed bill of rights a Trojan horse which could "conceal a knife for 'disembowelling the parliamentary system',"[47] he objected to the federal proposal. He maintained that such rights would be beyond the reach of legislatures, "leaving it up to a non-elected judiciary to interpret" and, as is the case in the United States, to legislate and set social policy through judiciary pronouncement,[48] a practice which was alien to parliamentary democracy and a departure from the current form of government.[49] Manitoba's premier also objected to any extension of language rights beyond federal institutions. In his view this would be an infringement on provincial jurisdiction.[50] He also thought that Ottawa should not be preoccupied with Quebec and language problems.[51] According to Lyon, more pressing issues such as energy, economic growth, inflation, unemployment and transportation had to be dealt with first.[52]

Notwithstanding the importance of these issues, the Société franco-manitobaine refused to leave needed constitutional reforms related to linguistic rights on the back burner. On November 18, 1980 it threw Manitoba's francophone community into the constitutional debate by organizing, together with fifteen cultural organizations, a provincial meeting. Armed with a mandate calling for public services in French from a province which claimed to be officially bilingual,[53] the society made an appearance the

following week before the Manitoba legislature's standing committee on statutory regulations, set up to study constitutional
reforms. It asked that Section 23 of the Manitoba Act be imple-
mented, not simply accepted and given effect. Its brief also called
for a constitution which would recognize the existence of an
association of two founding nations. Basing its case on historical,
economic, philosophical and political arguments, it further asked
that the constitution acknowledge collective rights to enable official minorities to enjoy a status equal to that of the majority.
Only with that recognition could minorities ever hope to achieve
their full potential. Finally, the society requested the creation of
mechanisms and services which, instead of "bilingualizing" the
province, would see to the immediate needs of the Franco-Manitoban community.[54]

During the committee hearings, the question of entrenching
rights into a new Canadian charter was discussed. Society spokes-
men were adamant that such rights "must be enshrined in a new
constitution to put them beyond the reach of less-sympathetic
governments."[55] The suppression of French language rights in
1890 and 1916 and the refusal of the province in 1892, 1909, 1976
and 1979 to accept court rulings declaring the Official Language
Act unconstitutional were sufficient proof that legislatures were
more likely to ignore and oppress minorities than to legislate on
their behalf.[56] Their arguments brought the point home that minorities have not been well served by the parliamentary system
where the will of the majority must prevail. An entrenched bill of
rights, on the other hand, would at least "afford a delaying period
... provide a clear avenue for redress ... and, over a period of
time ... tend to make governments more careful."[57]

The Société franco-manitobaine again spelled out its arguments in support of the entrenchment of linguistic rights in November 1980 when it appeared before a parliamentary committee
studying the federal government's constitutional proposal. It,
however, made its endorsement of Ottawa's proposed bill of
rights conditional "upon a guarantee of access to courts and
inclusion of an enforcement mechanism to ensure constitutional
behaviour by public authorities."[58]

The society also took exception to the federal government's
proposal that minority-language school rights be contingent upon
linguistic status and a population large enough within an area to
"warrant" creation of publicly financed facilities. Its brief criticized the charter for being evasive on the question of what constituted an area and a sufficient number of students to warrant a
minority-language education.[59] The society's position was that

"one either has rights or does not have them." The wording of the charter was also unclear as to how families were to be divided into French-speaking and non-French-speaking members. The definition of a French-speaking family would have to take into account mixed marriages and families where the parents had spoken French at one time, but after attending English schools because French schools were not available, or having worked in English for so long, they had not used their mother tongue for many years. It would be grossly unfair, the society argued, "to require Franco-Manitobans who had been submitted to unconstitutional assimilative pressure, to bear the onus that they first learned and still understood French."[60] The brief further called for the right to publicly funded minority-language schools[61] and immersion programs; the right of parents, irrespective of their background,[62] to choose the language of their children's education; and the right of the official minority to administer its French-language schools through a single school division which would control both the direction and the content of its educational program.[63] Instead of Ottawa's uniform proposal for school language rights, the Société franco-manitobaine was asking for a constitution which would recognize the social conditions and needs which differed from province to province.

Franco-Manitobans are certainly concerned about the outcome of the current constitutional discussions, but they are not waiting for a miracle. They will remember the observation made over sixty years ago by an archbishop of St. Boniface, Monseigneur Arthur Béliveau. Without dismissing the importance of legal guarantees in safeguarding the French language, he insisted that a proud people wanting to speak it remains the best guarantee of its survival.[64] And this has been the case with Franco-Manitobans over the years. As Winnipeg's English daily newspaper has pointed out to governments, "the French language in Manitoba is not going to go away. It is rooted in history ... and in contemporary social reality" and is "a permanent feature of the Manitoba linguistic landscape."[65] The *Free Press* consequently urged the Manitoba government to stop complaining about a "costly" and "huge translation burden."[66] Instead, it impelled it to find ways to carry out its duties. "The work to be done," it added:

> is much more than what the Supreme Court has outlined. Besides offering the service in French which the constitution requires, the Manitoba government must also make it possible for French-speaking citizens to deal with the government and its agencies in their own language wherever it is practical.[67]

It was not the first time that the *Free Press* had asked its readers to face reality. Following Winnipeg's decision to issue bilingual traffic tickets in May of 1980, it reminded ethnic groups, who wanted their languages to have at least as much consideration as the French, that Winnipeg could not:

> isolate itself from the country of which it is part. The council's decision acknowledges that language policy and practice in Winnipeg are one variable in the linguistic and cultural equation on which Canada is based. The thousands of Winnipeg parents who send their children to French immersion classes reached that conclusion long ago. French-speaking Winnipegers have a good claim to public services in their own language on the basis of history.[68]

Whatever the contentions over the concept of a "compact between two founding peoples," linguistic and educational duality was made explicit in the provisions for the entrance of Manitoba into Confederation. The Manitoba Act gave the francophone community fundamental constitutional guarantees that assured it "full participation in the machinery of government without the necessity of assimilation."[69] Franco-Manitobans cannot be considered an ethnic group, like any other, stemming from the mass immigration of the turn of the century. Nor can they give way to pressures inciting them to become part of the multicultural mosaic.

Franco-Manitobans are today calling for the official recognition of the existence of two linguistic communities and the equality of two founding nations. They are also asking for a guarantee of collective rights through distinct governmental institutions, touching all aspects of their educational, cultural and social life. In this way institutions would be designed to meet their needs. (The Bureau de l'éducation française is an example.) The setting up of such institutions would avoid the uneconomical, awkward and unwanted implementation of bilingual services in geographical areas where one language will suffice. Franco-Manitobans want to live their own lives. They do not want to "shove French down anybody's throat." They do, however, want to see their aspirations fulfilled in order to achieve a sense of purpose. For this reason they must regain a measure of control over the institutions important to their lives.

The government of Manitoba erred when it appealed the Manitoba Court of Appeal ruling which declared the 1890 Official Language Act "inoperative." Following the Supreme Court decision it acted unwisely by merely accepting the decision. Its latest response to the 1979 ruling has been the establishment of a section within the Department of Cultural Affairs and Historical Resources "to improve the capacity of the provincial government to respond to requests from the public in the French language." The section, according to an official communiqué, will provide an avenue of communication between the Franco-Manitoban community and government departments and will eventually recommend policies and priorities of services provided in the official minority language.[70]

The decision is a welcome one. By taking this step, the government of Manitoba can only contribute to all aspects of Franco-Manitoban life. By meeting the social, educational, cultural and economic needs of the community, it will not only guarantee its development and aspirations, it will give recognition to its rights. The process may be a long one but if the government is responsive, Franco-Manitobans will be reasonable.[71]

The linguistic conflict which has existed in Manitoba for over ninety years arose because of a denial of duality. Within the last decade, man has made progress in coming to grips with many issues such as the ecology, energy, conservation, women's rights, the Third World, human rights and native rights, to name a few. It would be a tragedy if within the next decade, a realistic formula, permitting two nations to live side by side, was not found.

The 1979 Supreme Court decision sounded like a cannon shot in a distant field. Its reverberations are just beginning to make themselves felt within the Franco-Manitoban community. Yesterday's generation sees itself vindicated for having fought for its linguistic rights. Today's generation is proud to see its mother tongue come out of the underground to become an official and living language. Tomorrow's generation will have the reflexes to demand its legal rights and to live as francophones.

The increased popularity of French immersion programs may be a sign that the anglophone community, with its law-abiding traditions, is beginning to feel that their children should be bilingual, and that unilingual anglophones may become a minority within the next generation.

Notes

1. *Le Devoir*, 14 December 1979.
2. *Manitoba News Services*, 14 December 1979.
3. The Georges Forest case started with a $5.00 parking ticket which was issued to the plaintiff in English only in February 1976. In July of that year, his attempt to have the parking offence dismissed was

rejected by a provincial court judge who ruled that parking tickets were part of the court process which the 1890 Official Language Act stated to be in English only. In November a notice of appeal was filed in French in the County Court of St. Boniface. A month later Judge Armand Dureault ruled the 1890 act unconstitutional. In February 1977, Georges Forest's lawyers requested four provincial statutes in French. The province's reply was a $17,000 bill to cover the cost of translation. In April of the same year, documents were filed to force the province to supply the statutes in French and without cost. The request was rejected by the Manitoba Court of Appeal because it had not been filed in English. A motion was subsequently filed in English to force the courts into accepting the initial documents written in French. The court of appeal sent Forest's case to the Court of Queen's Bench in June 1977. In July 1978, Chief Justice A.S. Dewar refused to rule on the constitutionality of the 1890 act on the grounds that the County Court of St. Boniface had already ruled on it. The following month Forest filed an appeal. In April 1979 the court of appeal unanimously ruled that the 1890 act was unconstitutional. In May the Manitoba government appealed the case to the Supreme Court of Canada. On December 13, 1979, the Supreme Court of Canada unanimously upheld the Manitoba Court of Appeal ruling.

4. *The Winnipeg Tribune*, 14 December 1979.

5. *Manitoba News Services*, 25 January 1980.

6. According to *Canada Census* (1971), Manitoba's population numbered 988,245, of which 86,515 were of French origin. The population of French mother tongue was listed at 60,550. An estimated 39,600 were said to speak French at home.

7. *Le Devoir*, 20 December 1979; *La Liberté*, 20 December 1979.

8. It replaced the Association d'éducation des canadiens français du Manitoba whose primary objective since its foundation in 1916 had been to fight for French language rights in the field of education. When the Manitoba government recognized the right to receive instruction in French on a half-time basis in Manitoba public schools, the AECFM was replaced by the SFM whose goals were "to encourage, promote, and further the economic, political, cultural and educational interests of the French-speaking population of Manitoba." Société franco-manitobaine Prospectus, n.d., see also the Society's Act of Incorporation (1970).

9. *The Winnipeg Tribune*, 14 December 1979.

10. *The Winnipeg Free Press*, 24 April 1980.

11. Ibid., 13 December 1980.

12. Ibid.

13. Ibid., 9 May 1980.

14. *Le Devoir*, 20 December 1979.

15. Joseph Eliot Magnet, "Validity of Manitoba Laws After Forest: What Is To Be Done," *Manitoba Law Journal* 10, no. 3 (1980), p. 244.

16. Jean-Charles Bonenfant, "La Dualité linguistique au Manitoba," *Mémoire de la Société royale du Canada* VIII (1970), p. 140.

17. *La Liberté*, 20 December 1979.

18. *Le Devoir*, 11 February 1980.

19. *The Winnipeg Free Press*, 3 April 1980.

20. *La Liberté*, 20 December 1980.

21. *The Winnipeg Free Press*, 14 December 1979.

22. *Le Devoir*, 2 September 1978. Since 1945, the conditions which had given the Franco-Manitoban community a language that was qualitatively and quantitatively adequate have largely disappeared. Following the Second World War, the community lost its rural character, becoming urbanized, establishing itself in areas where acculturation took place quickly. Other factors which brought about changes within the community involved the dramatic influence of television, the exodus of a potential ruling class to eastern Canada, and a certain loss of interest in the "cause" due to mixed marriages (according to the 1976 Census, such marriages occurred in 45 per cent of the cases involving Franco-Manitobans). During the 1960s, the less-used language was abandoned. The French language lost its importance in social interactions. With Franco-Manitobans marrying, divorcing, bequeathing, buying and working in English, the French language became largely folkloric, a museum object, a childhood memory to which was attached a sentimental value within the family framework. It was only a question of time before the French language ceased to be based on a normative syntax and grammar. Franco-Manitobans could not continue indefinitely to speak their mother tongue while living in English.

Today, without any institutions other than a limited number of schools and cultural organizations, with only a handful of individuals to sit on all the committees, not to mention the tension between rival groups, the community's fate appears to be a foregone conclusion. A minority segment made up of self-proclaimed intellectuals and petty elites, the remainder a group of second-class citizens, constituted a clandestine French-speaking community. For those wishing to retain their culture, one wonders if the government of Quebec should not be requested to invoke a law which would facilitate the return and integration of Franco-Manitobans to Quebec life, after the fashion of Israel when it first came into existence. See Paul-Emile Leblanc, "L'Enseignement français au Manitoba, 1916-1968" (Masters thesis, University of Ottawa, 1968), pp. 2-3; Robert Painchaud, "The Franco-Manitoban Communities of Western Canada

Since 1945," presented to Western Atlantic Canadian Studies Conference, Calgary, 1978; *Le Devoir*, 3 February, 14 March, 29 and 30 May, 3 September 1978; 3 January, 28 December 1979; 7 and 12 January, 8 February 1980.

23. *The Winnipeg Free Press*, 15 August 1980.

24. In 1970 the Manitoba Legislative Assembly adopted Bill 113 giving French, at least in principle, equal status with English as a language of instruction in public schools. Two years later, a French-language teacher-training institute opened. The year 1974 was highlighted by the official opening of the Centre culturel franco-manitobain (Franco-Manitoban Cultural Centre). In 1975 the Bureau de l'éducation française (Bureau of French Education) was established within the Manitoba Department of Education and the Collège communautaire de Saint-Boniface (St. Boniface Community College) was opened. The year 1976 saw the appointment of a French-speaking assistant deputy minister responsible for the Bureau de l'éducation française. In 1978 the Centre de ressources éducatives françaises du Manitoba (Manitoba French Educational Resource Centre) became operational, and Francofonds, an important fund raising organization, was set up.

25. See René Préfontaine, "Aux frontières de la francophonie: le Manitoba français," CEFCO (February 1980), pp. 6-7; *La Liberté*, 3 January 1980; *The Winnipeg Tribune*, 29 January 1980.

26. *The Winnipeg Free Press*, 22 December 1979.

27. *La Liberté*, 3 January 1980.

28. *The Winnipeg Free Press*, 24 March 1980.

29. The annual meeting is open to all Franco-Manitobans.

30. *La Liberté*, 22 March 1980.

31. The only tangible announcement to be made public at the annual meeting was the appointment of the Deputy Minister of Cultural Affairs and Historical Resources, René Préfontaine, as liaison between the Franco-Manitoban community and provincial government departments.

32. *The Winnipeg Tribune*, 3 April 1980. The words are those of Laurent Desjardins, MLA for St. Boniface.

33. *The Winnipeg Free Press*, 5 April 1980.

34. The community's business people and political leaders called the endorsement of the YES vote "an irresponsible act by a small group . . . who are not supported by the 60,000 French-speaking residents of Manitoba," *The Winnipeg Tribune*, 3 April 1980. Apprehensive about the attorney general's declaration that "French-speaking residents of Manitoba should not support the Parti Québécois in its referendum on sovereignty-association because separation could jeopardize their constitutional language rights," a member of Winni-

peg's city council, Georges Provost, accused the society's executive of adding "fuel to the fire for all the bigots in the city," and of ruining "the work he and other Manitobans have been doing to smooth over the French-English issue." In his words, "we were just getting it a little settled and this one stupid thing ... [put us] right back to the beginning." Ibid, 2 and 3 April 1980. Georges Provost was never regarded as a strong defender of francophone rights, nor is he perceived as a francophone leader. He is more noted as a strong defender of the letter of the law.

35. *The Winnipeg Free Press,* 2 April 1980.

36. *The Winnipeg Tribune,* 7 April 1980.

37. *La Liberté,* 10 April 1980.

38. La Société franco-manitobaine per Maurice J. Arpin, QC, "Presentation to the Intersessional Committee of the Legislative Assembly of Manitoba for Revision of the Public School Act," 22 October 1979.

39. *The Winnipeg Free Press,* 23 May 1980.

40. *La Liberté,* 8 May 1980.

41. *The Winnipeg Tribune,* 21 May 1980.

42. *The Winnipeg Free Press,* 22 May 1980; *The Winnipeg Tribune,* 27 May 1980.

43. *The Winnipeg Tribune,* 23 May 1980.

44. Ibid.

45. *The Winnipeg Free Press,* 26 November 1980.

46. *The Winnipeg Tribune,* 18 June 1980.

47. Ibid., 11 July 1980.

48. *The Winnipeg Free Press,* 9 June 1980.

49. *The Winnipeg Tribune,* 23 May 1980.

50. Ibid., 9 June 1980.

51. *The Winnipeg Free Press,* 10 June 1980.

52. *The Winnipeg Tribune,* 16 August 1980; *The Winnipeg Free Press,* 22 August 1980; *Manitoba News Services,* 15 August 1980.

53. *La Liberté,* 4 and 11 December 1980.

54. Ibid., 20 November 1980; see also La Société franco-manitobaine, "La langue française au Manitoba: ressource renouvelable de première importance," September 1980. The Société historique de Saint-Boniface, the Fédération provinciale des comités de parents and the Conseil jeunesse provinciale participated in the drafting of the brief.

55. *The Winnipeg Free Press,* 19 November 1980.

56. Ibid.

116   *Gilbert-L. Comeault*

57. University of Manitoba Law Professor Dale Gibson quoted in *The Winnipeg Tribune*, 18 June 1980.

58. *The Winnipeg Free Press*, 22 November 1980.

59. At present, the statutory rule in Manitoba is that school divisions must educate students in French whenever the parents of twenty-three children, who can be grouped in one class, ask for a French-language education. Under the proposed charter, a loosely-defined group of parents have the right to have their children educated in their mother tongue. It does not, however, compel the school authorities or the province to provide that education. Though it mentions educational establishments, it does not specify the word *school*, nor does it define what constitutes an area. To take advantage of the federal proposal, Franco-Manitobans would have to be quantifiable, compartimentalized, and have justifiable reasons. As such, it offers less than what is guaranteed in the Manitoba School Act.

60. *The Winnipeg Free Press*, 22 November 1980.

61. The proposed charter states that parents only have the right to have their children educated in the minority language. A school division could refuse public funding by arguing that parents could send their children to French schools as long as they paid for them and as long as provincial standards were met.

62. The Ottawa proposal would force immigrants and the linguistic majority to educate their children in the English language.

63. Société franco-manitobaine, "Mémoire de la Société franco-manitobaine concernant la constitution du Canada," November 1980; *La Liberté*, 27 November 1980; *The Winnipeg Free Press*, 29 October and 29 November 1980. If Ottawa's educational guarantees were "designed to protect Quebec's French-speaking majority against assimilation in the English culture," wrote the *Free Press* in its November 29 issue, "they are not helpful for protecting French-speaking minorities in other provinces, including Manitoba."

64. *La Liberté*, 5 February 1981.

65. *The Winnipeg Free Press*, 9 May 1981.

66. Ibid., 7 April 1981.

67. Ibid., 8 May 1981.

68. Ibid., 23 May 1980.

69. Magnet, "Validity of Manitoba Laws After Forest," p. 241.

70. *Manitoba News Services*, 20 March 1980. In commenting on the government's decision to appoint an official in the cultural affairs branch to help select services which ought to be available in French, the *Winnipeg Free Press*, in its issue of April 9, 1980, commented that experience "may soon show that one lone official is not enough for the job to be done, but it is a beginning. If Mr. Mercier thinks the government is in trouble now just complying with the constitu-

tion, he will be totally out of his depth when that official starts pointing to other areas where the French language needs to be introduced into government operations."

71. Following the November 1981 Manitoba provincial election, the New Democratic party, under the leadership of Howard R. Pawley, QC, formed a new government. On March 21, 1982 the premier, in an address to the Société franco-manitobaine, announced a series of policy guidelines concerning the implementation of French language services within the Government of Manitoba. The policy guidelines were as follows:

> Services provided by the Government . . . shall be made available to the extent possible, in both official languages in areas where the French-speaking population is concentrated. . . . All written correspondence received from members of the public, in French or English, shall be answered in the same language. Where feasible, forms, identity documents, and certificates for use by the general public, shall be in a bilingual format. Government information documents destined for the general public shall be either bilingual or separate language formats depending on cost efficiency and required distribution. Where practical, signs and public notices in the regions of the province (where the French-speaking population is concentrated) should be in both official languages. Priority in the introduction of French language services shall be given to departments which have a greater impact on the general population, in particular young people and senior citizens.

Manitoba News Services, 21 March 1982.

Bibliography

Primary Sources

I. Manuscripts

Archives de la Société Historique de Saint-Boniface.
    Fédération provinciale des comités de parents. "Une mise en situation en prévision d'une rencontre avec le gouvernement provincial suite au jugement de la Cour suprême." 26 February 1980.

Fox, Francis. "Notes pour une allocution à l'occasion du congrès de l'Association canadienne-française de l'Ontario." Ottawa, 27 September 1980.

Société franco-manitobaine. "Communiqué de la S.F.M. aux présidents d'associations provinciales." 5 March 1980.

————. Compte rendu d'une réunion convoquée par la S.F.M. pour échanger sur des alternatives d'action suite au jugement de la Cour suprême du 13 décembre 1979. 8 January 1980.

————. "La dernière chance." Conférence de presse livrée par Gilberte Proteau, présidente de la SFM. 1 April 1980.

————. "La discussion est entamée sur la constitution." Dossier spécial préparé pour le service d'information de la Société franco-manitobaine. December 1980.

————. "La Langue française au Manitoba: ressource renouvelable de première importance." Préparé pour le Comité des règlements statutaires. September 1980.

————. "L'évolution de l'affaire Forest." 1979.

————. "Mémoire de la S.F.M. concernant la constitution du Canada." November 1980.

————. "Mémoire de la S.F.M." présenté au Groupe de travail sur les minorités de langue française. 30 September 1980.

————. "Orientation générale de la S.F.M." n.d.

————. "Presentation to the Intersessional Committee of the Legislative Assembly of Manitoba for revision of the Public School Act." 22 October 1979.

————. "Sondage Communautaire." Rapport effectué par CERECO Inc. September 1980.

————. "Vers des services en langue française du gouvernement Manitobain." Document de travail no. 1. 10 April 1981.

II. Government Records

Agriculture Canada. *Plan des langues officielles.* 1978.

Archives publiques du Canada. *Votre guide des langues officielles.* March 1980.

Commission de l'unité canadienne. *Se retrouver: Observations et recommandations.* Ottawa: Ministère des Approvisionnements et Services Canada, 1979.

Manitoba News Services. 1979-1981.

Manitoba Legislative Library. *Political Scrapbooks.* 1978-1981.

III. Newspapers

La Liberté. 1978-1981.

Le Devoir. 1978-1981.

The Winnipeg Free Press. 1979-1981.

The Winnipeg Sun. 1980-1981.

The Winnipeg Tribune. 1979-1980.

Secondary Sources

I. Monographs

Association canadienne d'éducation de langue française. "The Evolution of the English Education System in Quebec," *ACELF,* 1978.

Dorge, Lionel. *Introduction à l'étude des Franco-Manitobains. Essai historique et bibliographique.* Saint Boniface: La Société historique de Saint-Boniface, 1973.

———. *Le Manitoba, reflets d'un passé.* Saint Boniface: Les Editions du Blé, 1976.

Jaenen, Cornelius J. *Glimpses of the Franco-Manitoban Community/Regards sur les Franco-Manitobains.* Winnipeg: The University of Winnipeg Press, 1976.

II. Unpublished Theses and Papers

Comeault, Gilbert-L. "Pour la reconnaissance linguistique et culturelle d'un peuple fondateur." Document ayant pour but d'amorcer un dialogue touchant les implications de la décision de la Cour suprême qui déclarait anticonstitutionnelle la loi de la langue officielle du Manitoba. Préparé pour la Société franco-manitobaine. May 1980.

Leblanc, Paul-Emile. "L'enseignement français au Manitoba, 1916-1968." Masters thesis, University of Ottawa, 1968.

Painchaud, Robert. "Multiculturalism: A Western French-Canadian Viewpoint." Unpublished paper, University of Winnipeg, 1975.

——. "The Franco-Canadian Communities of Western Canada Since 1945." A paper presented to the Western Canadian-Atlantic Canada Studies Conference. Calgary and Fredericton, 1978.

Rosco, Alexander Allan. "The Manitoba Act in Transition, 1870-90: The Transformation of Manitoba's French-Canadian Politico-Cultural Institutions." Masters thesis, University of Manitoba, 1969.

Turenne, Roger E. "The Minority and the Ballot Box: A Study of the Voting Behavior of the French Canadians of Manitoba." Masters thesis, University of Manitoba, 1970.

III. Articles

Association canadienne d'éducation de langue française. "Pour un plan de développement de l'éducation française au Canada: Manitoba, Saskatchewan, Alberta, Colombie-britannique." *Revue de l'ACELF* VI, no. 2 (November 1977), pp. 1-74.

——. "Pour un plan de développement de l'éducation française au Canada: Nouveau-Brunswick, Saskatchewan, Alberta, Colombie-britannique." *Revue de l'ACELF* VI, no. 3 (December 1977), pp. 1-60.

——. "Pour un plan de développement de l'éducation française au Canada: synthèse et recommandations." *Revue de l'ACELF* VII, no. 2 (February 1978), pp. 1-31.

——. "Les Média et la culture française." *Revue de l'ACELF* IX, no. 1 (October 1980), pp. 1-18.

——. "Les Média et l'école." *Revue de l'ACELF* IX, no. 2, (November 1980), pp. 1-22.

——. "Les Média et la société francophone." *Revue de l'ACELF* IX, no. 3 (December 1980), pp. 1-24.

Bertrand, Gabriel. "La Triglossie ou l'Ecartement linguistique au Manitoba français." *CEFCO* (May 1979), pp. 2-7.

Bonenfant, Jean-Charles. "La Dualité linguistique au Manitoba." *MSRC/TRSC* VIII, Fourth Series (1970), pp. 133-40.

Carlyle-Gordge, Peter. "Endangered Species: Has history caught up with Franco-Manitoba?" *Maclean's Magazine,* 18 April 1977, pp. 44-48.

Conseil de la vie française en Amérique. "Mémoire du Conseil de la vie française sur la révision de la constitution canadienne." *Vie française* 34, no. 11-11-12 (1980), pp. 3-14.

Dorge, Lionel. "Petite Histoire de la langue française au Manitoba." *Bulletin de l'ACELF* VIII, no. 3 (April 1980), pp. 1-3.

Falardeau, Jean-Charles. "La Langue française: la leur ou la nôtre?" *Forces* (1979), pp. 19-33.

Heintzman, Ralph. "The Spirit of Confederation: Professor Creighton, Biculturalism, and the Use of History." *CHR* 56, no. 2 (September 1971), pp. 245-75.

Jaenen, Cornelius J. "French Public Education in Manitoba." *Revue de l'Université d'Ottawa* 38 (1968), pp. 19-34.

Magnet, Joseph Eliot. "Validity of Manitoba Laws After Forest: What Is To Be Done." *Manitoba Law Journal* 10, no. 13 (1980), pp. 241-57.

Morton, W.L. "Confederation, 1870-1896: The End of the Macdonaldson Constitution and Return to Duality." *Journal of Canadian Studies* I (1966), pp. 11-24.

Painchaud, Robert. "Des Franco-Manitobains tiraillés. . . . " *Perception* (November/December 1977), pp. 15-17.

Préfontaine, René. "Aux frontières de la francophonie: le Manitoba français." *CEFCO* (February 1980), pp. 1-14.

Stanley, G.F.G. "French and English in Western Canada." In *Canadian Dualism: Studies of French-English Relations.* Edited by Mason Wade. Toronto: University of Toronto Press, 1960.

Le Patriote de l'Ouest and French Settlement on the Prairies, 1910-1930

André N. Lalonde

From 1890 to 1910 the Roman Catholic church played a leading role in the field of francophone settlement in the Canadian west. Its endeavours, seconded by those of prominent laymen and the federal government, resulted in the presence of approximately 100,000 French-speaking settlers in the three prairie provinces by 1910. Of that number, 23,000 resided in the newly created Province of Saskatchewan, with concentrations in the southeast, the southwest and the north along the fringe of the parkland area. The scarcity of French settlers and the isolation of Fransaskois* communities troubled most members of the clergy who feared that their flock's religious, cultural and linguistic survival was threatened by the arrival of hordes of foreign immigrants. A device was needed to unite and solidify the francophone parishes of Saskatchewan. The Fransaskois needed a French newspaper. The power of the press would serve to create a strong sense of solidarity and would help to increase the flow of French settlers from Quebec to the prairies.

After two years of intense discussions, a handful of clergymen created a company, La Bonne Presse, hired a manager-editor, Father Adrien Gabriel Morice, and arranged to have their newspaper printed in Duck Lake, Saskatchewan. The first issue of *Le*

*The francophones of Saskatchewan

Patriote de l'Ouest appeared on August 22, 1910.[1] Father Morice, in his first editorial, clearly enunciated the *raison d'être* of the new journal:

> Le titre de notre journal proclame assez haut que nous voulons servir nos concitoyens de langue française dans l'Ouest. Nous les défendrons quand ils seront attaqués. . . . Nous nous attacherons à contribuer de tout notre pouvoir, à la conservation de leur belle langue. . . . C'est dire aussi que ce qui tend à l'augmentation numérique de ceux qui la parlent dans les trois provinces du Manitoba, de la Saskatchewan et de l'Alberta est d'avance assuré de notre appui. En autres termes, nous voudrions être colonisateur autant que journaliste.[2]

Father Morice's career as editor was brief. He was dismissed within six months for using the newspaper to support the Liberal party. His successor Father A.J. Auclair, the former editor of *L'Etincelle* of Ottawa, had barely settled in when a fire destroyed the building housing the press in November 1910. The newspaper reappeared six months later[3] to resume its promotion of colonization.

From 1910 to 1918 the editor and directors of *Le Patriote* viewed the St. Lawrence River Valley as the chief source of francophone colonists. The prevailing myth that the west was inhospitable had to be countered. Once Quebeckers who were contemplating a move were made fully cognizant of the advantages and opportunities which the west had to offer, a more significant number would opt to homestead on the prairies:

> Pour attirer dans l'Ouest des colons français de Québec ou des Etats-Unis, qui ont décidé d'aller tenter fortune ailleurs, que faut-il faire? Mais tout simplement leur faire connaître l'Ouest. . . .
> Et comment faire connaître les immenses avantages de l'Ouest à ceux qui sont sur le point de se décider à aller tenter fortune quelque part? Par des conférences publiques, par des conversations à domicile, par des correspondances privées, et surtout par la grande voix de la presse.[4]

To publicize the west, the editor called upon the predominantly francophone parishes to create a *comité paroissial de colonisation* which would work in conjunction with a central *bureau de consultation* established by the newspaper. Through this mechanism, *Le Patriote* proposed to keep abreast of the advantages offered to prospective settlers within the multitude of scattered francophone communities.[5]

The monographs and other relevant material forwarded by the local committees and published in *Le Patriote* all praised the fertility of the soil and emphasized the healthy status of the western Canadian economy.[6] Glowing annual harvest reports and personal testimonies by francophone Saskatchewan residents, who had improved their economic status since their arrival in the west, abounded in the paper.

While the west was pictured as an agricultural paradise, life in the industrial centres of the eastern United States was described in detrimental terms. French Canadians who migrated to those *lieux de perdition* (places of downfall) lost their heart and soul, lost control of their own destiny, became the slaves of industry and could look forward to a bleak future for themselves and their children. The alternative was to occupy the fertile lands of the Canadian prairies which were awaiting *le soc de la charrue* (the plough's blade) to yield bountiful crops.[7]

To relay this information to prospective settlers, copies of *Le Patriote* were forwarded to the *missionnaires-colonisateurs* for distribution in Quebec and the United States. The local readers were asked to purchase additional subscriptions for friends and relatives in the east:

> Si chacun veut ainsi s'intéresser à la cause de la colonisation, nous avons vite fait de faire connaître les avantages de notre pays à plus de 25,000 personnes parmi celles précisément qui sont les mieux disposées à venir s'établir chez-nous.[8]

The staff of *Le Patriote* recognized that publicity depicting the Canadian west in glowing terms would produce negligible results unless a substantial segment of Quebec's intelligentsia supported the migration of the province's surplus population to the prairies. Ignorance of the advantages the west had to offer and the denunciation by a number of clerics and politicians of previous efforts to recruit settlers in eastern Canada were viewed as the main causes of the failure to generate a steady stream of francophone settlers to the Canadian west.[9]

To placate their eastern counterparts, Father Auclair and other periodic contributors to the newspaper repeatedly contended that they were not attempting to depopulate *la belle province*. On the contrary, the French-speaking minorities on the prairies could not hope to survive without *un Québec fort*. Quebec, as the past had illustrated, could not accommodate all of its people, and thousands of them were migrating yearly to the United States. It was this surplus population that the newspaper was trying to reach.

The eastern journalists, clerics, academics and politicians, who professed that Quebeckers venturing to the Canadian west would drown in a sea of foreigners, were misinformed according to *Le Patriote*. The 100,000 francophones on the prairies were preserving and would maintain their language, their culture and their faith. In the parishes of Saskatchewan, the French Canadians enjoyed all of the cultural, educational and religious advantages found in Quebec. Instead of disappearing, they were progressing:

> Nos paroisses, loin d'être étouffées sous la poussée de la population étrangère qui les environne, prospèrent et s'agrandissent. Nous assistons en quelque sorte à une répétition de ce qui s'est passé dans les Cantons de l'Est et dans certaines régions de l'Ontario.[10]

Quebec's own interests dictated that its surplus population remain in Canada instead of venturing south of the forty-ninth parallel. A strong contingent of French Canadians on the prairies could elect federal representatives who would endorse the efforts of Quebec's politicians to protect the interests of *la race*. Furthermore, the presence of numerous French Canadians across the prairies would ensure that the west would always remain Canadian culturally and politically.[11]

While the majority of articles intended for the elite of Quebec took the form of appeals and were highly conciliatory, there were instances where the detractors of the west as a potential field for French Canadian settlement were vehemently denounced. Such opponents were accused of denying their people the opportunity to exercise their true vocation, the cultivation of the soil. To restrict the slogan *emparons-nous du sol* (let us take over the land) to the Province of Quebec, where new land had to be cleared of brush and trees, simply prompted those who had lost the pioneer spirit of their forefathers to flock to the American industrial cities. With some encouragement, many of these people would opt to remain on the land by occupying a homestead on the prairies where the soil was easy to till.[12]

Similarly, individuals who insisted that *la patrie* was confined to the territory of Quebec were rebuked in *Le Patriote*. *La patrie* encompassed all French minority groups and extended across the whole of Canada. The prairies constituted part of their birthright, part of the patrimony bequeathed by the French explorers, fur traders and missionaries. The present generation of leaders in Quebec had no right to deprive *le peuple* of its patrimony. They had no right to limit the borders of *la patrie* to the shores of the St. Lawrence.[13]

Father Léandre Vachon, who had served as *missionnaire-colon-isateur* for the diocese of Prince Albert during the first decade of the twentieth century, used the columns of *Le Patriote* to accuse the opponents of French settlement in the west of thwarting God's will by opposing the messianic role He had conferred upon *le peuple canadien-français:*

> Nous sommes de ceux qui croient à la mission évangélisatrice du peuple canadien-français sur cette terre d'Amérique. Voulez-vous que le nom catholique et Canadien français soit glorifié et aimé par les races étrangères qui nous entourent, laissez nos compatriotes pénétrer cette masse hétérogène avec l'étendard de la croix qu'ils feront connaître.[14]

Modifying the traditional image many Quebeckers had of the west and countering the negative view which prevailed within a segment of the elite was only one facet of *Le Patriote*'s activities in the area of colonization. The newspaper also focused on activities in Saskatchewan. The Fransaskois were repeatedly reminded that they had to play an important role in the field of settlement to ensure their existence. Regional immigration offices were required to welcome and direct new settlers to francophone parishes which needed bolstering.[15] Too many colonists of various ethnic origins were occupying land in or near French communities. By pooling their financial resources and creating colonization companies, the Fransaskois could purchase this available farmland and sell it to incoming Franco-Catholic settlers.[16] *Le Patriote* even revived the concept of *la revanche du berceau* (the revenge of the cradle). In the best French Canadian tradition, the French-speaking residents of Saskatchewan were urged to readily accept "le fardeau parfois pesant de la paternité" to increase their numerical strength.[17]

Starting in 1914, the amount of attention devoted to colonization in *Le Patriote* declined substantially. Canada's degree of participation in the First World War and the conscription crisis in Quebec rendered attempts to recruit settlers east of the Ottawa River seemingly pointless. Throughout most of the war, the editor and his associates made use of the paper to deal with more pressing local problems. The outburst of nativist sentiment in Saskatchewan and the sequential attacks on the separate schools and the French language posed a serious threat to the Fransaskois' cultural survival. Every available tool, including the newspaper, was commandeered to repel the aggressor and defend the besieged minority's cherished institutions.

In the midst of this racial conflict, it became abundantly clear
that the French of this province resembled an army without a
commander. Except for the clergy, they had too few leaders. In
his private correspondence, the archbishop of Regina, O.E. Mathieu, spared few words to describe the problem:

> Ce que j'ai constaté en arrivant ici, ce que je constate encore, c'est
> que nos catholiques sont ignorants. Nous n'avons pas d'hommes
> instruits. . . . [18]

Without the educational facilities to prepare local lay leaders, the
Fransaskois again asked Quebeckers to come to their rescue. *Le
Patriote* exhorted the young members of the liberal arts professions to consider moving to Saskatchewan. Farmers were always
welcome, but the French minority also needed teachers, lawyers
and doctors:

> Nous invitons les jeunes gens des universités de Québec à venir se
> joindre à leurs confrères. Ils trouveront ici un vaste champ ouvert à
> l'exercice de leur profession, et l'occasion de rendre service à leurs
> compatriotes, dans les hautes sphères gouvernementales. [19]

The appeals fell, for the most part, on deaf ears. [20]

The francophones of Saskatchewan were fortunate to emerge
from the racial crisis virtually unscathed. The separate school
system remained intact; the use of French as a language of instruction was restricted to grade one; French could be taught as a
subject for one hour a day beyond grade one. However, by 1918,
the Fransaskois began to recognize that it was futile to rely almost
exclusively on Quebec to secure their future. It was too late.
There was an inadequate supply of prairie farmland now to accommodate any massive influx of settlers. The only homesteads
left were confined to the parkland area: [21]

> Si le courant qui alimente aujourd'hui l'émigration vers les centres
> manufacturiers américains avait été dirigé, il y a vingt ans, vers
> l'Ouest canadien, nous aurions gardé au pays plusieurs centaines
> de mille des nôtres, notre gouvernement n'aurait pas eu besoin de
> faire appel aux populations de l'Europe centrale pour venir mettre
> en culture nos prairies qui seraient restées entre nos mains, et les
> droits de la langue française seraient plus respectés qu'ils ne le sont
> actuellement. [22]

The efforts to recruit settlers in Quebec, nevertheless, were not
abandoned altogether after the war. The arguments used in the

past were rehashed, but the appeals for colonists and for young professionals printed in *Le Patriote* were less frequent and showed less fervour. They reflected a degree of hopelessness, a certain resentment, an element of bitterness. The author of one article, Donatien Frémont, attacked the intelligentsia of Quebec for encouraging its surplus population from the old parishes to farm rockland north of the St. Lawrence Valley. Unable to earn a living by cultivating unproductive soil, these poor souls ended up in the United States where they became the servants of industry. Frémont felt that, had they been encouraged to settle in the west, these people would have remained in Canada and lived comfortably. Only the blind still insisted that the French could not survive in this country outside Quebec.[23] In another instance, Quebec was denounced for abandoning its brothers in the west as France had abandoned her colony of New France in 1760.[24] One individual humourously ridiculed the attitude of Quebec's clergy towards the prairies:

> Je regrette de dire que le clergé catholique de la province de Québec ne néglige rien pour empêcher le Canadien français de venir s'établir dans l'Ouest sous prétexte qu'il y perdra sa langue et sa religion. Chose étrange, il ne parait pas s'alarmer autant lorsque des paroisses presque entières abandonnent le pays pour aller peiner dans les villes manufacturières des Etats-Unis. Cependant, il me semble que dans l'Ouest nous n'avons pas de Noël Trudeau qui se font appeler Christmas Waterhole, ni de François Leblanc qui laissent à leur progéniture le nom de Frank White.[25]

Having largely forsaken their dream of a large number of Quebeckers swelling their ranks and recognizing that the efforts of colonization missionaries working to repatriate Franco-Americans would produce negligible results, the French of Saskatchewan were determined to rely increasingly on their own resources to secure their future. In 1918 the Collège Mathieu of Gravelbourg opened its doors to create an elite *sur place*. Throughout the 1920s the articles on colonization which appeared in *Le Patriote* focused largely on local and regional issues. Francophone settlers residing in predominantly non-French districts were constantly urged to relocate in Franco-Catholic parishes. Suggestions were offered to facilitate the resettlement of these francophones in French parishes. Young people were advised to stay on the land in or near French communities. *Le Patriote* admonished those readers who were considering selling their lands to foreigners for a large profit.[26] Evidently *Le Patriote* no longer considered that survival depended on "l'apport de l'extérieur"—on numerical strength. During the 1920s, survival was "une question de regroupement, d'organisation et d'attachement au sol."[27]

Quebec's failure to respond to their cries for help in the form of settlers and the Fransaskois' ensuing recognition of the fact that their destiny rested on their own shoulders gave birth to a traumatic dichotomy. On the one hand, Auclair and his associates felt that no single French minority could survive without Quebec's tangible and moral support. The Fransaskois could not afford to completely sever the umbilical cord linking them to *le bercail* (the nest). *Le Patriote* sponsored annual train excursions to eastern Canada—referred to as "voyages de liaison et de survivance"—to maintain a communication link with the home province and to remind Quebeckers that the French of Saskatchewan still existed. On the other hand, the recognition that it was futile to depend on outsiders for help served to lessen the Fransaskois' emotional attachment to their place of origin.[28] As French Canadians they harboured a sentimental attachment to Quebec, but economic, political and social considerations compelled the French of Saskatchewan to identify increasingly with their adopted province. Throughout the 1920s they regarded themselves more and more as westerners.

This new regionalism was reflected in the columns of *Le Patriote*. For example, when the eastern French-language press attacked the Progressives of western Canada for recommending the adoption of radical agriculture and social reforms, *Le Patriote* rose to the defence of western regional interests:

> *La Presse, Le Soleil* et les autres journaux français qui mènent de ce temps-çi une campagne contre l'Ouest sont peut-être sous l'impression que leurs attaques visent un parti agraire anglo-saxon. Il ne s'agit pas de savoir jusqu'à quel point l'élément canadien-français chez-nous est progressiste, mais quelle que soit sa couleur politique, il est bien certain que, vivant dans l'Ouest, il y est profondément attaché, comme c'est son devoir, et montre peu de disposition à se laisser bourrer le crâne par les serviteurs à gages des gros intérêts de la finance et de l'industrie.[29]

While visiting Manitoba in 1928, the abbé Lionel Groulx discovered that factors other than distance now separated the French minorities of western Canada from their eastern compatriots:

> Point de survivance d'une minorité française qui soit pensable sans le Québec. Une tragique corrélation de sentiments s'aperçoit dans l'âme des dispersés: affaiblissement du lien sentimental avec la

vieille province d'origine, affaiblissement fatal après deux ou trois générations.... D'autre part, naissance fatale d'un régionalisme, ébauche d'une conscience adulte en ces rameaux détachés du tronc et presque devenus boutures autonomes.

J'observais la naissance d'un régionalisme légitime en soi, mais qui inclinait mal à supporter la collaboration des Québecois.[30]

This regionalism was still in its infancy when the depression hit the prairies. Immigration came to an abrupt end and emigration began. Several francophones, particularly lay members of the community's small intelligentsia, left the province. Others abandoned their farms and relocated in the northern area of the province where firewood was plentiful and the drought was less severe. Recruitment efforts devised and nurtured by *Le Patriote* were partly dismantled by the forces of nature during the 1930s. *Le Patriote de l'Ouest* itself became a victim of the depression. Economic considerations forced a merger with *La Liberté* of Manitoba. The only French-language newspaper published in Saskatchewan ceased to exist as a separate entity in 1941.

From 1911 to 1931 the French population of Saskatchewan more than doubled, increasing from 23,000 to over 50,000 people. At the same time, the total number of Saskatchewan residents also doubled. During these two decades of rapid demographic growth, the French managed to maintain their ratio of the provincial population at slightly more than 5 per cent.[31]

The numerical contribution of *Le Patriote de l'Ouest* to the growth of French settlement in Saskatchewan is difficult to assess. In one instance, the newspaper claimed that its subscribers were scattered in 572 different localities throughout Canada, particularly Quebec, and in over twenty American states.[32] It often boasted that hundreds of its eastern Canadian readers were moving to Saskatchewan. Such declarations might constitute slight exaggerations. The newspaper's list of subscribers was very limited: 2,500 in 1917, 5,000 in 1919 and 7,000 in 1922.[33] The company of La Bonne Presse was constantly teetering on the verge of bankruptcy. At best, *Le Patriote de l'Ouest* served to bolster the work performed by other individuals or agencies such as government immigration offices, francophone colonization societies and the *missionnaires-colonisateurs*.

In its attempts to attract settlers from Quebec in 1910 to 1918, *Le Patriote* made two erroneous assumptions. The editor, Father Auclair, and several of the other contributors believed that *faire connaître l'Ouest* would suffice to inspire a large segment of Quebec's population to venture to the Canadian prairies. They

chose to ignore many of the lamentations voiced by the colonization missionaries who repeatedly complained that their appeals
went unheard. These western newspapermen also assumed that
the elite of *la belle province* had the power to control the migratory movement of its people. If that was the case, the thousands
of French Canadians who crossed the border to settle in the
United States would have remained in Quebec. *Le Patriote* disregarded the fact that economic considerations had a more immediate impact on people than elitist exhortations and admonitions.[34]
It was more comforting to entertain the implausible dream of
creating francophone enclaves on the prairies out of a steady
migratory flow from Quebec.

The turning point came after 1918 when *Le Patriote* ceased to
regard Quebec as the sole key to the Fransaskois' salvation. The
French Canadians had missed a golden opportunity to establish
three mini-Quebecs on the prairies. Now it was too late. A mosaic
of ethnic groups had occupied most of the available land. The
recognition that it would have to face the future and weather
storms like the school question of 1918 with little or no support
from outsiders forced the French minority of Saskatchewan to
come to terms with reality, to mature quickly. Quebec's indifference, and the geographical distance and new social environment
for francophones on the prairies all combined to create "une
bouture autonome" during the 1920s. Instead of "Notre langue,
notre foi," "Fais ce que tu peux avec ce que tu as" would have
constituted a more fitting motto for *Le Patriote de l'Ouest* after
1918. Ironically, it was used to adorn the front page of *L'Eau vive*,
a newspaper created by the Fransaskois in 1971, thirty years after
the disappearance of *Le Patriote*.

Notes

1. R. Huel, "The French Language Press in Western Canada: *Le Patriote de l'Ouest*, 1910-41," *Revue de l'Université d'Ottawa* 46, no. 4
   (1976), pp. 476-99.

2. *Le Patriote de l'Ouest*, 22 August 1910. The newspaper will be
   referred to as *Le Patriote* in the remaining notes.

3. Huel, "French Language Press," pp. 480-82.

4. *Le Patriote*, 29 August 1912.

5. Ibid., 1 June 1912.

6. On June 13, 1912 *Le Patriote* published a special issue devoted to colonization which contained a multitude of monographs. The twelve delegates selected to attend le premier congrès de la Langue française, to be held in Quebec City in June, would use the issue to publicize the west.

7. *Le Patriote*, 20 June 1912; 12 February 1912.

8. Ibid., 5 September 1912. See also 5 December 1912; 9 October 1918.

9. Ibid., 29 March 1912.

10. Ibid., 11 December 1918.

11. Ibid., 6 July 1914; 16 July 1914.

12. Ibid., 20 June 1912; 9 February 1912; 6 July 1914.

13. Ibid., 14 September 1910; 6 July 1914.

14. Ibid., 6 July 1914.

15. Ibid., 29 August 1912.

16. Ibid., 21 March 1912.

17. Ibid., 20 July 1911.

18. Mathieu to the premier of Quebec, A. Taschereau, April 9, 1921, Archives of the Archdiocese of Regina, Affaires personnelles de Mgr. Mathieu, 1916-1921, Regina.

19. *Le Patriote*, 14 July 1914; see also 13 March 1918.

20. Raymond Denis, the president of the Association culturelle franco-canadienne, who had spearheaded a campaign to recruit bilingual teachers in Quebec during the height of the racial crisis in Saskatchewan, wrote in *Le Patriote* on March 5, 1919: "Et ces instituteurs, nous ne devons plus compter sur les autres groupes français du Canada, pour nous les fournir, mais sur nous mêmes."

21. W.J. White to the Canadian agents posted in the United States, September 30, 1914, Public Archives of Canada, Immigration Papers, RG 76, Vol. 75, File 5146, Part 4.

22. *Le Patriote*, 18 October 1922.

23. Ibid., 23 July 1919.

24. Ibid., 13 June 1923.

25. Ibid., 28 July 1920.

26. Ibid., 24 September 1919; 29 September 1920; 20 September 1922; 4 October 1922; 1 September 1926; and 11 January 1926.

27. Ibid., 4 August 1920.

28. Not all Fransaskois came from Quebec either directly or via the United States. A small minority of the francophones in this province came directly from France and Belgium.

29. *Le Patriote*, 2 August 1922; see also 23 July 1919; 26 July 1922; and 23 April 1924.

30. Lionel Groulx, *Mes Mémoires* 3 (Montreal: Fides, 1972), pp. 25-27.

31. *1911 Census of Canada* II, pp. 340-41; *1931 Census of Canada* II, pp. 294-97.

32. *Le Patriote*, 19 February 1919.

33. Huel, "French Language Press," pp. 487-89.

34. A. Lalonde, "L'Intelligentsia du Québec et la migration des Canadiens français vers l'Ouest canadien, 1870-1930," *RHAF* 33, no. 2 (September 1979), pp. 184-85.

Franco-Ontarians

Spatial Patterns in Franco-Ontarian Communities

Donald Cartwright

The objectives of this paper are to present the distributional patterns of major francophone communities in Ontario and to discuss certain spatial features that appear to be significant to the respective concentrations. Processes that are associated with human contact and interaction for Franco-Ontarians are also outlined to emphasize areal variation within the province. Such variations may be important to the formulation of policy and programs that are intended to accommodate the requirements of a diverse francophone population in Ontario. Analysis will emphasize location and situation and the significance of scale variation to ethnic research. An application of the *language intensity index* is used to determine the patterns of contact and interaction among francophones and between francophones and members of an anglo-dominant society.

At the outset, a short explanation of what constitutes spatial patterns, in the context of Franco-Ontarian settlements in the province, may help to clarify the theme of this paper. With developments in communications, the absolute location of such settlements remains, while the location of francophone communities relative to the core area of French Canada (Figure 1) can alter. This concept of location involves the element of distance and concomitant potential for human contact and interaction with Quebec society. This interaction can be in the form of regular radio and TV broadcasts, telephone conversations across the provincial boundary, subscriptions to French-language newspapers and magazines, and visits to Quebec to see friends and relatives. These aspects of location can be measured to ascertain whether relative distance is increasing or decreasing between a specific community and the core area, which is significant to language maintenance (through regular and varied usage) and the reinforcement of values that help to sustain a cultural heritage.

Another feature of spatial analysis of Franco-Ontarian communities is situation. In geographical terminology, situation is generally considered to be relative spatial position with respect to other places such as major service centres or other francophone-populated areas. One usually considers situation in relation to the specific feature of the human landscape. For example, if a major

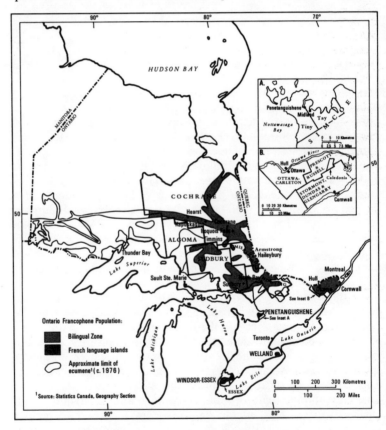

Figure 1. Major Concentrations of French Mother-Tongue Population, Ontario, 1976.

urban centre is situated beyond a large francophone area, regular visits necessitate entry into an English-dominant milieu and behaviour accords.

Another important feature of the spatial analysis of Franco-Ontarian settlements is to develop some measure of the strength and pervasiveness of the French language among the francophones in their daily routine of local contacts and interaction. Since the language-of-the-home question was incorporated into the 1971 Census, it is possible to relate this statistical population (those who are currently using the language) to the mother-tongue population: those who first learned the language as children (although they may not necessarily speak it). This relationship will provide researchers with an indication of the tenacity of the mother tongue in a community or among various members of that community. But beyond the home, it is difficult to know to what degree a Franco-Ontarian enters and functions in an English-dominant environment.

Any bilingual population (those who responded "both" to the official-languages question) can be analysed to determine whether it consists mainly of anglophones or francophones, thereby providing a useful measure of "balanced" or "unbalanced" bilingualism.[1] There are, however, two weaknesses in using bilingual population data to ascertain the level of ascendancy of one language within a bicultural community. The definition of ability to speak both official languages ("... well enough to conduct a conversation") is perhaps the most vaguely defined and most subjective of the language-related census questions. Distance from the core area of French Canada may exacerbate the confusion in responding to this question. A citizen from British Columbia or Newfoundland who responds "yes" to this section of the official-languages question may wish to alter the response after a four-week sojourn within the bilingual zone of Ontario or Quebec. Also, a respondent who answers "French" to the mother-tongue question and "English" to the language-of-the-home question, or vice versa, is classified by Statistics Canada as bilingual *regardless* of the response to the official-languages question.[2] It is not hard to envisage a person who learned French as a child, and who may still understand a small portion of the language, no longer feeling competent to *speak* the mother tongue because he or she has linguistically intermarried and has lived in an English-dominant environment for decades. Nevertheless, for the 1971 Census that individual was classified as bilingual by Statistics Canada.

To provide an indicator of the potential for language usage

beyond the home, it was decided to use the unilingual population
—those who replied "English only," or "French only" to the
official-languages question—in a cross-tabulation with responses
to the home-language question. The former must be considered
the least subjective of the language-related questions in the census; while the language-of-the-home question can be confusing to
respondents who were raised in a home where more than one
language was used.[3] However, it does provide a measure of those
who are currently able to speak their mother tongue. Thus, when
the unilingual population of any geostatistical unit is cross-tabulated with the home-language population, we can establish an
index that will range from 1.00 to 0.00. This has been termed the
index of language intensity:

$$\frac{\text{official-languages population} \quad \begin{matrix}\text{French} \\ \text{or} \\ \text{English}\end{matrix} \quad \text{only}}{\text{home-language population} \quad \begin{matrix}\text{French} \\ \text{or} \\ \text{English}\end{matrix} \quad \text{only}} = \text{Index of language intensity}$$

Any geostatistical unit that has an index close to 1.00 may be
considered one in which persons can function well in their mother
tongue during their daily interactions in the home and beyond.
When the index approaches 0.00, the opposite occurs. Then people must switch to the other official language to obtain most
services, to function at work, and in many of their daily human
interactions.

A low scale on the index should not suggest that francophones
do not use French in specific places beyond the home, such as
cultural centres or service clubs. A high proportion of French
home language to French mother tongue for any francophone
area that has a low index of language intensity would indicate
patronage of French-language institutions but English usage
throughout the rest of their community. The following tabulation,
therefore, may be applied, in association with the index, to the
Franco-Ontarian communities as another aspect of spatial research.

$$\frac{\text{French home-language population}}{\text{French mother-tongue population}} \times 100$$

This form of tabulation has been used elsewhere to delimit language zones in Canada. Franco-Ontarian communities were designated as within a *bilingual zone* or a *language island,* based upon the results of the tabulations and their distance from the core area of French Canada.[4] The spatial analysis that follows will be applied separately to the bilingual zone and to the language islands of Ontario. In this paper there will be no spatial analysis of the Franco-Ontarians in metropolitan Toronto. This area could accommodate a separate study but would require more space than can be provided at this time. In 1976 the census recorded 39,805 people of French mother tongue in Toronto, but the Bilingual Districts Advisory Board (1975) was unable to denote a specific district in Toronto because this population was so dispersed.[5]

Throughout this paper, reference will be made to changes in mother-tongue populations. There are some social scientists who believe that caution must be taken before relying on the historical comparability of such data.[6] It is the contention of this writer, however, that with the scale utilized in the following spatial analysis, problems of comparison have been minimized.[7] It also should be noted that comparisons are used to identify trends in population change.

The Bilingual Zone of Ontario: Northern and Eastern Ontario

Although administrative boundaries are delimited between Quebec and the English-dominant provinces to the east and west, no such boundary can be established for language communities. Between the dominant English and French language areas of Canada, there is a zone of transition, the bilingual zone, in which people use both official languages. For the purpose of spatial analysis, this zone in Ontario can be divided into the northern and eastern part of the province.

Northern Ontario has been classified as a region of moderate economic disparity. Reliance upon extractive industries and primary production has created a local economy that is at the mercy of the vagaries of external market conditions and, accordingly, suffers higher unemployment than other parts of the province.[8] Its dissatisfaction with policies and programs from Queen's Park to develop secondary industry is perennial, and the question of separate provincial status seems to be constantly under discussion.

Table 1: Language-Related Data for Selected Census Divisions, Northern Ontario, 1941, 1971, 1976

Census Division FHL/FMT/LI*	Cochrane 91% 0.34	Nipissing 83% 0.27	Sudbury 82% 0.21	Timiskaming 82% 0.35	Total
1941					
total population	80,730	43,315	80,815	50,604	255,464
EMT population	33,471	19,997	34,280	33,042	120,790
FMT population	31,728	20,453	30,262	10,223	92,666
1976					
total population	96,825	81,740	194,990	43,760	417,315
EMT population	42,155	53,340	113,400	29,485	238,380
FMT population	46,355	24,385	59,670	11,655	142,065
Change:					
1941-1976					
total population	16,095	38,425	114,175	−6,844	161,185
EMT population	8,684	33,343	79,120	−3,557	117,590
FMT population	14,627	3,932	29,408	1,432	49,399

EMT   English Mother-Tongue Population
FHL   French Home-Language Population
FMT   French Mother-Tongue Population
LI   Index of Language Intensity
*   Based on 1971 Census Data

Source: *Census of Canada*, Population Data

The population data presented in Table 1 for part of northern Ontario reveal that the French mother-tongue population is less than half of the total population in the four districts that constitute this portion of the bilingual zone. Furthermore, between 1941 and 1976, the English mother-tongue population increased by 97 per cent, while the French mother-tongue population grew by 53 per cent. In this time period, the anglophones increased as a percentage of the total population (47 per cent to 57 per cent), while the francophones decreased (36 per cent to 34 per cent). Although there are approximately 142,000 people of French mother tongue in the four districts in 1976, this figure must be placed in the context of spatial analysis outlined above to ascertain the significance of their magnitude.

When one changes the scale of analysis to plot the location of these Franco-Ontarians according to the distribution of permanent settlement (the ecumene), it is possible to demonstrate that, in this northern environment, situation tends to inhibit regular contact and interaction among the francophones.

There is an areal separation between two dominant francophone areas: the Sudbury-North Bay agglomeration, and the railway orientation of the Timmins-Iroquois Falls-Cochrane-Kapuskasing axis. Large tracts of uninhabited land lie between them. Furthermore, the distribution pattern of permanent settlement appears to be undergoing a significant process of change. There seems to be an increase in the growth and concentration of the Franco-Ontarians in the vicinity of the Sudbury census metropolitan area in the district of Sudbury and within the Timmins-Cochrane-Kapuskasing axis in the district of Cochrane. Between these two growth areas, the francophone population has declined, mainly in Nipissing and Timiskaming, particularly since 1961. This change in the scale of investigation of areal distribution is another important aspect of spatial analysis.

If one can rely on the census data for mother tongue and for changes in distributional patterns, the polarity of the French population in northern Ontario has intensified in and around those centres in which the strength of the English language is very high on the index of language intensity (0.85 to 0.95). For the French language in these centres, the index is 0.25 and lower. And if the trend to urban or urban-oriented locations (i.e., rural non-farm) has become as prominent as in southern Ontario, the linguistic environment for the francophones will alter and become closely linked to centres that may be classified as English dominant. A variation in the application of the index may illustrate the significance of such a trend.

The index of language intensity was applied, through a special tabulation of age cohorts, to selected Franco-Ontarian communities.[9] Tabulations of French mother-tongue populations were obtained from responses to home- and official-languages questions and to age and sex categories in the 1971 Census. An index of language intensity was calculated for grouped cohorts then plotted on a line graph. Representative francophone areas were selected from within the bilingual zone (Figures 2 and 3) and from one language island (Figure 4). In Armstrong Township and in the town of Haileybury, both in the Timiskaming district, the proportion of the French mother-tongue population who use French in the home is quite high—87 per cent (Figure 2). The index of language intensity for both communities, however, is relatively low—0.44 and 0.32 respectively. Nevertheless, this indicates that some services and human interactions beyond the home are performed in French.

For each community the index is relatively high for the 5 to 14 age cohort, particularly in rural Armstrong Township. This probably reflects the large proportion of elementary school-age children, many of whom attend unilingual French schools, who speak French in the home and with playmates and have a narrow range of interactions beyond the home. The index declines markedly for the next cohort (15 to 24 years), probably reflecting their greater movement in the neighbourhood and exposure to English. After this decline, however, the index rises for each successive cohort. An increase in the index of language intensity for those in the labour force, particularly those in the age cohorts 25 to 44 and 45 to 64, may indicate a neighbourhood place of employment. If the place of work is proximal to the place of residence, it may be considered by some as an extension of the neighbourhood, and so the mother tongue is used accordingly. Associated with this is the possibility of a lower socio-economic level among these cohorts, so that workers do not have the occasion to interact beyond a rather narrow range of fellow employees. Involvement in the labour force, consequently, may be highly unilingual. If a large proportion of these older cohorts are housewives, their involvement with neighbours may be French dominant or exclusive. In Haileybury, even though they constitute only 9 per cent of the French mother-tongue population, those over 65 years of age have an index almost as high as the youngest cohort. Beyond the standard age of retirement, daily movements and interactions decrease, and the need to use English may decrease with them. Do these profiles suggest that ability gained in speaking English provides mobility to those in the 15-24 age group, leaving behind

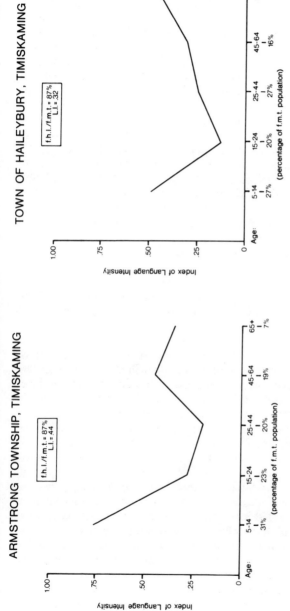

ARMSTRONG TOWNSHIP, TIMISKAMING

f.h.l./f.m.t. = 87%
L.I. = .44

Index of Language Intensity

1.00
.75
.50
.25
0

Age: 5-14   15-24   25-44   45-64   65+
     31%   23%   20%   19%   7%
(percentage of f.m.t. population)

TOWN OF HAILEYBURY, TIMISKAMING

f.h.l./f.m.t. = 87%
L.I. = .32

Index of Language Intensity

1.00
.75
.50
.25
0

Age: 5-14   15-24   25-44   45-64   65+
     27%   20%   27%   16%   9%
(percentage of f.m.t. population)

(f.h.l. = French home–language population; f.m.t. = French mother–tongue population; L.I. = index of language intensity)

FIGURE 2. INDEX OF LANGUAGE INTENSITY BY AGE COHORTS FOR SELECTED COMMUNITIES, NORTHERN ONTARIO, 1971.

a neighbourhood work-force of whom the greater proportion consider themselves to be unilingual? If so, this may indicate that most francophones who leave northern Ontario are in the young, bilingual, wage-earner category.

In eastern Ontario there are a number of similarities to the patterns and processes of northern Ontario. The use of the mother tongue by Franco-Ontarians as the language of the home in some eastern Ontario census divisions is even stronger than in northern Ontario. Beyond the home, however, they function largely in English except in Russell and Prescott Counties (Table 2). These two counties are closest to the census metropolitan area of Montreal—the most densely populated area of Quebec. Many francophones in these counties are descendants of the first settlers in eastern Ontario and enjoy a strong cultural tradition.[10] These factors may help to explain a relatively low index of language intensity for the anglophone population of Russell and Prescott. At 0.73 and 0.62 respectively, it is the lowest throughout the bilingual zone of Ontario.

With the exception of Ottawa/Carleton, population growth in this region has been below the provincial average. Although agriculture has been dominant (in contrast to mineral and forest exploitation in northern Ontario), the area was characterized by low incomes and considerable land abandonment. Much of the population growth in Russell County, for example, can be attributed to an increase in dormitory centres and in the number of rural non-farm residents who have moved there from the Ottawa metropolitan area.[11] This population growth is reflected in the decline of the proportion of Franco-Ontarians in the country—from 80 per cent of the total population in 1941 to 64 per cent in 1976—a trend that is likely to continue. Since 1961 the rate of increase of the French mother-tongue population has been below that of the anglophone population in each of the five census divisions; and the proportion of the former to the total population has dropped accordingly.

The significance of proximity to the core area of French Canada and of a high proportion of Franco-Ontarians to the total population is revealed when the index of language intensity is applied to various age cohorts in two communities within the bilingual zone of eastern Ontario (Figure 3). Caledonia Township in Prescott County has a high proportion of francophones who use the mother tongue in the home (98 per cent) and a relatively high index of language intensity (0.65). The profile for the index by age cohorts in this community is almost identical to Armstrong Township in northern Ontario. We may assume that the same

Table 2: Language-Related Data for Selected Census Divisions, Eastern Ontario, 1941, 1971, 1976

Census Division FHL/FMT/LI*	Glengarry 89% 0.25	Stormont 82% 0.19	Prescott 99% 0.48	Russell 99% 0.50	Ottawa Carleton 84% 0.22	Total
1941						
total population	18,732	40,905	25,261	17,448	202,520	304,866
EMT population	9,495	24,311	4,452	3,397	137,250	178,905
FMT population	8,736	15,230	20,642	14,006	56,586	115,200
1976						
total population	19,270	61,175	29,100	32,115	508,155	649,815
EMT population	10,700	39,370	5,595	10,565	360,178	426,768
FMT population	7,835	18,830	22,850	20,550	94,120	164,185
Change: 1941-1976						
total population	538	20,270	3,839	14,667	305,365	344,949
EMT population	1,205	15,419	1,143	7,168	222,928	247,863
FMT population	−901	3,600	2,208	6,544	37,534	48,985

EMT   English Mother-Tongue Population
FHL   French Home-Language Population
FMT   French Mother-Tongue Population
LI   Index of Language Intensity
*   Based on 1971 Census Data

Source: *Census of Canada*, Population Data

processes are operative here, and that Ottawa and Montreal attract young wage-earners who are proficient in both official languages. For example, the percentage of the French mother-tongue population in the 15 to 24 age cohort is only 18 per cent in Caledonia Township, compared to 23 per cent in Armstrong Township. Approaching the western margin of the bilingual zone in Ontario, a dramatic change in the profile occurs. In Charlottenburg Township, Glengarry County, for example, the francophones constitute only 31 per cent of the total population. The graph profile (Figure 3) for the township indicates the pervasiveness of the English-language population and the necessity to function accordingly. This applies to all but a few who are over 64 years of age and have a small range of daily contacts beyond the home.

For the five-county area that constitutes the western region of the bilingual zone, concern must be expressed for the slow rate of growth of the francophone population relative to the total increase since 1961 (8 per cent versus 36 per cent). The distribution of Franco-Ontarians appears to be diminishing areally as well.[12] If the government of Ontario is in earnest when it promises improved French-language services for the area, those francophones who continue to live in this region should sustain their language and cultural heritage. Those who are conscious of a trend towards language transfer should be concerned with provincial policies that will promote the location of small industries in these five counties to exploit the market potential of Ottawa and Montreal. Such policies, coupled with recent improvements in road transportation, may accelerate this trend. Branch plant operations that may locate in eastern Ontario in response to such programs and/ or to exploit the metropolitan markets are likely to function internally in English. For residents of French mother tongue any advance in this type of local employment opportunity would consequently occur in an English-dominant work environment. It is important to monitor the changes in land-use activity and industrial development in eastern Ontario, for such changes could have a negative impact on the potential for language usage beyond the home by Franco-Ontarians.

Language Islands in Ontario

For the francophone language islands of Windsor/Essex, Welland and Penetanguishene, distance from the core area of French Canada has, to a degree, been overcome by their size and sense of

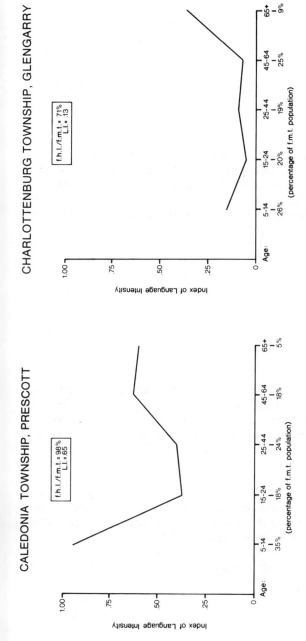

CALEDONIA TOWNSHIP, PRESCOTT

f.h.l./f.m.t. = 98%
L.l. = .65

CHARLOTTENBURG TOWNSHIP, GLENGARRY

f.h.l./f.m.t. = 71%
L.I. = .13

(f.h.l. = French home-language population; f.m.t. = French mother-tongue population; L.I. = index of language intensity)

FIGURE 3. INDEX OF LANGUAGE INTENSITY BY AGE COHORTS FOR SELECTED COMMUNITIES, EASTERN ONTARIO, 1971.

community. Within each island there are opportunities to use French at various neighbourhood centres; and community leaders have worked to sustain elements of their cultural heritage.[13] Each island has benefited from periodic in-migration of French-speaking families from Quebec and northern Ontario. In their ethnic persistence, these Franco-Ontarians satisfy the conditions of critical mass and community structure that Vallee (1971) identified as crucial.[14] Unfortunately, there is evidence that in recent years, the French mother-tongue population has been declining in some areas of the islands. Even where growth is occurring, it is at a rate below that of the dominant anglophone population. This process can be attributed, in part, to the geographical location of these Franco-Ontarian communities and to their local characteristics.

In 1976, 80 per cent of the population of Essex County lived within the census metropolitan area of Windsor. Of the 21,795 Franco-Ontarians in the county, 83 per cent were within the boundaries of the metropolitan area. The index of language intensity for French in the county was low for both urban and rural francophones (0.13). The proportion of those who continued to use the mother tongue in the home varied only slightly between the two locations. (No profile was provided for this centre, as plotting the index for each cohort produced almost a straight line very close to the horizontal axis of the graph.) In Windsor, 44 per cent of the French mother-tongue population used French in the home, whereas the percentage rose to 52 for rural francophones.

Mercer (1974) found that there was a correlation between the length of residency in this urban environment and the predominance of French in the homes.[15] (He maintains that as length of residence increases, there is a trend for English to become the dominant language of the home.) He also found that, in general, there was a relationship between higher economic status and a shift to the use of English in the home. The in-migration of French-speaking families did not appear to be sufficiently numerous to offset these processes. Furthermore, as the economic growth of a region faltered or went into recession, there was a marked decline in the movement of families into this urban centre—Windsor. As a consequence, the Franco-Ontarian community of Essex was denied the necessary infusion of French-speaking families from Quebec or other parts of Ontario. This trend should be reflected in the 1981 Census for Windsor/Essex.

There is a tendency for the significance of the neighbourhood to diminish with each generation in such urban environments. As young families move to suburban areas, they lose contact with ethnic parishes and local social organizations. But Mercer did find statistical evidence that clustering still exists for many francophone families in Windsor, and that a social structure, which he identifies as vital to ethnic persistence, can be found. The size of the francophone population, the richness of their local history and heritage, the efforts of community leaders and the persistence of a variety of ethnic organizations cannot be disregarded in the face of the assimilative processes. While evidence of an ethnic heritage may persist in Windsor, the use of language as one element of this persistence appears to be giving way to other spatial and socio-economic processes.

The geographical configuration of Essex County is confining the growth of Windsor. Rural Franco-Ontarian communities are in the path of this growth and one by one appear to be engulfed by the expanding urban environment.[16] Although more than half of the Franco-Ontarians in the rural environment use their mother tongue in the home, they practise what has been described as a patterned evasion of language usage in the community.[17] Although it is possible to use French in social contact beyond the home, there appears to be a selective process in this. According to a pilot study conducted in the area,[18] French was used most frequently to patronize the elementary schools, the church and doctors' services. The study showed a decline in the use of French for all other services, so that about one-quarter of the total French mother-tongue population used their language to obtain municipal services or to patronize various social clubs. In households in which French was used exclusively as the home language, evasion was less pronounced; but even here only 52 per cent attempted to use French to obtain municipal services. In households in which English was used predominantly, evasion was pronounced.

When asked if services in French were adequate for their community, over 82 per cent of the respondents declared that they were. The pattern of language usage for Franco-Ontarians found in rural Essex County was mirrored in Penetanguishene and in neighbouring Tiny and Tay Townships. When asked if services in French in these areas were adequate, 81 per cent of the French mother-tongue respondents answered "yes."

Mindful of the weakness in comparing mother-tongue data over time (Lachapelle, 1977), it is nevertheless, useful to observe the change in this population for an indication of trends and for juxtaposition with migration processes within language islands. In the early decades of settlement, the francophone population of the Penetang/Tiny-Tay community benefited by its distance from the growth centres of southern Ontario. Rural francophones did not face absorption into an expanding metropolitan area as did their counterparts in Essex County. Journey-to-work movements apparently did not necessitate entry into an English dominant environment. The use of the mother tongue in social situations beyond the home was reinforced by church, financial (Caisse Populaire) and educational institutions that provided services in French. These factors of heritage, geographic location, occupational and cultural services are manifest in the encouraging proportion, in the Penetang region, of French mother-tongue persons who speak it in the home (60 per cent).

Since 1941, however, there has been an alteration in the migration processes in Simcoe County that may be eroding the home-language population. Part of the county now functions as dormitory for daily commuters to metropolitan Toronto. Between 1941 and 1976 the total population of the county grew by 142 per cent with more than one-third of the growth occurring since 1961. The French mother-tongue population increased by almost 16 per cent between 1941 and 1961, but the rate has not been constant for each decade. The pilot study conducted in Essex and Penetang revealed that the French mother-tongue population had experienced greater magnitude in out-migration from the county than people of English mother tongue. Education and employment opportunities in other areas, particularly metropolitan Toronto, appear to be attracting young Franco-Ontarians from this Georgian Bay community. There are local attractions for retirement families and wealthier commuters, although the study shows that most of them are anglophones.

In-migration of both francophones and anglophones has occurred in Windsor/Essex, so that loss through out-migration for the francophones there does not appear to be as currently severe as for those in Penetang. One implicit aspect in the geography of Essex County is the strong attraction of Windsor as an employment centre. For those who live in a rural, French-language environment, employment in Windsor necessitates daily entry into an English-language milieu. This may be a more potent factor in the attrition of the French language and attitudes toward language maintenance than the actual change of residence that appears to be taking place in Penetang.

If the proportion of francophones in Simcoe County, particularly those in rural areas who continue to use French in the home, is encouraging, then the proportion found in Welland may be startling. In this city, over 77 per cent of the French mother-tongue population speak the language most often at home. The majority of these people are located in two census tracts in the centre of the city. Analysis of large-scale settlement patterns within the city reveals that people of French mother tongue live in close proximity to each other (Bennett, 1980). Constituting a high proportion of the total population, these people can patronize and maintain a variety of social and institutional activities which in return encourage continued usage of the language in the home and neighbourhood.

Although the index of language intensity for the two census tracts is low (0.20 and 0.14 respectively), analysis of the age-cohort composition reveals an interesting profile (Figure 4). The index is low for the youngest age groups but begins to rise rather markedly for those over 45 years of age. This tends to support the findings of Bennett (1980), who has suggested that the late arrival of relatively large numbers of French-speaking families into a community that had a social infrastructure to accommodate them accounts, in large part, for the success of language maintenance. According to the Census of 1901, there were sixty-seven people of French mother tongue in Welland. By the census year 1921, this minority group had grown to 499 people. Bennett found that this rapid growth could be explained mainly through the hiring policy of the Empire Cotton Company. In 1918-1919 the company recruited experienced textile workers from Montmorency, Quebec and offered them higher wages and accommodation in company-owned housing near the mill. In the 1920s people had a narrower range of social interaction than at present. Consequently, French would have been relatively easy to maintain within the neighbourhood. Since the majority were mill workers, social class was not a factor that would create segregation among the francophones (Vallee, 1971). An ethnic parish was established in 1920 under the guidance of a French-speaking priest. This and the subsequent development of French-language services in cultural and commercial institutions helped to stabilize the use of French within the community. A new wave of francophone in-migrants settled within and near the parish during and after the Second World War. Industrial expansion occurred throughout the region (the Niagara Peninsula), and this expansion was associated with a wartime and postwar economy. The francophone community apparently experienced cultural rejuvenation with the arrival of new French-speaking neighbours. A significant numerical threshold and a locational pattern were thereby sustained to provide support and expansion of various cultural and educational institutions. One example was the establishment of a French-language secondary school in 1959. Educational opportunities were thereby extended for students of the unilingual French elementary school. According to Bennett, this was accomplished, in part, because of the goodwill and cooperation of the majority of the anglophone population.

Welland has suffered in recent years because of its distance from the core area of French Canada. (This can be said of all the language islands in southern Ontario.) The profile in Figure 4 will probably begin to level off as age cohorts advance. Without regular contact with the core area, periodic in-migration of French-speaking families and daily contact with French-language media, it is likely that the processes of maintenance will give way to the processes of assimilation. The strength of the extended family and the significance of institutions wane in the face of movements away from the neighbourhood hearth and improvements in mass media and transportation. With an extended range of movement and interaction, Franco-Ontarians work and recreate further from their neighbourhood. Bilingual and bicultural accommodation in these enclaves may increase the incidence of mixed marriages, but it also enhances community cooperation and reduces ethnic conflict. For generations, the minority population within most language islands appears to have developed a form of accommodation and balance in co-existence with the majority. In part, this process of accommodation can be found in the patterns of language usage that occur in the regular routine of interaction within each community. These areas are not static, and awareness of processes that effect change through spatial, socio-economic and demographic analysis should assist in monitoring alterations in community structure and interaction that may be detrimental to the cultural heritage of all Franco-Ontarians.

Each of the areas with a Franco-Ontarian concentration, illustrated in Figure 1, have enjoyed the "critical mass" necessary to sustain those activities and institutions that have reinforced their cultural attributes. Those within the bilingual zone of Ontario have the added advantage of proximity to the core area of French Canada and concomitant contact and interaction across the provincial boundary. These features plus the duration of settlement appear to have minimized the instances of patterned evasion of language usage that was prevalent in two of the French-language islands of southern Ontario. Further research on the bilingual zone is required, however, to determine whether selectivity of

Spatial Patterns   155

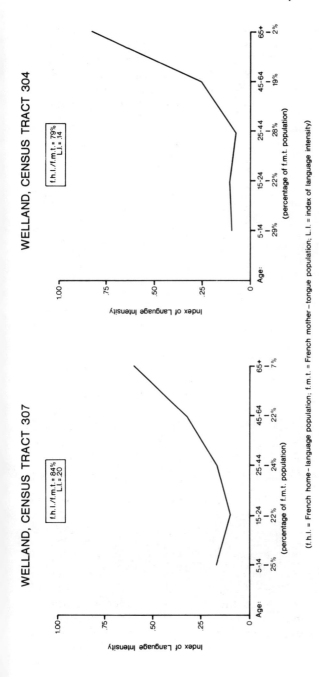

WELLAND, CENSUS TRACT 307

f.h.l./f.m.t. = 84%
L.i. = .20

Age: 5-14 15-24 25-44 45-64 65+
      25%   22%   24%   22%   7%
(percentage of f.m.t. population)

WELLAND, CENSUS TRACT 304

f.h.l./f.m.t. = 79%
L.i. = .14

Age: 5-14 15-24 25-44 45-64 65+
      29%   22%   28%   19%   2%
(percentage of f.m.t. population)

(f.h.l. = French home-language population; f.m.t. = French mother-tongue population; L.i. = index of language intensity)

FIGURE 4. INDEX OF LANGUAGE INTENSITY BY AGE COHORTS FOR CENSUS TRACTS 307 AND 304, WELLAND, ONTARIO, 1971.

language usage is entrenched or shifting. Franco-Ontarians within this zone appear to be experiencing a process of areal concentration, particularly in northern Ontario. Again, large-scale analysis could determine the impact of this upon the range of interaction among francophones and the magnitude of out-migration for the young, incipient wage-earners.

In eastern Ontario several features of the cultural environment require large-scale analysis. Is the movement of urbanites into Russell County (near Ottawa) and into Prescott County (proximal to Montreal) a harbinger of an ethnic population shift at the expense of the Franco-Ontarians? Is the purchase and amalgamation of farm units in these counties by in-migrants from Switzerland and Germany indicative of a trend or only a short-term movement that will not significantly affect the composition of the ethnic population? Will secondary industry develop in the counties, providing added impetus to the inroads already in progress? It has been suggested that this *could* introduce an English-dominant work environment into a portion of the bilingual zone that now enjoys a relatively high usage of French beyond the home as measured by the index of language intensity.

Encouraged by community leaders, programs sponsored by l'Association canadienne-française d'Ontario and educational, religious and financial institutions, the Franco-Ontarians in Windsor/Essex, Welland, and Penetanguishene and environs have done well in sustaining attributes of their cultural heritage. Certain processes appear to be eroding some of the accomplishments of these groups, however. The movement of families, including francophones, into Windsor/Essex and Welland may be retarded as employment opportunities wane. Such family movement may be a minor obstacle if the concentrations of Franco-Ontarians can be sustained in the face of the attraction of suburban living for young families (Welland), absorption by the census metropolitan area of Windsor (Essex County) and an increase in the proportion of English-speaking families in all neighbourhoods (Penetang and Essex County). Bennett's work in the Franco-Ontarian community in Welland revealed cultural, business and religious French-language institutions that were well patronized but uncovered an element of pessimism because many were unable to attract young members.

Further research into patterns of household movement within or away from the original settlement area should help forecast the future of many of these institutions. There is a need for large-scale research in each of the areas discussed to determine variations in the migration process, the patterned evasion of language usage and adherence to cultural traits by different age groups. Policies and programs to assist the Franco-Ontarians in retaining elements of their heritage will be more effective if they are designed to accommodate these variations.

Notes

1. Frank G. Vallee and Albert Dufour, "The Bilingual Belt: a Garotte for the French?" *Laurentian University Review* 6, no. 2 (1974), pp. 19-44.

2. John Kralt, *Languages in Canada,* Profile Studies No. 99 (Ottawa: Statistics Canada, 1976), p. 707.

3. Charles Castonguay, "Quelques remarques sur les donées du recensement de 1971 concernant la langue et l'origine ethnique," *Cahiers québécois de démographie* 5, sp. no. 3 (1976), pp. 211-41.

4. Don Cartwright, *Language Zones in Canada,* a reference supplement to the Report of the Second Bilingual Districts Advisory Board (Ottawa: Information Canada, 1976).

5. Canada, Bilingual Districts Advisory Board, *Report* (Ottawa: Information Canada, 1975).

6. See John Kralt, *A User's Guide to 1976 Census Data on Mother Tongue,* mimeographed (Ottawa: Statistics Canada, 1978); Réjean Lachapelle, "Quelques notes à propos de la comparabilité de la composition par langue maternelle aux recensements de 1971 et de 1976," *Cahiers québécois de démographie* 6, sp. no. 3 (1977), pp. 93-137; and, Paul Lamy, "The Validity of the 1971 Census Language Data," in *Language Maintenance and Language Shift in Canada: New Dimensions in the Use of Census Language Data,* edited by Paul Lamy (Ottawa: University of Ottawa Press, 1977).

7. Kralt and Lachapelle have analysed the methods used in gathering and processing mother-tongue data for 1961, 1971 and 1976 and are concerned with the accuracy and comparability of self-enumeration data (1971, 1976) against responses to direct enumeration (1961). They also point out that persons raised in a bilingual environment may be confused over which language was "first learned" and is "still understood." Lamy discovered that respondents of French origin had a greater incidence of parents who spoke different languages at home than those respondents of Anglo-Celtic origin. Between 1961 and 1971, Statistics Canada altered processing techniques to take advantage of new computer facilities and this variation has also made comparability subject to error. Through large-scale analysis (census subdivisions, enumeration areas and census tracts) errors

may be lessened but not eliminated as Lamy discovered. It is possible to focus upon areas of strongest mother-tongue concentration through scale variation. If one is confused about their mother tongue in this scale of analysis he/she may be considered "lost" to the respective group. Furthermore, in this paper consideration is given only to French and English while those of "other" mother tongue have been omitted. Nevertheless, the writer is aware of the concerns over comparability and for that reason has stressed *trends* only in mother-tongue population changes.

8. J.U. Marshall, "The Urban Network," in *Ontario,* ed. R. Louis Gentilcore, Studies in Canadian Geography (Toronto: University of Toronto Press, for the twenty-second International Geographical Congress), pp. 64-82.

9. The writer would like to express appreciation to Professor Charles Castonguay, University of Ottawa, for suggestions regarding the application of the index of language intensity.

10. Don Cartwright, "Institutions on the Frontier: French Canadian Settlement in Eastern Ontario in the Nineteenth Century," *Canadian Geographer* 21 (1977), pp. 1-21.

11. L.G. Reeds, "The Environment," in *Ontario,* edited by R. Louis Gentilcore, Studies in Canadian Geography (Toronto: University of Toronto Press for 22nd International Geographical Congress, 1972), pp. 45-63.

12. Don Cartwright, *Official Language Populations in Canada: Patterns and Contacts,* Occasional Paper No. 16 (Montreal: The Institute for Research on Public Policy, 1980).

13. John R. Bennett, "Cultural Maintenance in a Language Island: Welland, Ontario" (B.A. thesis, Department of Geography, University of Western Ontario, London, 1980).

14. Frank G. Vallee, "Regionalism and Ethnicity: the French Canadian Case," in *Immigrant Groups,* edited by J. Elliott (Scarborough: Prentice-Hall of Canada Ltd., 1971), pp. 153-67.

15. Warwick M. Mercer, "The Windsor French: Study of an Urban Community" (Masters thesis, Department of Geography, University of Windsor, Ontario, 1974).

16. John D. Jackson, "French-English Relations in an Ontario Community," in *Minority Canadians: Immigrant Groups* 2, edited by Jean Leonard Elliott (Scarborough: Prentice-Hall of Canada, 1977), pp. 160-74.

17. Gordon F. Streib, "The Restoration of the Irish Language: Behavioral and Symbolic Aspects," *Ethnicity* 2 (1974), pp. 72-89.

18. Don Cartwright and Harry W. Taylor, "Bilingual Accommodation in Language Islands: Essex County and Penetang, Ontario," *Canadian Ethnic Studies* II (1979), pp. 99-114.

The Role of the Church in French Ontario*

Robert Choquette

In presenting this paper, my intention is, first, to provide you with a brief sketch of Ontario's French Catholic history, focusing primarily on the nineteenth century, and second, to draw some conclusions and make some statements based in part on the initial overview.

Catholic evangelizing and ecclesiastical activity in the seventeenth and eighteenth centuries is a well-known and well-understood dimension of Canadian history. As far as Ontario is concerned, this period is almost exclusively made up of missionary endeavours, beginning with the voyage of the Recollet friar Joseph Le Caron to Huronia in 1615. The Jesuit missions to this same area around Lake Simcoe, beginning in 1626, culminated in the construction of Fort Sainte Marie (burned to the ground by the Jesuits themselves in 1649). Sainte Marie was the foremost missionary endeavour in seventeenth-century Ontario. A number of other outposts did exist, such as Quinte (1668-1682), Sainte Marie du Sault (from 1665), Fort Frontenac (from 1673). They were, however, primarily relay stations, harbouring a missionary on a temporary basis. French colonial administrators were almost exclusively concerned with the fur trade and related military ac-

---

* The following is a presentation based upon an ongoing research project. While I stand by what I will say, I reserve the right to adjust some of my statements if and when new evidence warrants. Since the topic is quite broad, I have avoided couching my paper in a web of footnotes.

tivities against the Indians or the English. Indeed, many so-called missionaries were really explorers or adventurers.

This pattern of settlement continued during the eighteenth century with one exception. Detroit was founded by Cadillac in 1701. A permanent resident priest arrived in 1728. Armand de la Richardie initially settled on the right bank of the Detroit River (today's Detroit), but in 1742 he moved his mission to the south bank (Windsor) in order to better serve the Indian people. In 1744 another Jesuit, Pierre Potier, succeeded de La Richardie. Potier supervised the building of the first chapel on the south shore of the Detroit River in 1749, the year successive governors of New France began to officially encourage the migration and settlement of white men on the south shore. The mission of L'Assomption, beginning in 1743, was the only permanent and uninterrupted mission in Ontario established under the rule of New France. At the time of the British conquest in 1760, then, there was only one established Catholic mission in Ontario, with the priest and all the parishioners either French or Indian.

When Loyalists began coming to Canada from the United States after 1775, several successive groups of Scottish Catholics settled in Glengarry County at the easternmost tip of Ontario. They were accompanied by their priests, Roderick Macdonell and Alexander Macdonell, who founded the missions and subsequent parishes of St. Raphael, St. Andrews and St. Regis. The only francophones in Ontario (Upper Canada) at the time were those in the Detroit peninsula; in fact, the total Ontario population in 1790 was only some ten thousand souls. The American Loyalists were followed, in their move to Canada, by Irishmen, Englishmen and Scotsmen. This led the bishop of Quebec to appoint a local administrator or vicar general for Upper Canada in 1807. Father Alexander Macdonell was chosen; he was consecrated a bishop in 1820, becoming bishop of Kingston upon the formation of the diocese in 1826. Macdonell's immediate ecclesiastical superior was in fact, although not in theory, the bishop of Quebec. Many of his clergy in Upper Canada were obtained through the auspices of the successive bishops of Quebec (Plessis, Panet and Signay), and he himself was fluent in French.

In 1833 the first working coadjutor to the bishop of Kingston (two others were appointed without ever occupying the office) was Rémi Gaulin, a Canadian priest who had ministered in Kingston between 1811 and 1815 before becoming a missionary to the Acadians in Cape Breton and on the Atlantic coast of New Brunswick. In 1821 Gaulin became the pastor of a series of parishes in the Montreal area before he became coadjutor. Gaulin immediately assumed a major share of the burden of administering Catholic church affairs in Upper Canada. He travelled extensively to the Catholic outposts in the Windsor area, Penetanguishene, Lake Huron, Toronto and the eastern counties. Gaulin even travelled up the Ottawa River as far as Allumette Island and through the Lake Nipissing region. Many of his priests were francophone: Father Proulx in Penetanguishene after 1835, Jean Charles Prince in Kingston in 1840 and even Vicar General Angus Macdonell in Sandwich and Bytown.

Upon the death of Bishop Macdonell in 1840, Gaulin automatically became bishop of Kingston. Deteriorating health, however, forced him to make use of a coadjutor/administrator (who would exercise the real administrative power). The chosen priest was Patrick Phelan, a Sulpician from the diocese of Montreal and pastor to Montreal's Irish Catholics. Phelan had been vicar general to Bishop Bourget and in 1840 had officially established (on behalf of Bourget) many parishes along the Ottawa River, such as Buckingham, Templeton, Chelsea and Aylmer. Phelan became vicar general to Gaulin and pastor of Bytown in 1842-1843. He was also fluent in French, and he had lived most of his adult life in a francophone ecclesiastical milieu. Gaulin, for his part, was also perfectly bilingual, according to Alexander Macdonell. Both men died within a month of each other in 1858.

The next bishop of Kingston was Edward John Horan (from 1858). A native of the British Isles, he had spent the last decade teaching at the Quebec seminary. He was another case of a "Frenchified" anglophone. The diocese of Kingston thus remained, until 1874, under French Canadian influence.

The diocese of Toronto (the western half of Upper Canada) was established in 1841 at the request of Bishop Gaulin. Its first bishop, beginning in 1842, was Michael Power. Power, of Irish origin, had been a missionary on the Ottawa River (separating Upper and Lower Canada) at Notre Dame de Bon Secours in the early 1830s before becoming a pastor in the Montreal area under Bishops Jean Jacques Lartigue and Ignace Bourget. Upon learning of Power's appointment (on his own recommendation), Gaulin was overjoyed, commenting to Bourget that Power was "just Irish enough" to do the job while being French Canadian enough to see things in the same light as Bourget and himself. Power immediately set about obtaining Jesuit missionaries for his diocese. The first three Jesuits arrived in 1843 and established themselves in Sandwich (Windsor). Operating from this base, they sent other missionaries throughout southwestern and northern Ontario. Most of these Jesuits were French speaking as was, for many years, the vicar general of Toronto.

In 1847 Michael Power died suddenly during an epidemic. An Irish Jesuit, stationed in New York, was appointed his successor but refused the job even after the apostolic letters of appointment had been issued. The choice then fell, in 1850, to Armand François Marie de Charbonnel, a Frenchman who ignited the Toronto ecclesiastical scene. Charbonnel was an either/or man, to whom most things appeared either black or white, but rarely grey. Father Bruyère was his vicar general, and Pierre Adolphe Pinsoneault—a former Montreal Sulpician now organizing the diocese of Toronto's secretariat—was appointed first bishop of London when that diocese was established in 1856. Toronto remained under francophone control until late 1859, when John Joseph Lynch became coadjutor to the bishop. Upon Charbonnel's resignation in the spring of 1860, Lynch became third bishop of Toronto.

The Ottawa Valley, however, was far removed from both Kingston and Toronto. It was first settled above the Long Sault by an American immigrant Philemon Wright. His growing colony at Chaudiere Falls (opposite Ottawa), within a few years included sawmills, gristmills, tanneries, and the like. The Ontario side of the Ottawa River (Upper Canada) was under the ecclesiastical jurisdiction of Alexander Macdonell in Kingston, while the Quebec side (Lower Canada) was under that of Jean Jacques Lartigue in Montreal. In 1824 Lartigue sent his first missionary up the river—the Sulpician Jean Baptiste Roupe—who repeated the voyage in 1826 and reported to Lartigue on the Indian bands and inhabitants of the shanties and lumber camps that existed in the valley.

Bytown (Ottawa) began with the construction of the Rideau Canal and the accompanying influx of workers in 1826. A priest stationed in Richmond, a military settlement west of Ottawa dating from 1816, began visiting Bytown in 1827. The bishop of Kingston permanently stationed priests there after 1829, but he found it difficult to maintain all his Ottawa Valley missions. Bishop Macdonell was not only understaffed, but communications were exceedingly difficult through the hinterland between Kingston and the Ottawa Valley. He thus rejoiced at any opportunity to have the church of Montreal handle the Ottawa Valley missions. For Montreal was not only a longer-established and better-staffed church, it was also the main departure point for travel up the Ottawa Valley (with Hudson's Bay Company canoes, servicing their trading posts, regularly journeying along the river as did winter travellers with horses and sleighs).

Thus in 1836 Bishop Lartigue sent Father de Bellefeuille to service the missions along the river. He repeated his trip in 1837 and 1838, just prior to his death. In the early 1840s Father Hippolyte Moreau became the primary missionary in the Ottawa Valley. Both de Bellefeuille and Moreau had usually travelled with another priest (either Poiré, Brunet, Cannon, Bourassa or Brady), preferably English speaking. Bourget himself had gone as far as Allumette Island in 1841, consecrating churches and confirming the young along the way.

The congregation of Bytown at this time was roughly 60 per cent English speaking (Irish) and 40 per cent French speaking. A succession of moral and disciplinary problems troubled its clergy throughout the 1830s until 1842, when Vicar General Patrick Phelan took over. He found many instances of ethnic rivalry and fighting within the community, which he tried to stop. Pressured by Bourget, Phelan accepted the coming of the French Oblates of Mary Immaculate in 1844 as well as the Sisters of Charity of Montreal General Hospital (Grey Nuns) in 1845. This was the beginning, for both of these religious orders, of a major network of religious houses throughout the French Canadian diaspora (Ontario). By 1846 concerned churchmen had already agreed that a new diocese should be formed in Bytown. Bourget carried the request to Rome along with the recommendation that Father Joseph Eugène Bruno Guigues, provincial superior of the Oblates, be made first bishop of Bytown. The diocese was officially constituted by Rome in 1847, Guigues being appointed its bishop. I should mention that Bourget had pressured Phelan into accepting the Oblates for Bytown, even though they were Frenchmen charged with an Irish majority congregation. By 1850-1851 the Oblates had been given exclusive jurisdiction over the missions among the Indians and the shanty dwellings of the valley (the latter, being financially profitable, made the Oblate exclusivity a point of controversy among some pastors in the Ottawa Valley). The Oblates were also given control of St. Joseph's College in Bytown, founded by Guigues in 1848 (now the University of Ottawa). One can see in these events a clear case of French Canadian ecclesiastical imperialism. It is probably because of this that Patrick Phelan, after 1843, had such difficult relations with the Grey Nuns and the Oblates (having to endure such men as Bishop Gaulin who refused to allow him, as diocesan administrator, access to diocesan papers).

Quite a number of priests and missionaries on the Ottawa River, from the 1830s to the 1850s, were English speaking. I wish to underline, however, that most if not all of these were Frenchified. A French Canadian today is surprised to find ordinary priests in obscure interior parishes, with names like Cannon, Brady, Lynch and Moore, all writing and speaking fluent and colloquial French.

By mid-nineteenth century, therefore, all the leading churchmen in Ontario were francophile or fluent in French. Bishop Bourget of Montreal had entrenched his real power and influence over the church in Canada; and the archbishop of Quebec, as metropolitan of the only ecclesiastical Canadian province, was the legal head of the Canadian church. Clearly, church projects, submitted to Rome for approval, as well as the selection of bishops were to be in the interests of French Canada.

This is a time of major expansion for Catholic institutions in the wake of Canada's ever increasing population due to large-scale immigration. The population of Ontario went from 120,000 in 1819, to 950,000 in 1850, to over 2,000,000 in 1900. Roman Catholic territorial administration had to keep pace. The following is a list of such developments: three dioceses existed in 1850, namely, Kingston (1826), Toronto (1841) and Bytown (1847); the dioceses of Hamilton and London were established in 1856, followed by the elevation of Toronto to archdiocese in 1870, the creation of the apostolic vicariate of northern Canada in 1873 and the apostolic vicariate of Pontiac in 1882; Ottawa was made an archdiocese in 1886, and in 1890 the tiny diocese of Alexandria was formed, and the vicariate of northern Canada became the diocese of Peterborough in 1882; Kingston became an archdiocese in 1890, while the vicariate of Pontiac became the diocese of Pembroke in 1898; the Sault Sainte Marie diocese dates from 1904 and the apostolic vicariate of Temiskaming from 1908 (the latter became the diocese of Haileybury in 1915 and then the diocese of Timmins in 1938); the apostolic prefecture of Hearst, created in 1919, was made a vicariate in 1920 and a diocese in 1938 (the same year as James Bay); and Thunder Bay and St. Catharines formed dioceses in 1952 and 1958 respectively.

Drawing some conclusions from the above: Ontario's Catholic church was under French Canadian control for most of the nineteenth century. Some Ontario dioceses have virtually always been under francophone control, such as Ottawa,Temiskaming/Haileybury/Timmins and Hearst. One diocese, Alexandria, went from anglophone to francophone control. Many others did the reverse —Toronto, London, Peterborough (northern Canada), Kingston (except under the first bishop) and Pembroke (Pontiac). The only

Catholic diocese in Ontario created during the nineteenth century that completely escaped French control was Hamilton. This was true of Sault Sainte Marie, Thunder Bay and St. Catharines in the twentieth century. However, Sault Sainte Marie proved to be a point of contention in French-English relations, and during the last two decades it has been given francophone auxiliary bishops. The Catholic hierarchy in Canada, as a whole, was dominated by French Canada during all of the nineteenth century and the early part of the twentieth century; that is to say, the French Canadian hierarchy outnumbered, outranked and outweighed the English Canadian hierarchy (almost without exception of Irish lineage). Some of these English-speaking bishops, such as Lynch of Toronto, Fallon of London and McNally of Calgary (particularly the latter two) made every effort to reverse the situation.

The francophone Catholic hierarchy and clergy constituted the main bulwark of Franco-Ontarian interests during that period. Bishops Bourget and Guigues did all in their power to favour French Canadian settlement in eastern Ontario. When the Ontario school crisis erupted in the first quarter of the twentieth century, the leading militant Franco-Ontarians were more often than not priests, like the Oblate Charles Charlebois, or bishops like Elie Anicet Latulipe or Arthur Béliveau. The clergy never shrank from exercising its political influence to its own advantage —whether it be for land grants, Catholic schools, settlers' railways or French schools.

In terms of theology and spirituality, the church of French Ontario was a popular and conservative church. When the school crisis developed over linguistic rights in Ontario, Irish Canadian Catholics and French Canadian Catholics proved to be bitter enemies. Their religious bond took a back seat to ethnic rivalry in all areas of activity. From Cornwall to Windsor, via Ottawa, North Bay and Sudbury, Franco-Ontarians fought for the right to bilingual schools. Irish Canadian Catholics sided with the Ontario government and the Orange lodges in denying these rights. The scars of the wounds inflicted during this battle of half-century ago still endure.

In closing, I wish to say that the Catholic church has been the most important social institution in nineteenth-century French Ontario. Franco-Ontarians owe a great deal to their clergy. This is perhaps the reason why the aggiornamento in international Catholicism—the movement spearheaded to reconcile the church with modernity—did not unleash the scepticism and anticlericalism in French Ontario that was part of its legacy in Quebec.

Today Catholics account for one-third or close to three million of the eight and one-half million people of Ontario. Of these three million Catholics, half a million have French as their mother tongue, while some 800,000 are of French origin—close to one-third of Ontario's Catholics—and their strength now seems to be recognized and accepted by the church hierarchy. For, while in the early 1900s English-speaking bishops in Ontario lobbied against French-education rights, they now petition for the extension of minority-language rights, such as those envisaged in Article 133 of the British North America Act, to Ontario.

The Franco-Ontarian Collectivity: Material and Symbolic Dimensions of its Minority Status*

Danielle Juteau-Lee

Si l'on me demande aujourd'hui: "Faut-il aider les Tziganes (ou les Catalans, les Basques, les Bretons, les Indiens, les Slovènes, les Juifs, les Arméniens...) à survivre en perpétuant et en approfondissant leurs différences?", je dirai qu'il le faut. Je ne chercherai pas à savoir—car il y a trop de haine et d'arrogance dans une telle curiosité—si ce groupe est un peuple, une nation, une tribu, une ethnie, une classe, une caste, une secte, un fossile ou un vestige. Ni si l'obstination qu'il met à s'éterniser convient au progressisme du moment. Les cultures ne sont pas des toupies. Il me suffit que le groupe existe, qu'il travaille à maintenir, à renouveler, à recréer son identité, et qu'il ne le fasse pas exclusivement en parasite. La volonté de vivre n'a pas à prouver son droit à la vie. C'est la volonté de détruire, c'est l'acquiescement à la mort qui doivent désormais fournir leurs preuves. Et je ne sais si ces preuves existent.

Richard Marienstras,
Etre un peuple en diaspora (1975)

The purpose of this article is to shed some light on the present condition of the Franco-Ontarian collectivity. In order to achieve this goal, we will outline the major parameters underlying our analysis, examine the factors which have affected its historical evolution and explore the ways in which this minority, committed

*I would like to thank Hélène Régnier and Jocelyne Talbot for their excellent research as well as Raymond Breton, Ann Denis, Paul Lamy and Jacqueline Pelletier for their useful comments on an earlier draft.

to boundary-maintenance, is reacting to changes such as industrialization and urbanization. These changes, it will be argued,
have broken down former mechanisms of boundary-maintenance
and modified the relationship between the dominant and the
subordinate groups. Consequently, new issues are raised, new
strategies are developed, new elites appear as members of the
collectivity endeavour to formulate a collective project in keeping
with the emerging Franco-Ontarian identity. The dynamics of this
process—an expression of the vitality of an ethnic community—will
be determined by the respective assets of the groups involved.

Underlying Parameters

The basic parameters[1] underlying our analysis will now be stated:

(1) An ethnic community is more than the number of individuals who possess certain common traits, whether biological (origin),
legal (residence or citizenship), or cultural (behaviour). Ethnicity
is not a natural attribute, there is no central core which creates
unalterable behavioural patterns specific to the members of a
particular ethnic community.[2]

(2) Although ethnic groups usually strive to delimit the space
where origin, legal status, culture and identity coincide, it is im-
possible to arrive at a definition of an ethnic group that applies to
all those who identify with it.[3]

(3) When examining an ethnic community, one should focus
on its material foundations, the historical process which has produced it. As pointed out by Bauer (1974), there exists an observa-
ble system, manifested by common language, customs, mores,
laws, institutions and religion. But this system, this form, emerges
because individuals share a common past and common experiences (their struggle to survive). Their distinctive shape, their
different cultural and structural features are a consequence of
their adaptation to diverse historical circumstances.

(4) The differences between historical-cultural communities become relevant only under certain conditions, namely, when they
engender a common orientation between the people sharing a
common destiny. In his discussion on communalization, Weber
states that "it is by no means true that the existence of common
qualities, a common situation, or common modes of behaviour
imply the existence of a communal social relationship."[4] He goes
on to argue that the crucial element is not the difference, but the
consciousness of a difference:

> It is only with the emergence of a consciousness of difference from third persons who speak a different language that the fact that two persons speak the same language, and in that respect share a common situation, can lead them to a feeling of community and to modes of social organization consciously based on the sharing of the common language.[5]

Clearly, what Weber suggests is that an ethnically determined social action is not produced automatically by "ethnic" traits; it emerges in the context of a relationship with another community. Furthermore, it is in this context that we can understand why certain traits and not others are chosen as a basis of communalization. If religion constitutes the main difference between the two collectivities, it will become the trait which determines an ethnically based social action; in other cases, it can be language or colour, for example. I also think that it is not the difference *per se* which should be taken into account; we should be able to specify those aspects of the community's life which are perceived as being threatened. They will become the traits around which the action of a community crystallizes; they will also be considered as its centre and its basis. That is why we cannot enumerate, once and for all, the traits which constitute an ethnic group, or a nation, for that matter.

(5) The relationship between ethnic communities usually involves a dominant group and a subordinate one. In such cases it is a social relationship of domination, as one of the communities is oppressed by the other. The oppressed collectivity is a minority, and its minority status comprises two interrelated components: first, this status rests upon a material basis, as the collectivity possesses a smaller share of economic and political resources; second, this objective status manifests itself at the symbolic level, as the minority is perceived as different, since the majority represents what is universal, the norm.[6] In other words, the subordinate group is defined by the dominant group or, at least, in terms of the dominant group. Since the dominant group and the subordinate group are united within a common system, changes in their relationship will affect the minority, its goals and its strategies.

(6) An examination of ethno-national minorities should address itself to the following questions: Does the community seek assimilation or does it prefer to maintain distinctive boundaries? What are the factors which determine the choice of a specific end-state and the capacity to attain it? Such an analysis could take into account past historical experiences, namely, the se-

quence of interaction (Schermerhorn, 1970); the amount of resources, namely, the level of organizational capacity (Breton,
1974); and the attitudes of the dominant group vis-à-vis the goals
of the minority (Schermerhorn, 1970). When a community
chooses boundary-maintenance, how does it go about reaching
this goal? Does it try to achieve various amounts of institutional
completeness without questioning the legitimacy of the existing
political order? Or does it define a historical and political project
of its own? If so, what form does this collective project take?
Political independence, federalism, regional autonomy, or other
types of structural pluralism?

According to these options, one can differentiate between various types of historical and cultural communities—ethnic groups,
"groupes nationalitaires" and nations (Simon, 1975). Ethnic
groups, Simon argues, occupy one end of the spectrum. They
have a history, but no historicity; that is to say, they are located
in the sphere of tradition and are not active historical agents,
since they do not seek to restructure the political order. At the
other end of the spectrum, one finds nations. These communities
possess a historical and political dimension, as they formulate a
very specific political project aiming at the establishment or re-
establishment of a national state. The "groupes nationalitaires" fall
somewhere between the ethnic groups and the nations. In this case,
the group also possesses a historical and political dimension, as it
challenges the existing political order. In this process of historical
self-realization, a "groupe nationalitaire" does not seek political
independence, nationhood. Its attempt to restructure the political
order so as to achieve its ultimate goal of boundary-maintenance
can take on many forms. In some cases, there emerges a collective
project which clearly proposes a blueprint for the redistribution of
political power, such as federalism, decentralization, local autonomy; in other cases, the community cannot define an overall project but attempts, in a variety of ways, to exercise greater control
over its destiny. Franco-Ontarians have reached that stage; incapable of formulating a clear collective project, the members of this
community are nevertheless constantly defining numerous, and
often heterogeneous, goals and strategies.

These six parameters will have the following implications for
our study: (1) Our analysis of the Franco-Ontarian community
will not involve a fruitless search for essence, nor will it limit itself
to a detailed and static enumeration of the community's institutional contour, number of churches, schools, etc.; (2) By focusing

on process, it will emphasize the ways in which an ethnic community constantly defines and redefines its name, its institutional rules, its conventions and its visible structures in the face of a changing situation.[7] In this case, it means examining the struggle carried on by the French community in Ontario in order to maintain, affirm and control its existence;[8] and, (3) These organizational changes experienced by the community are brought about by modifications affecting its relationship to the dominant group. Its new material situation will determine the presence, the shape and the extent of its collective project and will express itself at the symbolic level, manifested in new forms of social identification and consciousness. More precisely, this implies that boundary-maintenance can no longer be achieved through isolation, that it necessitates some struggle in the political arena. It is suggested that while high levels of organizational capacity (Breton, 1974) give birth to independentist movements, low levels will tend to be associated with the absence of a clear, well-articulated, comprehensive collective project.

Historical Evolution

In keeping with the conceptual framework outlined previously, we will now examine the historical forces which have affected the evolution of the French community in Ontario.

The French Canadians who settled in Ontario during the middle of the nineteenth century attempted to recreate the patterns of social organization they had left behind in Quebec.[9] The emphasis on a rural way of life usually led to the development of a relatively self-sufficient agricultural economy; the low income from the farms was supplemented by part-time work in the logging and lumbering industry. The life of the community was organized around a central core, the village *qua* parish. This more or less complete social formation was only marginally integrated into the capitalist economy;[10] its reproduction was mainly ensured by the family and the church, and this process was controlled by the local petty-bourgeois and clerical elites. The socio-cultural world of this collectivity was a closed one; its leaders perceived the state as an outsider and put all their effort into developing intermediary institutions such as cooperatives and credit unions.[11]

By the end of the nineteenth century, the French Canadian nation comprised a great number of French-speaking communities, which spread out from Quebec to the west coast. The church constituted the controlling apparatus of this nation. As manager-in-chief it had a vested interest in opposing and reducing the power of the state. While it could and did achieve this goal in Quebec, it occupied a subordinate position in Ontario, where it was usually struggling against an Anglo-Saxon Protestant political elite and the English-speaking Catholic elite (Choquette, 1980). Thus, the major difference between the French Canadian communities in Quebec and Ontario was to be found in the unequal amount of power held by their respective managers. This weak position manifested itself in 1912 during the Ontario school crisis. This event clearly demonstrated that the fate of French Canadians in Ontario was largely in the hands of a dominant group intent on assimilating its minority. But on the whole, the community maintained distinct boundaries as a result of its relative isolation. However, this could not last forever.

The minority's situation is modified by changes in its concrete base and its relationship with the dominant group. Such transformations affect the boundaries of the community, as reflected in new social identities (we the French Canadians as opposed to we the Quebecois) and contribute, in some cases, to the emergence of new collective projects (i.e., Souveraineté-Association). The expansion of Anglo-American capitalism has engendered the industrialization and urbanization of French communities in Canada (Lee, 1974; Juteau-Lee, 1979). Both in Quebec and Ontario, these processes have undermined the communities' material foundations. As a result, their former managers—the French clerical elite —lost their power base and their control, leaving a vacuum. Also, by integrating into the capitalist economy, the communities lost their isolation, and the mechanisms which had ensured their relative stability were eroded.

In Quebec the control shifted from the hands of the clergy to the state, as an emerging political-bureaucratic elite presided over the destiny of the community. Political modernization was the essence of the Quiet Revolution. The state became an agent of social transformation. Its projects, reforms and interventions affected those who lived in Quebec and accentuated the territorial basis of social identification. In a way, it is this state that has given birth to the Quebecois nation and identity. The former controlling elite had emphasized pattern-maintenance as a means of boundary-maintenance; the new elite fostered the implementation of change—the ideology of conservation gave way to the catching-up ideology (Rioux, 1971). "Nous les Québécois" was linked to a new collective project, aimed at socialism, independentism and secularization which excluded all francophones living outside of Quebec. The initial tensions between the Quebecois and the other French Canadian communities lead to the emergence of parallel systems of solidarity as manifested in the "Etats généraux."[12]

In addition to these factors, the Franco-Ontarian community was subject to other forces. Here too, industrialization and urbanization transformed the basis of the community and its relationship to the dominant group. Assimilative pressures increased as members of the collectivity migrated, for economic reasons, to the urban centres of central and southwestern Canada, where they represented a minimal proportion (1.9 per cent) of the total population,[13] thus increasing the marginalization and "émiettement" described by Savard (1978).The provincial state has also become centralized in Ontario. Its scope has increased to include areas such as education, health and welfare, and culture. The public sector expanded at the expense of the community level, and local elites (both francophone and anglophone) saw their power wane as their basis crumbled. In the French Canadian community, the clerical elite was replaced by civil servants, teachers, media commentators and other members of the new petty-bourgeoisie.[14] In Ontario as in Quebec, the traditional francophone elites were replaced by those in the political sphere. But while those in Quebec control and use the state apparatus in order to implement reforms, the new francophone elites in Ontario face a state controlled by another historical and cultural community. Therefore, the collectivity is more dependent than ever on public funds and on officials of a state that has not always accepted the collectivity's goal of boundary-maintenance and that often rejects its demands, such as the recognition of French as an official language and the establishment of a Conseil homogène de langue française. Thus, the nexus of control has shifted from the cultural and ideological sphere to the political, and this underlined the precariousness of a community that does not control a state apparatus essential to its development.

These changes as well as their present status are reflected in the emergence of a new collective identity, as the French Canadians of Ontario became Franco-Ontarians. This term implies that the collectivity defines itself in terms of its relationship to a state and its territory, Ontario, but it also emphasizes its specificity, its particularism. On the one hand, there are Ontarians who embody the norm, on the other, there are those who are different, the

Franco-Ontarians. This minority status, which embodies both a concrete and a symbolic dimension, will have a bearing on the way the community seeks to maintain and affirm its existence.

Present Situation

We shall now examine how the Franco-Ontarian community has reacted to its changing situation; how it is creating new patterns of social relationships on the basis of existing concrete solidarities; how it is developing new ways of being. The general pattern is one of struggle, struggle for the recognition of the legitimacy of its goal of boundary-maintenance, for the implementation of its fundamental rights, for the acceptance of those means deemed essential to its existence. This struggle has deep historical roots, as pointed out by Cook when he argues that Ontario has always fought against French domination and papal supremacy—opposing group rights and proposing a system of unilingual schools.[15] The imposition of Règlement XVII in 1912 gave birth to a bitter conflict between the French and English in Ontario, and it should be remembered that it was only after fifteen years of struggle that it was withdrawn.

Of course, attitudes have evolved during the century, but Franco-Ontarians have not yet achieved full equality. As pointed out in a document prepared by the Fédération des Francophones hors Québec (FFHQ), *Deux poids, deux mesures,* the English minority in Quebec is far better off than the French in Ontario. Every gain made by the latter requires the expenditure of vast sums of energies because the dominant group rejects the idea of greater institutional control for and by the Franco-Ontarian community. For example, the North Bay District Chamber of Commerce (1971) asserted its support for bilingualism but rejected Bill 141, passed in 1968 by the Ontario provincial legislature, because the creation of "racial" schools would weaken Ontario. Such attitudes brought about the school crisis in Sturgeon Falls and in Cornwall, as well as many other conflictual situations, some of which will now be mentioned.

Although we shall not analyse them in detail, we would like to mention that all these cases are examples of a struggle in which the dominant group disagrees either with the goals of the subordinate group or, at least, with its choice of means:

a)   Between June 1975 and June 1976, thirty-two people were jailed because they refused to pay unilingual parking tickets.

b)   In 1977 the Essex County school board rejected the demand
      for a French secondary school in Windsor.
c)   In 1978 le Comité consultatif de langue française (CCLF)
      recommended to the Simcoe Country Board of Education
      that a French language secondary school be built. This was
      accepted only in April 1980, after petitions, marches and the
      mobilization of support given by numerous groups, such as
      artists, student associations, the Association canadienne-
      française de l'Ontario (ACFO), the premier of Quebec, etc.
d)   The establishment of a French language school in Elliott
      Lake was approved in 1979, after eight years of negotia-
      tions.
e)   In 1979 Queen's Park rejected a demand for a Conseil hom-
      ogène de langue française for Ottawa-Carleton.
f)   In 1979 the premier of Ontario rejected Bill 89, dealing with
      the official recognition of French in Ontario.

Because of their relatively low degree of organizational capacity, Franco-Ontarians cannot hope to control their provincial state
and cannot formulate a project akin to that of the Quebecois.
They cannot even define a well-articulated collective project to
redistribute political power between ethnic communities in Ontario. Each groupe nationalitaire fends for itself in a more or less
haphazard fashion, and this is reflected in the multiplicity and
heterogeneity of its interventions.

To summarize, Franco-Ontarians have not disappeared from
Ontario. They are trying to express and maintain their collective
existence. These efforts have not led to the elaboration of a
political project but, nonetheless, manifest themselves in a variety
of ways. First of all, a community manifests itself in the search
for its historical roots. The work accomplished by the DOPELFO
(Documents pédagogiques en langue française pour l'Ontario)
team is a step in the right direction. The diffusion of their excellent study will allow all Franco-Ontarians to become familiar with
the events that shaped their collectivity and will facilitate our
analysis of its present and future. For too long the history of
French Canada was restricted to that of Quebec.

Second, a collectivity manifests itself by assessing its present
situation in order to find adequate answers to existing problems:
The *Rapport Bériault* (1968), the *Rapport St-Denis* (1969), the
Rapport Symons (1972), the Report of the Social Planning Coun-
cil of Ottawa-Carleton, the numerous publications of the FFHQ
(*Les Héritiers de Lord Durham, Deux poids, deux mesures*), the
Rapport Savard (1977), the Bordeleau et al. study on French

secondary schools are all examples of this endeavour; their recommendations aim at ensuring the continued existence of this community. Others do not write reports or make recommendations but seek to make the Franco-Ontarian experience visible and to understand how it expresses itself on a daily basis: journalists, radio and television reporters, researchers in the media (Radio Canada; Office de télécommunication éducative de l'Ontario), in universities (Ottawa, Laurentian, Glendon College and the Ontario Institute for Studies in Education) and community colleges (Algonquin). Others express this reality in their songs, their poems and their plays. Théâtre Action (1972), les Editions Prise de Parole (1980), l'Institut Franco-Ontarien (1977) and its journal *La Revue du Nouvel-Ontario* (1978), le Centre de recherche en civilisation canadienne-française (University of Ottawa) all attempt to encourage and facilitate this process.

Third, the collectivity is struggling for the recognition of its rights, mainly linguistic. These demands are articulated by many people and associations, such as members of Parliament, the FFHQ, the ACFO, the Comité de Planification des Services de langue française en Ontario, the Commissariat aux Langues officielles, and through different mechanisms—briefs, communiqués and research. They are addressed to various levels of government and to private organizations. Their main objectives, at this stage, consist of the application of the dispositions of Article 133 to all provinces and the development of bilingual services in Ontario. In this sphere at least, there are some visible consequences, namely, the creation of a "Bureau du Coordinateur provincial des Services en langue Française," (Coup d'Oeil), the establishment of a "politique des services en langue française" (Ministère des services sociaux et communautaires, 1980) and the granting of certain limited services in French in courts and hospitals. Finally, the FFHQ has published, in January 1981, a critical analysis of the federal programs dealing with the teaching of the official languages and has proposed a series of recommendations to improve the educational system of the French minority outside of Quebec.

Fourth, at the institutional level, the efforts of the collectivity to create new forms of social existence are reflected in the disappearance of some associations, the changes in structure and objectives of others and the emergence of new ones. One immediately thinks of ACFO because of the major role it has played. Guindon's article (1979) helps us understand its evolution as well as that of the leadership of the community in general. But there are many other examples, such as Direction-Jeunesse, which has modified its objectives, and the FFCF (Fédération des femmes canadiennes-françaises), which seeks to rejuvenate its membership. The analysis of the institutional order, yet to be done, would contribute greatly to our understanding of the present dynamics. One could discover which sectors have lost their importance (disappearance of certain associations) and which ones have emerged (appearance of new interest groups, such as the ROE (Rassemblement des Ontaroises de l'Est)). One could examine the relative importance of each one, their respective power bases and amount of control (in education or the work world, and so on), and the conflict within each group between the traditionalists and the change-prone.

Interventions in the institutional order can range from the community level to that of the state. At the community level, the aim is to promote various forms of cultural life, to recreate social relationships equivalent to those maintained in the context of the parish community. The cultural centres and the programs of social-cultural animation sponsored by the Secretary of State (1969) constitute examples of this type of action. At the other end of the spectrum lies the state. Since the collectivity has no hope of seizing the state apparatus, it has tried to exert some kind of influence on the central agencies of decision-making by naming a "responsable des Affaires franco-ontariennes," as in the case of the Ontario Arts Council (1970), and by the establishment of the Conseil Consultatif des Affaires franco-ontariennes (1974), which "is allowed on its own initiative to review, comment and make recommendations to the Government."

Somewhere between the two poles of the continuum one finds institutions which are under the direction of the state but organized at the level of the community. The educational system is the prime example. I will not relate its evolution here, but it constitutes "l'événement-matrice" of the collectivity. It drains most of the communities' energies for decades and represents the battleground where they are engaged in a power struggle (Conseils Homogènes de langue française). It should also be remembered that a tremendous effort is now being made not only to teach in French and in French schools, but to develop and transmit material that is produced by the community which reflects its past and present situation. The Centre franco-ontarien de ressources pédagogiques, created in 1974, fulfills such a function (Grisé, 1980).

The four types of activity examined above (search for historical roots, assessment of the present, struggle for the implementation of rights and the creation of a new institutional order) all constitute a concrete manifestation of a will to live and, as such, define the collectivity and reflect its objective position, i.e., its minority status. Indeed, what surfaces is a struggle against the increasing pressures of the dominant historical-cultural community. What also emerges is the difficulty to outline a coherent plan of action since the "second dérangement" (to use the expression of the Comité économique de la FFHQ) has destroyed the former patterns of social relationships as well as their basis. As the community has acquired a new social identity, it has become the bearer of a new form of consciousness which, in turn, has influenced its primary orientation—Franco-Ontarian, rejection of tradition, conservatism and pattern-maintenance; recognition of the central influence of the state (Ontario) in its everyday life, expression of "la différence." It expresses a reality, the concrete and symbolic dimension of its minority status. It does not foster a coherent project, but it does bring about a multiplicity of activities which express the community's existence and give birth to a number of pressure groups which constantly reaffirm the right of the collectivity to exist.

It is interesting to note that all these activities are primarily located in the social-cultural sphere and that the legitimacy of the state is never challenged. Controlled by another historical-cultural community, this state (and the nation state in general) exerts tremendous assimilative pressures. The minority responds by taking a jab here, another one there, gaining some concessions, when the political context is favourable, but which are not sufficient to combat the bulldozing effect of the majority culture. Haphazard production in the socio-cultural sector and sporadic battles against the state, such is, in my opinion, the destiny of a minority that does not question the overall framework which defines its existence. Yet, the impasse will not be broken until there is more profound discussion concerning the economic and political bases of the community.

The two reports published by the FFHQ (Pour ne plus être ... sans pays, 1979; Un espace économique à inventer, 1981) are an attempt in this direction. Although we can ask ourselves how to survive in the context of capitalism and statism, it is obvious that the situation of a collectivity that does not control the means of production and/or the state apparatus is bound to be precarious. Maybe the solution lies in the direction of *l'autogestion* (self-management) *both* in the economic and political sphere. Eventually, it is the existence of the state itself that has to be questioned, since in both capitalist and socialist countries it pursues its efforts at homogenization in order to increase its control.[16] We accept as normal only the collectivities which have a state of their own, or at least, a possibility of achieving that goal. As a result, the diaspora existence is considered a shameful disease, or something artificial.[17] The model of the nation state, as the unique form of normal existence, must be contested. The factors which are responsible for the minority being a minority would then disappear. Because Franco-Ontarians are incapable of following the example of the Quebecois, they are obliged to innovate, and that might lead to a project of control by and for the community. We already have the example of the Ontarois:

> ... La communauté veut fixer ses propres objectifs et contrôler son devenir. Dans l'impossibilité de formuler les vieux rêves de l'Etat-Nation, elle se voit, fort heureusement, contrainte à l'élaboration de solutions nouvelles. Dans ce sens, la définition et l'adoption d'un projet autogestionnaire apparaissent des plus souhaitables puisqu'il est le seul susceptible d'éliminer, ici et ailleurs, les rapports inégaux entre les communautés d'histoire et de culture. Tant que la régulation de la communauté repose entre les mains de l'Etat, même d'un Etat géré par les membres de sa communauté, elle ne peut définir d'une manière autonome son développement. Il s'agit donc d'un projet autogestionnaire visant à l'abolition de la situation concrète de minoritaire.
>
> Parallèlement à la définition de ce projet (il est en effet trop tôt pour parler de lien causal), certains membres de la collectivité se sont appelés des Ontarois. Cette nouvelle désignation reflète des transformations profondes. Elle exprime le refus de la situation symbolique de minoritaire. La collectivité ne veut plus se définir par sa différence (Franco-ontarien) mais veut exister en dehors de ce rapport d'oppression. A quand la rencontre de ce nouveau projet autogestionnaire et de cette nouvelle conscience ontaroise?[18]

Notes

1. For a more detailed presentation of these parameters see D. Juteau-Lee, "Français d'Amérique, Canadiens, Canadiens français, Franco-Ontariens, Ontarois: qui sommes-nous?" in *Pluriel-Débat* 24 (1980), pp. 21-42.

2. R. Marienstras, *Etre un peuple en Diaspora* (Paris: Maspero, 1975), p. 51.

3. Ibid., p. 49.

180   *Danielle Juteau-Lee*

4. M. Weber, *Economy and Society,* ed. G. Roth and C. Wittich (Berkeley: University of California Press, 1978), p. 42.

5. Ibid., p. 43.

6. For example, until recently, the dominant group did not consider itself as an ethnic group. Ethnic applied to the other groups, those who were different, i.e., ethnic food, ethnic dances, etc. Also see C. Guillaumin, *L'idéologie raciste. Genèse et Langage actuel* (Paris/La Haye: Mouton, 1972), p. 86ff.

7. Marienstras, *Etre un peuple en Diaspora,* p. 52.

8. We are using the word struggle because the dominant and subordinate groups did not share, to use Schermerhorn's terminology (1970), similar beliefs concerning the final goals of the relationship. The centripetal aim of the dominant group has conflicted over the years with the centrifugal option of the minority. (For ample illustration of this fact, see R. Cook, 1966.) In spite of changes in recent years, the two groups have been unable to agree on the nature and extent of means required by the minority in order to maintain its boundaries.

9. Juteau-Lee, "Français d'Amérique, Canadiens, Canadiens français, Franco-Ontariens, Ontarois: qui sommes-nous?" p. 30.

10. D. Dennie, "De la difficulté d'être idéologue franco-ontarien," *Revue du Nouvel Ontario* (1978), no. 1, p. 74.

11. C. Archibald, "La pensée politique des Franco-Ontariens au XXe siècle," *Revue du Nouvel Ontario* (1979), no. 2, p. 20.

12. These meetings, held in Montreal in November 1966, November 1967 and January 1969, brought together representatives of French Canada as a whole. The Quebec delegates then voted for their right to self-determination, thus creating a split between the Quebecois and the other French Canadians.

13. Juteau-Lee, "Français d'Amérique, Canadiens, Canadiens français, Franco-Ontariens, Ontarois: qui sommes-nous?" p. 39.

14. Dennie, "De la difficulté d'être idéologue franco-ontarien," p. 74.

15. R. Cook, "Quebec, Ontario and the Nation," in *Canada and the French-Canadian Nation* (Toronto: MacMillan of Canada, 1966), pp. 32-36.

16. Marienstras, *Etre un peuple en Diaspora,* p. 62.

17. Ibid., p. 88.

18. Juteau-Lee, "Français d'Amérique, Canadiens, Canadiens français, Franco-Ontariens, Ontarois: qui sommes-nous?" p. 42.

Bibliography

Bauer, O. "Le concept de nation." In *Les marxistes et la question nationale, 1848-1914.* Edited by G. Haupt, M. Lowy and C. Weill. Paris: Maspero, 1974, pp. 233-57.

Bordeleau, G. et al. *Les écoles secondaires de langue française en Ontario: Dix ans après.* Toronto: Ministry of Education and the Ministry of Colleges and Universities, 1980.

Breton, R. "Types of Ethnic Diversity in Canadian Society." Paper read at the Eighth World Congress of Sociology, 1974.

Choquette, R. *L'Ontario français, historique.* Montreal/Paris: Editions Etudes vivants, 1980.

Fédération des Francophones Hors Québec. *Les Héritiers de Lord Durham* I. Ottawa, 1977.

———. *Deux poids, deux mesures: Les francophones hors Québec et les anglophones au Québec: un dossier comparatif.* Ottawa, 1978.

———. *Pour ne plus être... sans pays.* Rapport du Comité politique de la FFHQ. Ottawa, 1979.

———. *Un espace économique à inventer.* Rapport du Comité économique de la FFHQ. Ottawa, 1981.

———. *A la recherche du milliard....* Ottawa, 1981.

Grisé, Y. "A la découverte de l'identité franco-ontarienne par la création pédagogique." Communication presentée le 6 novembre, 1980.

Guindon, R. "Pour lever les contradictions structurelles de l'ACFO," *Revue du Nouvel Ontario* (1979), no. 2, pp. 35-40.

Juteau-Lee, D. "The Evolution of Nationalism in Quebec." In *Two Nations, Many Cultures: Ethnic Groups in Canada.* Edited by J.L. Elliott. Scarborough: Prentice-Hall of Canada, 1979, pp. 60-75.

Lee, D. "The Impact of Modernization and Environmental Impingements upon Nationalism and Separatism: the Quebec Case." Ph.D. dissertation, University of Toronto, 1974.

North Bay and District Chamber of Commerce. *Brief to the Ministerial Commission on French Language Secondary Education.* 1971.

Rapport Bériault. Rapport du Comité sur les écoles de langue française en Ontario. 1968.

Rapport St-Denis. La vie culturelle des Franco-Ontariens. 1969.

Rapport Savard. Cultiver sa différence. 1977.

Rapport Symons. Commission ministérielle sur l'éducation secondaire en langue française. 1972.

Rioux, M. *Quebec in Question.* Toronto: James Lewis & Samuel, 1971.

Savard, P. "De la difficulté d'être franco-ontarien." *Revue du Nouvel Ontario* (1978), no. 1, pp. 11-22.

Schermerhorn, R.A. *Comparative Ethnic Relations.* New York: Random House, 1970.

Simon, P-J. "Propositions pour un lexique des mots-clefs dans le domaine des études relationnelles." *Pluriel* (1975), no. 4, pp. 65-76.

The Franco-Ontarian Experience

Gaetan Vallières

Whether referred to as French-speaking Ontario (*l'Ontario français*), Franco-Ontarians (*Franco-Ontariens*), or in earlier days as
French Canadians of Ontario (*Canadiens français d'Ontario*), or
again more recently as *Ontarois* (without a translation), Ontarians
of French mother tongue are usually considered a fairly unified
collectivity sharing a common aim for a viable culturally-differen-
tiated future. Nevertheless, after a brief examination of their 1976
spatial distribution and of the main historical factors accounting
for such in the following paper, I will illustrate how diversity is
also an important part of the Franco-Ontarian experience.

In 1976 Ontarians of French mother tongue totalled 462,050 or
5.6 per cent of the 8,264,350 inhabitants.[1] Concentrated in the
easternmost tip of the province, you will find 37.9 per cent of
Franco-Ontarians along the Ottawa River. Central Ontario has an
18.9 per cent concentration in the Golden Horseshoe, from Toronto to the Niagara Peninsula. Close to 8 per cent (7.9) of all
Franco-Ontarians live in southwestern Ontario, mostly around the
city of Windsor and in Kent County. Only 2 per cent are scattered in the vast northwestern region. Northeastern Ontario accounts for 33.3 per cent of Franco-Ontarians, situated along the
two main axis of communication from North Bay west to Sault
Ste. Marie and north to Hearst.

When you consider Ontario's total population by region and
accompanying proportion of Franco-Ontarians, you will find the
following distribution: in eastern Ontario, where 13.9 per cent of

Ontarians live, 15.3 per cent are of French mother tongue, while in central Ontario, with 61.1 per cent of the population, only 1.7 per cent are French-speaking. Southwestern Ontario accounts for 15.5 per cent of the population, with 2.9 per cent French-speaking. In the northwestern part of the province, representing only 2.8 per cent of Ontario's population, 3.9 per cent are of French mother tongue. Finally, 26.3 per cent of northeastern Ontario, which accounts for 7.1 per cent of the provincial population, are Franco-Ontarians.[2]

The present Franco-Ontarian population is a result mainly of nineteenth and twentieth century French Canadian migration from Quebec. This unity of origin is a major characteristic of French-speaking Ontario. The 1971 Census seems to confirm that, even in periods of economic prosperity such as the one that followed the Second World War, relatively few French-speaking immigrants came to Ontario: out of 482,000 Ontarians of French mother tongue, less than 16,000 were born outside Canada. Moreover, even in southwestern Ontario, few present-day Franco-Ontarians can trace their ancestry to the Detroit River settlement left by the French regime in 1760.

Indeed, although the French experience west of the Ottawa River originated with Etienne Brûlé's voyage in 1610, there was little permanent settlement. Some colonization schemes were begun, but few had more than an existence on paper in the colonial administrators' reports. In fact, the number of French people in *les pays d'en haut* did not amount to more than was required for the fur trade, military defence and missionary work among the Amerindians. The collapse of the French empire in North America resulted in commissioned officers, soldiers and colonial administrators returning to France. In 1763 a small agricultural community (established since 1701 in the Detroit area), missionaries and a floating population of *coureurs de bois* were all that remained to bear witness to a century and a half of French colonial presence in what was to become, in part, present-day Ontario. Indeed, the American Revolution, less than twenty years later, left the smaller part of the Detroit settlement to Ontario. Some French settlers, loyal to the British, did, however, move to the east bank of the river.[3] But, in order to survive culturally among a growing population of British descent, this originally French-speaking community of less than a thousand souls needed the additional influx of French Canadians, which it was to receive throughout the nineteenth century, and then again in the twentieth.

Rural out-migration from the old seigneurial parishes of the Saint Lawrence Valley was responsible for the first French Canadians that came to settle in Ontario. Much has been written about the crisis that plagued Quebec's agriculture as early as the first decades of the nineteenth century.[4] Over-farming mixed with poor agricultural methods and crop diseases, over-division of land and a high birth rate combined to produce a relative rural over-population. Marginal lands were gradually put to use, only to be abandoned later. Rural out-migration followed, seasonal at first, as seen by the growing number of French who spent the winter in logging and timber operations usually up the Ottawa Valley. By the 1840s, emigration had become a noticeable fact in Quebec's rural parishes. Urban growth and infant industrialization in the province, hindered after 1870 by more than two decades of economic depression, simply could not absorb the demographic surplus. Emigration continued to grow, reaching a peak in the 1880s.

The most common destination for the emigrants was New England where employment could be found, notably in the textile factories. Up to 340,000 French Canadians moved there permanently in the second half of the nineteenth century; another 700,000 went there temporarily.[5] Southwestern Ontario, to a much smaller extent, also offered work to the emigrant on railroad construction; farmland was limited but still available and new French-speaking parishes were established in Pointe aux Roches, Saint Joachim and Paincourt. In Essex and Kent Counties, growing French-speaking communities attracted Quebec professionals in search of clientele. South of Georgian Bay, around Penetanguishene Bay, a particularly dynamic priest, as early as the 1830s, convinced parishioners of his native Batiscan and the surrounding area to join the remnants of an agricultural colony formed earlier by French-speaking *voyageurs* who had come there in the 1820s after Drummond Island had been declared American territory.[6] Finally, to some French Canadians who were not inclined towards agricultural settlement, Toronto offered employment, especially in its public works; a French national parish was created in 1887.[7] But, above all other regions of the province, eastern Ontario proved to be the most attractive.

By the mid-nineteenth century, much land still remained vacant in eastern Ontario, especially along the Ottawa River. Loyalist settlers had developed farms along the upper Saint Lawrence from New Johnston (Cornwall) to Kingston. Subsequent British immigrants had settled along the Ottawa, in the counties of Prescott and Russell, but had bypassed large poorly irrigated areas,

moving beyond to the counties of Carleton, Lanark and even
Renfrew. In Prescott, Russell and the adjoining counties, French
Canadians began to acquire vacant land in the 1840s.[8] Moreover,
in 1826 the construction of the Rideau Canal joining the Ottawa
River to Kingston on the Saint Lawrence had prompted the birth
of Bytown. Renamed Ottawa as the nation's capital, the city
attracted French Canadians to its lumber industry, construction
projects and various commercial enterprises.

In 1871 francophones in eastern Ontario numbered 41,000;
forty years later, in 1911, there were 102,000. During that time,
the total population of the province had risen from 392,000 to
508,000. From a mere 10 per cent of the population in 1871, the
French Canadians represented 20 per cent in 1911. Furthermore,
they were highly concentrated east of Ottawa and Cornwall,
where, in rural counties, they had become the largest ethnic
group. In Ottawa, they continued to maintain 30 per cent of the
population. Indeed, an observer termed the French Canadian
migration into eastern Ontario as "peaceful invasion," noting that
some rural inhabitants, mainly Scottish and Irish, had moved out
west after the completion of the Canadian Pacific Railway (CPR).
"Incredibly jealous of their predominance," he added, "they
could not accept the idea of being outnumbered."[9]

Nevertheless, French Canadian immigration to the manufacturing centres of New England continued, reaching a peak in the
last two decades of the nineteenth century. Nationalist leaders
and clerics became increasingly concerned with this "continuous
bleeding of the vital forces of the nation." Along with some local
newspaper editors, they shared a view of the American Republic
as an abyss where the "moral, religious and national values of
French Canada" were being lost. City life and work in unhealthy
factories were also blamed. In short, they claimed an alternative
to immigration to the United States did exist. It was agricultural
colonization.

For awhile during the 1870s, Manitoba was looked upon fa-
vourably by colonization promoters as suitable for French Canadian settlement.[10] But neither the encouraging pastoral letter of
1871 signed by every bishop in Quebec and read in every parish,
nor the diligent work of colonization missionaries brought French
Canadians to Manitoba and the west in numbers approaching the
thousands of settlers that did come from Ontario. Numerical
equality between French and English in the west was already
slipping away by the 1880s. Riel's hanging in 1885 and the Manitoba school question of the 1890s were final blows to Quebec's

hope of maintaining their advantageous position in the west. In the meantime, new territory was opened up to colonization within Quebec, notably in the foothills of the Laurentians and in Témiscamingue. To French Canadians who felt obliged to leave Quebec, the colonization promoters proposed settling in New Ontario. Indeed, establishing a chain of French Canadian parishes across northern Ontario from Mattawa through New Ontario could, in their opinion, reach Saint Boniface's French-speaking community in Manitoba.[11]

As the CPR was being constructed in the early 1880s from Mattawa west to Sudbury and then northwest to the Lakehead, with a branch line joining Sudbury and Sault Ste. Marie, the French started to migrate from Quebec and from already crowded rural eastern Ontario to Mattawa, Lac Talon, Corbeil, North Bay, Sturgeon Falls, Verner, Sudbury, Blind River and Sault Ste. Marie.[12] Not only were they involved in opening up agricultural land, they also worked in woodcutting operations, sawmills, pulp and paper mills, transportation and mines. They started local businesses and opened shops; professionals and parish priests also came. But they remained outside the group of entrepreneurs who had amassed fortunes in the industrial ventures of the new north. French investors did not answer Romanet du Caillaud's repeated appeals for investment in Sudbury's future, which he sent to his native France during the first decade of the century.[13] American investors, however, did not neglect New Ontario as exemplified by the formation of the International Nickel Company in 1902 and the ventures of Francis Clergue in Sault Ste. Marie.

By the end of the 1880s, Toronto was finally linked by rail to the CPR line in North Bay. There in 1902, a government-owned and operated railway—the Temiskaming and Northern Ontario Railway (TNO)—was started, designed to reach Lake Temiskaming and promote the agricultural development of Ontario's share of the Little Clay Belt. Across the lake, agricultural colonization was already well established in Quebec's Témiscamingue.

In 1903 as the TNO tracks were approaching mile 103, silver was discovered south of Haileybury, and the town of Cobalt was born. Hordes of prospectors and adventurers converged on the area, pushing through the rough rocky terrain. More silver was found and then gold in the Porcupine area and near Kirland Lake. As a result the Temiskaming and Northern Ontario Railway was pushed northward, branching off secondary lines wherever important mines were being excavated. It reached Cochrane in 1908, where a second transcontinental railway under construction was crossing the Great Clay Belt, promising future agricultural development in the region. For the time being, the Little Clay Belt was experiencing rapid growth. Better transport facilities and closer markets for agricultural products now favoured Ontario's side of Lake Temiskaming, where new opportunities were offered in farming, mining, lumbering, commerce and service industries. And French Canadians participated in the prosperity. They represented close to 30 per cent of Cobalt's 5,600 residents in 1911 and almost 20 per cent of Haileybury's 3,900 residents. In fact by 1911, with the Great Clay Belt still awaiting its share of settlers, French Canadians numbered almost 43,000 in northeastern Ontario (25 per cent of the population). East of Sudbury they represented as much as 35 per cent of the 74,000 inhabitants. In the northwestern region of the province there were not 5,000 in all. So with 31,500 living in the southwest, 21,500 in central Ontario and 102,000 in the eastern region, there were more than 202,000 Franco-Ontarians in 1911 (8 per cent of the provincial population).

French Canadian colonization movements only just survived during the First World War. Extraordinary demand for farm produce momentarily brought relative prosperity to rural Quebec. But the end of the war found industries unprepared to convert to a peace-time economy; the demobilization of soldiers swelled the labour force; and agricultural prices fell sharply in the early 1920s. Again nationalists and clerics denounced immigration to the United States. "Back to the land" movements emerged as an alternative to emigration and to work in the morally and physically unhealthy urban factories. Agricultural colonization in the Great Clay Belt, as advertised by promoters, held the promise of a high return.[14]

Now accessible by two railways—the east-west National Transcontinental, recently absorbed into the government-owned Canadian National Railway, and the south-north Temiskaming and Northern Ontario—the Great Clay Belt of Quebec's Abitibi and Ontario's Cochrane districts received a steady flow of new settlers in the 1920s. Remembering earlier speeches, some clerics and nationalists believed that French Canadian "back to the land" movements would effect a northern connection with Saint Boniface along the east-west railway. By the time the Great Depression hit Canada, agricultural settlement was brought to a halt just west of Hearst (almost half-way to Saint Boniface). Although government colonization schemes in the 1930s did convince some unemployed city-dwellers to settle in the Clay Belt, Hearst remained the western limit of agricultural settlement.

Beginning with the early development of Abitibi, the Quebec government had adopted various programs of financial assistance to colonizers. During the 1930s, not only did it participate in the federal-provincial Gordon's Plan of assistance to unemployed city-dwellers-turned-settlers, but it devised its own program—Vautrin's Plan—to promote colonization in Témiscamingue and especially Abitibi. Much to the despair of many French Canadians who were still arriving to settle in Ontario's share of the Clay Belt, the Ontario government decided not to go beyond Gordon's Plan. Indeed, in 1935 Premier Mitchell Hepburn declared that Ontario was withdrawing from all colonization programs.

Nevertheless, Ontario's Great Clay Belt (roughly corresponding to the census division of Cochrane) did receive many French Canadian settlers. In 1931 its total population, with Timmins being by far the largest town (14,200), reached 58,000; 39 per cent were of French origin. Within the rural population, 42 per cent were of French origin. Ten years later, while Timmins had doubled its population to 28,800, the census division of Cochrane had grown to 80,700 inhabitants. Ontarians of French origin now represented 40 per cent of the total, and 44 per cent of the rural population. During the decade, the number of operating farms increased from 2,489 to 3,061, although 1,130 farms were abandoned.

With the ebbing of the depression, the advent of the Second World War and the ensuing rapid industrial growth, agricultural colonization movements subsided. In French Canada the ideology of colonization survived into the 1950s, but fewer and fewer calls to settle in the Clay Belt were answered.

By 1940 French-speaking Ontario was largely a product of French Canadians who, for almost a century, had left Quebec in search of a more promising future in agricultural settlement. Such colonization had been the most important single factor to explain the Franco-Ontarian presence. Of course, French Canadians had also gone directly to urban centres like Ottawa or Sudbury, Toronto or Welland. Rural out-migration in eastern Ontario and abandonment of colonization farms throughout the northeastern part of the province had, by 1940, already brought Franco-Ontarians into cities and regional industrial centres. But during the following thirty years, through internal migrations and the arrival of other francophones, French-speaking Ontario was to experience significant changes in its spatial distribution.

On examination of the regional distribution of the Franco-Ontarians (of French mother tongue) in 1941 and 1971, the most notable is the increase in central Ontario's share of the total French-speaking population: from less than 8 per cent in 1941 to nearly 20 per cent thirty years later.[15] Eastern Ontario's share has decreased from 43 per cent to 36 per cent; the southwestern region also experienced a decrease from 13 per cent to 8 per cent. Northern Ontario, both its western and eastern regions, remained stable. Many factors contribute to an explanation of these considerable shifts in the spatial distribution of the Franco-Ontarians.

The migrations of Franco-Ontarians within the province should first be considered. Regional differences in birth rates, although an interesting subject of study, would probably not be very significant in explaining the shifts in spatial distribution, especially since the francophones did favour central Ontario, the most industrialized and urbanized part of the province. Moreover, the population under study here is defined by its mother tongue—a characteristic that is not permanent from one generation to the next. It is also an accepted fact that linguistic transfers in favour of English have been considerably more numerous in central and southwestern Ontario than in the eastern and northeastern regions. In fact, regional differences in the birth rate and especially in linguistic transfers appear to have shadowed the internal migrations favouring central Ontario. Further research would probably indicate that central Ontario received, through natural increase, inter-regional migrations, new arrivals from French Canada and immigration, more than the 71,400 francophones that our figures suggest.

Out-migration of Franco-Ontarians from eastern and northeastern Ontario accounted for a significant portion of the increased number of French-speaking citizens of central Ontario. By 1911 the easternmost tip of Ontario had reached its maximum rural population. From then on, rural out-migrations to neighbouring towns and cities, new colonization areas such as northern Ontario and the industrial centres of Canada became increasingly apparent. From 1941 to 1971, departures must have been numerous in the counties of Glengarry and Prescott whose combined population only rose by 2,300; Russell County was in a similar position until Ottawa's urban expansion reached its western limit. Indeed, Ottawa—and Cornwall—benefited from the rural out-migrations. Cornwall became a city of 47,000 in 1971, escalating from a mere 17,000 in 1951; its proportion of French-speaking residents rose from 27 per cent to 39 per cent. Ottawa grew from a city of 202,000 in 1951 to a metropolitan area of 453,000 in

1971, while its proportion of Franco-Ontarians slightly decreased from 25 per cent to 21 per cent. Moreover, Ottawa was not only the Canadian capital attracting English- and French-speaking citizens from across the country to the civil service; it was also the Franco-Ontarian capital where one would come to attend a bilingual educational institution and then stay; another would find employment with one of the various Franco-Ontarian provincial associations; and yet another would simply benefit from the job opportunities to be found in the largest urban centre in Ontario where he was most likely to feel culturally at home.

In northeastern Ontario, corresponding more or less to the Little Clay Belt, Temiskaming actually declined from 50,600 inhabitants in 1941 to 46,500 in 1971. Cochrane—or the Great Clay Belt—only grew from 80,700 to 95,800 residents. The number of operating farms dwindled from more than 3,000 in 1941 to a mere 900 twenty years later. Comparatively, however, the Franco-Ontarians who left the clay belts were fewer in number than their compatriots. In Temiskaming, from 1941 to 1971, they went from 20 per cent to 28 per cent of the population. In Cochrane they rose from 39 per cent to 49 per cent. Lacking mobility because of little schooling, lower income and, perhaps, a more obstinate belief in agricultural colonization; feeling secure in a region where their numbers protected their language and their faith, they stayed, but in the regional industrial centres.[16] For example in 1971, Timmins and Kapuskasing accounted for 60 per cent of the population of the county of Cochrane, as compared to 40 per cent in 1941. Similarly, in the census division of Nipissing and Sudbury, where out-migrations have not been as significant, the growth of regional industrial cities has attracted Franco-Ontarians. In 1951, 18,000 of Nipissing's 50,500 residents were living in North Bay, with 22 per cent of them French-speaking; while in 1971, North Bay accounted for 49,200 of Nipissing's 78,900 inhabitants, with 17 per cent French speaking. The Sudbury census division had 109,500 inhabitants in 1951, with the city of Sudbury having 42,400; of the latter's population, 35 per cent were French speaking. Twenty years later, the metropolitan area of Sudbury, where 32 per cent were Franco-Ontarians, accounted for 155,500 of the 198,000 residents of Sudbury's census division.

Further research is necessary on northeastern Ontario's population changes: out-migrations of the earlier Franco-Ontarians may have been more numerous than suggested here, since a steady flow of new arrivals from Quebec and New Brunswick have probably shadowed their magnitude.

Finally, our data suggest that there was out-migration from

southwestern Ontario, as the French-speaking population only increased from 37,300 in 1941 to 41,000 in 1971. However, from the personal history of many French-speaking families presently living in southwestern Ontario, there is evidence of Franco-Ontarians migrating into that region after 1945, especially to Windsor and Sarnia. However, probably due to a high rate of linguistic transfer, our figures are not representative of such migrations. Let me simply add that, by 1971, only 9,000 of the 35,000 Franco-Ontarians of Essex, Kent and Lambton Counties resided outside the urban centres of Windsor and Sarnia.

Out-migration from Quebec and New Brunswick was also instrumental in raising the French-speaking population of Ontario from 289,100 in 1941 to 482,000 in 1971. As opposed to the pre-Second World War movements, the industrial core of central Ontario was not neglected. Welland, for example, which had started to attract francophones after the First World War, had 2,400 French-speaking citizens in 1951, 15 per cent of its 15,400 residents; in 1971, within the city limits, 7,600 residents out of 44,400, or 17 per cent, were French speaking. In 1951, the city of Toronto was home to 10,000 Franco-Ontarians, 1.5 per cent of its 675,800 residents. Twenty years later, the metropolitan area of Toronto, with 2,698,100 residents, had 44,800 French-speaking citizens—1.7 per cent. Besides the 330,000 Ontario-born Franco-Ontarians in 1971, there were almost 108,000 born in Quebec, 17,500 in New Brunswick, 11,000 elsewhere in Canada and close to 16,000 outside Canada. Moreover, 72,500 French-speaking Ontario-born citizens were, at that time, living in another province, in particular Quebec, which accounted for 63,000.[17]

This brief exposé of the main historical factors contributing to the present spatial distribution of the Franco-Ontarian community suggests a few conclusions. The current spatial distribution of French-speaking Ontario has evolved from two major occurrences. The first was characterized by agricultural settlement in eastern Ontario and agricultural colonization in the northeastern region of the province up until the 1940s. This movement often had the aspect of a collective endeavour. Leaving Quebec, the French Canadians came in groups with religious leaders, some professionals and merchants. They formed villages or parishes; and in regions lacking pre-established structures and institutions, they transplanted social and economic institutions that were familiar or became known to them through frequent contacts with their native province. In short, the French Canadians, including those who opted for urban life in cities like Ottawa and Windsor, who came to settle in Ontario, were moving within a French Canada that was not so much a territorial concept but a powerful cultural entity.

The second movement has become increasingly important since the 1940s. Internal and external migration has modified spatial distribution in favour of industrial and urban centres. Largely rural in the early 1940s, by 1971, 35 per cent of French-speaking Ontarians were living in cities of more than 100,000 inhabitants, another 27 per cent in cities of 10,000 to 100,000, and towns of 1,000 to 10,000 claimed 15 per cent. Only 23 per cent were classified as rural, with less than 5 per cent dwelling on farms. This movement was more individualistic in nature than the previous agricultural influx. Better knowledge of English, either from living in Ontario or from better schooling, increased individual mobility. The experience of urban life and industrial work gradually made it easier to move from one city to another. Improved communications and transport facilities were also important.

Urbanization of the Franco-Ontarian population had far-reaching consequences for their institutions and way of life. The relatively homogeneous socio-cultural and, in many instances, socio-economic milieu of the Franco-Ontarian villages, neighbourhoods, parishes, schools, work situations and leisure activities became difficult to maintain. Even in cities where they had established an active community life—Ottawa's Basse-Ville and Plaines Le Breton, Sudbury's Moulin à fleur, or even Toronto's Paroisse du Sacré-Coeur—urban renewal often forced dispersion to the suburbs where seldom could be found a familiar social and cultural setting. Moving to an urban centre where institutions and complex social structures already existed invited integration instead of transplantation. In the factories, mills and services of urban centres, the individual and personal conflict between cultural and socio-economic interest became increasingly critical. Often dispersed and representing a small proportion of the population, limited as to organizational possibilities, the urban Franco-Ontarians could carry on their social life in English all the more easily since their individual bilingualism could adjust to the unilingualism of a greater number of English-speaking citizens, just as it could adjust to the unilingualism of public administration, employment—companies and labour unions—and the media. Finally, gradual laicization in the urban centres made religion less important as a factor of cultural cohesion.[18]

On the one hand, French Canada slowly shifted from a cul-

194   *Gaetan Vallières*

tural concept to territorially-oriented Quebecois nationalism. On the other hand, in Ontario as well as in Quebec, the increasing role of the province in devising and implementing its own complex network of government, affecting the citizens residing within their boundaries stimulated the notion of territory in one's identity.[19] The increasing number of Ontario-born francophones and the individualistic nature of the new arrivals were also important in fostering the development of a new term to define the francophone-living experience of Ontario—Franco-Ontariens.

The gradual shift from Canadiens français to Franco-Ontariens is not complete. The older generations still define themselves as Canadiens français, while a new term has appeared recently—Ontarois—without a translation. Although it seems to have been proposed at first for aesthetic reasons, it is being adopted more and more by groups of young politically-minded francophones and intellectuals. The un-hyphenated and "un-translatable" Ontarois can be seen as an attempt to stress the full *appartenance* of the francophone community to Ontario's past, present and future. In fact, the concurring terms, Canadiens français, Franco-Ontariens and Ontarois bear witness to the historical factors that have contributed to the survival French-speaking Ontario.

Notes

1. Figures used in this paper are taken from or calculated from *Census of Canada,* different decennial or half-decennial editions. See also the map on the spatial distribution of French-speaking Ontarians in 1976 and the figure illustrating the percentage of French mother-tongue population by regions in Ontario in 1976, in Gaetan Vallières and Marcien Villemure, *Atlas de l'Ontario français* (Montreal: Editions Etudes vivantes, May 1981), plate 1.

2. See figure on the total population by regions and the proportion of French mother-tongue population by regions in Ontario in 1976, in Vallières and Villemure, *Atlas de l'Ontario français,* plate 2.

3. Cf. Ernest J. Lajeunesse, *The Windsor Border Region. Canada's Southernmost Frontier. A Collection of Documents* (Toronto: The Champlain Society for the Government of Ontario, University of Toronto Press, 1960); Télesphore Saint-Pierre, *Histoire des Canadiens du Michigan et du comté d'Essex* (Montreal: La Gazette, 1895).

4. Cf. Fernand Ouellet, *Histoire économique et sociale du Québec, 1760-1850* (Montreal/Paris: Fides, 1966); Gilles Paquet and Jean-Pierre

Wallot, "Crise agricole et tensions socio-ethniques dans le Bas-Canada, 1802-1812: éléments pour une ré-interprétation," *Revue d'histoire de l'Amérique française* 26, no. 2 (Sept. 1972).

5. According to Ralph D. Vicero in a presentation made at Premier colloque de l'Institut français du Collège de l'Assomption, Worcester, Massachusetts, 15 March 1980 and summarized by Claire Quintal in *Vie française,* revue trimestrielle du Conseil de la vie française en Amérique (Quebec, 1980), p. 6. Ralph Vicero has devoted his Ph.D. thesis to that subject, "Immigration of French Canadians to New England, 1840-1900: A Geographical Analysis" (University of Wisconsin, 1968).

6. D.A. Gobeil, "Epopée française à la baie Georgienne. 1610-1956," unpublished paper, Centre de recherche en civilisation canadienne-française, Archives, University of Ottawa, n.d.

7. Danielle J. Lee, "The Evolution of an Ethnic Urban Parish" (Masters thesis, University of Toronto, 1967).

8. Cf. D.G. Cartwright, "French-Canadian Colonization in Eastern Ontario to 1910. A Study of Process and Pattern" (Ph.D. thesis, University of Western Ontario, London, 1973); D.M. Ray, "Settlement and Rural Outmigration in Easternmost Ontario, 1783-1956," (Ph.D. thesis, University of Ottawa, 1961).

9. Father Pie Jutteau to the director of "L'Année dominicaine" (review), 31 December 1884, in J. Antonin Plourde, *Dominicains au Canada* II, p. 180.

10. A.-N. Lalonde, "L'Intelligentsia du Québec et la migration des Canadiens français vers l'Ouest canadien, 1870-1930," *Revue d'histoire de l'Amérique française* 33, no. 2 (Sept. 1979).

11. Gabriel Dussault, "Un Réseau utopique franco-québécois et son projet de reconquête du Canada (1860-1891)," *Relations Franco-Canada au XIXe siècle,* Les Cahiers du Centre culturel canadien, no. 3 (April 1974).

12. La Société historique du Nouvel Ontario has published since 1942 "Historical Documents" on the beginnings of many New Ontario communities, pointing out the French Canadian presence.

13. Frédéric Romanet du Caillaud, *Le Nouvel Ontario* (Paris: Société de géographie commerciale, 1906). Reprinted in the "Documents historiques, no. 38" (Sudbury: Société historique du Nouvel Ontario, 1960).

14. Cf. Benoit-Beaudry Gourd, "La Colonisation des Clay Belts du Nord-Ouest québécois et du Nord-Est ontarien. Etude de la propagande des gouvernements du Québec et de l'Ontario à travers leurs publications officielles (1900-1930)," *Revue d'histoire de l'Amérique française* 27, no 2 (Sept. 1973); Pierre Biays, *Les Marges de l'oekoumène dans l'est du Canada* (Quebec: Presses de l'Université Laval, 1964).

15. The percentage figures for 1941 and 1971 on the Ontario French mother-tongue population by region are taken from Statistics Canada, *Census of Canada 1941,* vol. II and *Census of Canada 1971,* vol. 13 and are cited in Gaetan Vallières, *L'Ontario français par les documents* (Montreal: Editions Etudes vivantes, 1980), p. 216.

16. S.D. Clark, "The Position of the French-Speaking Population in the Northern Industrial Community," *Canadian Society: Pluralism, Change and Conflict,* ed. R.J. Ossenberg (Scarborough: Prentice-Hall, 1971).

17. An illustration of the movements of the Ontario francophone population through an examination of the formation of French Catholic parishes from 1800-1978 can be found in Vallières and Villemure, *Atlas de l'Ontario français,* plate 10.

18. Pierre Savard et al., *Arts with a Difference: A Report on French-Speaking Ontario* (Toronto: Ontario Arts Council, 1977).

19. Danielle Juteau-Lee and Jean Lapointe, "Identité culturelle et identité structurelle dans l'Ontario francophone: analyse d'une transition," unpublished text submitted to the Study Group on the Arts in French-Speaking Ontario (cf. supra), Centre de recherche en civilisation canadienne-française, Archives, University of Ottawa.

Contributors

Raymond Breton is Professor of Sociology at the University of Toronto. His writings have included several books, journal articles and research reports on sociology and ethnicity. His latest publication is *La langue de travail au Québéc.*

Donald Cartwright is Associate Professor of Geography at the University of Western Ontario. His most recent publication is *Official Language Populations in Canada: Patterns and Contacts.*

Charles Castonguay, Associate Professor of Mathematics at the University of Ottawa, has written extensively on French language maintenance in Canada and is author of *Exogamie et anglicisation dans les régions de Montréal, Hull, Ottawa et Sudbury.*

Robert Choquette is Associate Professor of Religious Studies at the University of Ottawa. He has published many books and articles on various aspects of religious and social history in Canada, including *Language and Religion. A History of English-French Conflict in Ontario.*

Gilbert-Louis Comeault, Assistant Archivist for the Province of Manitoba, did his post-graduate work at the University of Manitoba. He has been a member of several historical and archival societies since 1971, acting as Vice-President for la Société historique de Saint-Boniface. He has also written articles on language and education in Manitoba.

Jean Daigle is Professor in the Department of History-Geography at the University of Moncton as well as Director of the Centre d'études acadiennes. He has published widely on Acadian history and is editor of *Les Acadiens des Maritimes: études thématiques.*

Frances H. Early is Assistant Professor of History at Mount St. Vincent University in Halifax. She has published studies on the working class of Lowell, Massachusetts and is currently editing the reprint edition of *Félix Albert, Histoire d'un enfant pauvre.*

Madeleine Giguère is Professor of Sociology at the University of Southern Maine. She has written extensively on Franco-American history as well as edited two volumes of *A Franco-American Overview.*

Gerald L. Gold is Associate Professor of Anthropology at York University in Toronto. He has created and produced programs for educational television and has authored many studies on social anthropology, French Louisiana and French Canada. He is co-editor of *Communities and Culture in French Canada.*

Robert F. Harney is Professor of History at the University of Toronto. He is Academic Director of the Multicultural History Society of Ontario and has written numerous works on ethnicity, primarily on Italian emigration and settlement in North America. He is co-author of *Immigrants: A Portrait of the Urban Experience, 1890-1930.*

David M. Hayne is Professor of French at the University of Toronto. He was General Editor of the *Dictionary of Canadian Biography* for four years and has written a multitude of articles, bibliographies and book reviews relating to Quebec literature.

Danielle Juteau-Lee is currently Associate Professor of Sociology at the University of Montreal, specializing in ethnic relations and the sociology of women. Her present research concerns the status of French communities outside of Quebec today. She has published many articles dealing with a feminist critique of sociological theory, the development of sociological theory in ethnic relations and the evolution of the Franco-Ontarian community.

André N. Lalonde is Professor of History at the University of Regina. He has undertaken the historical research and preparation for several radio programs on the French national network, as well as been a participant. He has published articles on French immigration to western Canada and is author of *Le Règlement XVII et ses repercussions sur le Nouvel-Ontario.* His current field of research is francophone immigration to the Canadian prairies, 1880-1930.

Pierre Savard is Professor of History at the University of Ottawa and Director of its Centre de recherche en civilisation canadienne-française (French Canadian Cultural Research Centre). His most recent book is *Aspects du catholicism canadien-français au 19ième siècle.* He has also written for scholarly journals and has co-authored a series of textbooks on general history and one on French Canadian literature.

Gaetan Vallières received his Masters degree in history and has been continuing his post-graduate studies at the University of Ottawa. He is presently Coordinator of the DOPELFO projects (French Language Teaching Texts for Ontario). He has authored and co-authored many books on French Ontario, including *L'Ontario français par les documents* and *L'Ontario français par l'image* respectively.